WOMEN AT WORK
IN
WORLD WARS
I & II

WOMEN AT WORK IN WORLD WARS I & II

Factories, Farms and the Military and Civil Services

PAUL CHRYSTAL

PEN & SWORD HISTORY
AN IMPRINT OF PEN & SWORD BOOKS LTD.
YORKSHIRE - PHILADELPHIA

First published in Great Britain in 2023 by
PEN AND SWORD HISTORY
An imprint of
Pen & Sword Books Ltd
Yorkshire – Philadelphia

Copyright © Paul Chrystal, 2023

ISBN 978 1 39907 126 0

The right of Paul Chrystal to be identified as Author of this work has been asserted by him in accordance with the Copyright, Designs and Patents Act 1988.

A CIP catalogue record for this book is available from the British Library.

All rights reserved. No part of this book may be reproduced or transmitted in any form or by any means, electronic or mechanical including photocopying, recording or by any information storage and retrieval system, without permission from the Publisher in writing.

Typeset in Times New Roman 10/12 by
SJmagic DESIGN SERVICES, India.
Printed and bound in the UK by CPI Group (UK) Ltd.

Pen & Sword Books Limited incorporates the imprints of Atlas, Archaeology, Aviation, Discovery, Family History, Fiction, History, Maritime, Military, Military Classics, Politics, Select, Transport, True Crime, Air World, Frontline Publishing, Leo Cooper, Remember When, Seaforth Publishing, The Praetorian Press, Wharncliffe Local History, Wharncliffe Transport, Wharncliffe True Crime and White Owl.

For a complete list of Pen & Sword titles please contact
PEN & SWORD BOOKS LIMITED
George House, Units 12 & 13, Beevor Street, Off Pontefract Road,
Barnsley, South Yorkshire, S71 1HN, England
E-mail: enquiries@pen-and-sword.co.uk
Website: www.pen-and-sword.co.uk

or
PEN AND SWORD BOOKS
1950 Lawrence Rd, Havertown, PA 19083, USA
E-mail: uspen-and-sword@casematepublishers.com
Website: www.penandswordbooks.com

Contents

About the author		vi
By the same author		vii
Acknowledgements		viii
List of Illustrations		ix
Preface		xiv
Introduction		xv

PART ONE: WORLD WAR I

Chapter 1	Women at work in World War I – women as temporary men	2
Chapter 2	Women in the services	19
Chapter 3	Women nurses, physiotherapists and doctors	25
Chapter 4	Women working on the land: farms, forage and forests	61
Chapter 5	Other wartime women's organisations	70
Chapter 6	Women in industry in World War I	75
Chapter 7	Small arms manufacturing	85
Chapter 8	Munitionettes – the canary girls	88
Chapter 9	Balloons and policewomen	105
Chapter 10	Between the wars	108

PART TWO: WORLD WAR II

Introduction		112
Chapter 11	Women workers in the military services – here we go again	114
Chapter 12	Women workers in the civilian services	134
Chapter 13	Nursing and other health care workers	149
Chapter 14	The Emergency Services	154
Chapter 15	Women on the farms, in the fields and in the forests	157
Chapter 16	Women in the war factories	160
Chapter 17	Prostitution in the World Wars	176
Chapter 18	The Day the war ended	182
Appendix 1	Marie Curie's War Effort	184
Appendix 2	Stamford Military Hospital, Dunham Massey and	
	The Carrel-Dakin Treatment	186
Notes		188
Further Reading		201
Index		217

About the author

Paul Chrystal was educated at the universities of Hull and Southampton, and at Sorbonne University, Paris, where he took degrees in classics and then for the next 35 years worked in medical publishing, much of the time as an international sales director for one market or another and creating medical education programmes for global pharmaceutical companies.

More recently he has been history advisor to Yorkshire visitor attractions, writing features for national newspapers, and broadcasting on talkRADIO, History Hack, BBC local radio, on Radio 4's PM programme and on the BBC World Service.

He is contributor to a number of history and archaeology magazines and the author of numerous books on a wide range of subjects including social and industrial history, classical history, the BAOR, the 'Troubles', pandemics (including COVID-19) and epidemics, biowarfare and many local histories. He is author of *Factory Girls: The Working Lives of Women and Children* (2022) which covers the working lives of women and children before and during the Industrial Revolution and in the years to 1914 where the present book resumes through to 1945.

He is past editor of *York History*, journal of the York Archaeological & York Architectural Society and of *Yorkshire Archaeological Journal*. His books have been translated into Chinese and Japanese.

By the same author

A History of Britain in 100 Objects (2022)

Factory Girls: The Working Lives of Women and Children (2022)

Woman at War in the Classical World (2020)

The Troubles (2018)

The British Army of the Rhine (2018)

A History of the World in 100 Pandemics, Plagues & Epidemics (2021)

Bioterrorism and Biowarfare: Weaponising Nature (2023)

Gunners from the Sky: The 1st Airlanding Light Regiment in Italy and at the Battle of Arnhem (2023)

For a full list please go to www.paulchrystal.com

Acknowledgements

No book is ever the work of one woman or man. This one certainly is not. It has been improved and enhanced by the invaluable help and assistance of librarians and archivists, of researchers and historians, and of friends. I am grateful to Christine Chalstrey and Graham Crossley for alerting me to 'Women and War: From the Fringes to the Front Line' - An exhibition telling the story of women in the Armed Forces in September 2023 in Woodstock. They visited on my behalf and provided much interesting information and many images. They also introduced me to Christine's mother, Alma Careswell, who was in the ATS Signals Corps in Harrogate and the Isle of Man. Alma and her story add that all-important personal element which often is disregarded. She is also proof of the sterling work taken on by women in a fiercely male world, and yet more evidence of the way in which women have been erased from history and received scant recognition and thanks for many decades.

Thanks to Dick Robinson who has kindly allowed me to use extracts from Edith Appleton's diaries. Edie was his great aunt. There is a lot of information about Edie on her website, http://anurseatthefront.org.uk/about-edie/. For more information on the book that came out of Edie's diaries see http://anurseatthefront.org.uk/the-book/.

Richard West kindly gave permission for me to use the photograph of his three great aunts who served as VADs.

Thanks to Emma Gilliland, curator at the Devil's Porridge Museum, for permission to use images, showing women workers at Gretna, 'stirring the porridge' and bale breaking. Images courtesy of The Devil's Porridge Museum.

Every effort has been made to contact copyright holders to seek permission for use of images and to quote from text. However, sometimes things slip through the net or no response is forthcoming; if you find this to be the case then please contact the publisher who will ensure that the proper accreditation is given in subsequent reprints or new editions.

List of Illustrations

1. **Sheffield's Women of Steel, Women of Steel, Sheffield.**
   This bronze sculpture is a wonderful tribute to the thousands of Sheffield women who worked in the steel and munitions factories during both World Wars. By Martin Jennings, it was unveiled in June 2016.
   Holly Hinchcliffe puts it well in https://www.ourfaveplaces.co.uk/where-to-go/women-of-steel/:

   The Women of Steel statue is not only a testament to these women's inner strength and unwavering resolve, but is also a welcome step in redressing the gender imbalance in historical statues that Laura Bates referred to [when she pointed out in a talk titled Everyday Sexism in which Bates revealed that out of 573 commemorative statues in the UK only a staggering 15% celebrate the achievements and lives of women]. Councillor Dore said the women wanted their statue to "reflect the friendships that they created while working together". Two steelworkers, standing arm in arm – the Women of Steel statue is a powerful symbol of solidarity between women, one that will no doubt remain a source of inspiration for generations to come.

2. **Sister Edith (Edie) Appleton, Queen Alexandra's Imperial Military Nursing Service.**
   Thanks to Dick Robinson, Edith (Edie) Appleton's great nephew for providing, and giving permission to use, the photograph of Edie. A book version of her diaries was published 10 years ago, *A Nurse at the Front;* you can see more about it on the book's website: http://anurseatthefront.org.uk/the-book/ and more about Edie on Edie's website http://anurseatthefront.org.uk/.

3. This photograph is of three sisters, May Winifred, Maud Elizabeth and Dorothy Evelyn née Lewis who served as Voluntary Aid Detachments for the British Red Cross during the World War I. Their three brothers saw active service where two sadly died in France and Belgium and the survivor was injured. Thanks to Richard West, their great nephew for permission to use it. See https://www.qaranc.co.uk/VAD-WW1-Uniform-Photo-Three-Sisters.php and www.qaranc.co.uk for more details. May was born in Hartlepool in 1883.

4. **Women workers at Gretna, 'stirring the porridge' and bale breaking.**
   (Images courtesy of The Devil's Porridge Museum)

5. **A VAD poster appealing to the patriotism of the people.**

Women at Work in World Wars I & II

6. **Queen Mary's Army Auxiliary Corps Tending graves in the cemetery at Etaples, 1919.**
Temporary grave markers, made of rough cut timbers bearing metal strips engraved with the name and regiment of the dead stand at the head of each of the graves. One of the graves, that of an airman, has been marked with a propeller as temporary headstones. In due course, all of these markers would be replaced by standard Imperial War Graves Commission headstones.
One of five photographs associated with Queen Mary's Army Auxiliary Corps, 1915-1919. (NAM. 1994-07-239-5 National Army Museum, Out of Copyright)

7. **The grave being tended by the Women's Army Auxiliary Corps (WAAC) gardener was that of Betty Stevenson.**
After the war, the wooden crosses over the graves were replaced by official white stone markers.
From an album containing 21 photographs and ephemera relating to the Women's Army Auxiliary Corps and Queen Mary's Army Auxiliary Corps, 1917-1919. (NAM. 1995-01-24-1 National Army Museum, Out of Copyright)

8. Vital war work at the London Rubber Company to help reduce the rampant spread of STIs which had afflicted military personnel in London and other ports and cities where troops, sailors and pilots mustered in WWII. On the left we have inflation testing and on the right electronic testing of condoms on the Automated Protective Line. (Both copyright Waltham Forest Archives and Local Studies Library, Vestry House Museum and published in *Protective Practices: A History of the London Rubber Company and the Condom Business* by Jessica Borge, McGill-Queen's University Press, 2020)

9. **A member of the Women's Land Army (WLA) operating a single-furrow plough on a British farm.** (Public Domain)

10. **Preston Army Pay Office Ladies' Football Team, 1918.**
Munitions factories, especially in the north of England formed highly skilful teams and played each other in league and cup competitions before huge crowds and in big stadiums such as Middlesbrough's Ayresome Park and Newcastle's St James's Park. (NAM. 1994-07-249-1 National Army Museum, Out of Copyright)

11. **Women's Army Auxiliary Corps typing pool, 1918.**
The Women's Army Auxiliary Corps (WAAC) was established to free up male soldiers for front line service. Clerical duties were one of its main roles, but its personnel also cooked for and waited on officers, served as typists, telephone operators, store-women, drivers, printers and bakers.
From an album containing 55 photographs relating to the Women's Army Auxiliary Corps, 1917-1918. (NAM. 1995-01-23-3 National Army Museum, Out of Copyright)

List of Illustrations

12. A number of ATS women were selected for training as radio operators and undertook Special Operator Training at Trowbridge and, in 1942, the Isle of Man.

    One such member of the ATS selected was Alma Marion Careswell (seen here on the right) who worked as a radio operator and/or interceptor. Once the required standard of Morse Code was reached and the women were conversant with German procedure signals, they joined the men of the Royal Signals at secret listening and intercept stations across Britain, including Harrogate at Forest Moor Y station.

13. and 14. Much work in and around the World War I years was focussed on chemical warfare and mainly involved toxic, asphyxiating and blistering gases. The associated images, artworks, memoirs, novels, films and poetry all remain etched on our minds. And it wasn't just soldiers who had to be protect, as these stunning images show us. Dogs, horses, donkeys and mules all benefited from specially adapted gas masks throughout the war.

15. **Two VADs performing first aid on a patient on a stretcher, surrounded by four men wearing gas masks and three curious young boys.**

16. **'The lady window cleaners of Newcastle-upon-Tyne'.**

17. A WW1 fitter of the Women's Royal Air Force working on the Liberty engine of a De Havilland 9A. The de Havilland DH9A, known as the 'Ninak', was developed as a medium bomber.

18. **The Hospital Supply Depot at Newport, Essex with nurses.**

19. **Women carriage cleaning.**

20. **Women of the Women's Mounted Emergency Corps, 2nd Field Artillery.**

21. **Auction sale aboard a Red Cross barge - selling a German helmet, Peronne, June 1917.**
    British nurses auction captured equipment to raise funds for the Red Cross. Similar auctions were sometimes held when a soldier was killed. His belongings would be auctioned to raise money for his next-of-kin. From an album of 76 official photographs. (NAM. 1999-11-70-48 National Army Museum, Out of Copyright)

22. **Munitionettes boring and milling in the Hartlepools National Shell Factory.**
    The following is taken from an Introduction to a publication featuring a series of photographs taken during a Royal visit to the Shell Factory on June 14th, 1917.

23. **Gas masked baby.**
This chilling, dystopian image from World War II remind us that war is all-encompassing and spares no one and nothing.

24. **One of the Stockport Air raid tunnels.**

25. **Women's Land Army Women on their knees thinning turnips on a farm near Kendal.**

26. **Two graphic posters aimed at US military personnel warning of the epidemic of STIs which afflicted after their arrival in Britain in preparation for D Day 1944.**

27. **Auxiliary Territorial Service personnel manning an anti-aircraft searchlight, 1940.**
Members of the Auxiliary Territorial Service (ATS) operated search lights and radar equipment. Others staffed anti-aircraft batteries as gunners, range finders and sound detectors. (NAM. 1994-07-279-58 National Army Museum, Out of Copyright)

28. **Auxiliary Territorial Service personnel at an anti-aircraft gun station, 1942.**
(NAM. 1994-07-279-45 National Army Museum, Out of Copyright)

29. **A West Indian member of the Auxiliary Territorial Service, 1943.**
In October 1943 a group of 30 women from across the Caribbean arrived in Britain. Motivated by loyalty to the 'mother country', they were the vanguard of over 100 West Indian women eventually recruited to the ATS in Britain. Despite the wartime personnel shortage these pioneers faced a long struggle to be accepted, as War Office officials were often hostile to the recruitment of black women. Racist then.
One of 69 photographs relating to the West Indies Auxiliary Territorial Service, 1943-1947. (NAM. 1994-07-283-1 National Army Museum, Out of Copyright)

30. **Women welding, probably in a shipyard.**
One of 58 Official photographs depicting scenes from the British Home Front, 1940-1941. (NAM. 2006-12-102-52 National Army Museum, Out of Copyright)

31. **October 1942: ATS women working on a Centurion tank at a Royal Ordnance Corps depot.**

32. **WAAF women in May 1944 packing parachutes for the impending Normandy landings.**

List of Illustrations

33. **Naafi break: tea, biscuits and buns.**

34. **Women war workers grinding lenses October 1916. Note the complete absence of eye protection.**

35. **WWII National Fire Service firefighters in action; twenty-three** NFS firewomen lost their lives.

36. **Members of QAINS arrive at the Normandy bridgehead, June 1944.** Nurses of Queen Alexandra's Imperial Nursing Service (QAINS) were the first women to arrive at the Normandy beach head seven days after the initial landings to set up of a hospital to house 600 patients. (NAM. 2006-12-103-18 National Army Museum, Out of Copyright)

Preface

This book is about women in World Wars I & II - women working in factories and on farms, or toiling perilously in field stations just behind the front lines, in inhospitable hospitals and convalescent homes. It is, therefore, about the prodigious contribution women made to the war efforts from 1914-1918 and 1939-1945, standing in for the men who had left their places of work for the various theatres of war from Greece and Italy to Belgium, from Mesopotamia to France. Their tasks were many and various: keeping the troops supplied with shells, bullets and explosives, keeping the nation from starving to death, keeping hundreds of thousands of wounded troops alive so that they might fight another day. This book is, in short, the uplifting but often tragic story of the many women who stepped up to work in the factories, hospitals, field stations, in transport and in civil defence, on the farms and shipyards of Britain, or signed up to the various military and civil services during the two world wars of the 20th century, wars to end all wars...

These women showed an indomitable determination and steely resolve to succeed in every area they encountered: industry, business, health care and numerous services from fire-fighting and policing, from tram driving to train cleaning and in doing so challenged and helped eradicate ingrained and enduring stereotypes relating to the ability of women to do heavy and complicated work, to accomplish physically and intellectually challenging tasks and to do it superbly well. As it turned out, little was beyond their capabilities and it is reasonable to suppose that without their huge efforts both wars might have turned out very differently for us.

How did it come to this? The story of women's work from earliest times to the early twentieth century via the Industrial Revolution, is told in my earlier book, *Factory Girls: The Working Lives of Women and Children* published in 2022. This present book continues the arduous but triumphant journey made by women (and sometimes their children) at work during the two world wars; it clearly shows their courage, determination, patriotism and success – success which has often been too long in the appreciating and in the acknowledging.

Introduction

Women's experiences in the workplace in the early 20th century are inextricably bound up with their contemporaneous struggle to win recognition as citizens in their own right, to achieve political and social parity with men. To do this they needed to win an earlier war they had been waging for the right to vote in public elections and have a say in the running of their country, a privilege thus far exclusive to men. The situation at the outbreak of war in 1914 was that women still had no voting rights, and there were no women MPs, which meant that there were no women sitting in the House of Commons to represent them and fight for their particular causes and issues. The first female MP came in 1919 in the shape of Nancy Astor, a rich American married to a British aristocrat. Astor could not have been more unrepresentative of the women of Britain – there were no Nancy Astors to be found in domestic service or in the sweatshops or munitions factories of the United Kingdom, or indeed in the Wrens, the WRAAF or the ATS or VAD; there were no Nancy Astors in the field stations of France, Belgium or in the Dardanelles up to their arms in blood, filling buckets with shattered body parts[1].

Indeed, women were, of course, discriminated against in most walks of life before and during World War I; the war was run by Edwardian men, the sons of Victorian men, many of whom took some persistent persuading to allow women to take over (so-called) men's work or to permit them to go to France and other foreign war-torn lands to save the lives of their compatriots. Procuring that elusive vote was seen by many, mainly women, as a way to mitigate the prevailing male superiority and as a passport to greater equality in all walks of life, not least in the workplace, in academia and in scientific endeavour. The cause was taken up with verve, determination and courage by the Women's Social and Political Union (WSPU), one of a number of militant suffrage societies active at the time. It was formed in February 1903 in the Manchester house of Emmeline and Christabel Pankhurst, who had become frustrated by the flaccid impact the National Union of Women's Suffrage was having on the cause[2].

Restrictions imposed on women in education did nothing to help women to progress in the higher echelons of the professions, science and industry, the military or the national bureaucracy: girls went to school of course, but in higher education women had been excluded from universities until the 1870s and were, by and large, for decades after, deprived of degrees in the attempt to prevent them gaining voting rights in their universities, a jealously guarded male bastion. The two august universities of Oxford and Cambridge had been dishing out degrees to men for hundreds of years before they finally rewarded women in the same way, even though women had been sailing through university examinations all the while, unrewarded with the degrees they deserved. The breakthrough finally came when women were awarded degrees in 1878 at the University of London, 1895 at Durham, 1905 at Sheffield, 1920 at Oxford, and 1948 at the late to the party Cambridge. Today we rightly gasp with horror when we see girls and women denied an education in Taliban Afghanistan but 100 years ago we were complicit in the same barbarism.

In 1914, however, a change of sorts was about to come. The film adaptation of Vera Brittain's autobiographical exercise *Testament of Youth,* illustrates this well. Brittain is a perfect example of the women who volunteered in their thousands to help with the war effort in a nursing or similar health care capacity[3]. These young middle class women, who before the war were required to be chaperoned on every social outing, now found themselves more or less on their own just behind the front lines, often learning on the job. They were speedy learners and they saved many lives, despite the worst intentions of some trained nurses to demoralise and belittle them.

Many of these volunteers had never worked in their lives before, never mind saved a life: Brittain explains that like most of her comrades, she possessed no domestic skills: she had never lit a fire, boiled an egg or made a bed. Now she was expected to assist in major trauma surgery, at amputations and in laying out corpses for burial. It is likely that most of these women had never seen a naked man before and now they spent their days attending to men's intimate needs in the most horrific conditions. Jan Nielsen (2015) points out how many women war workers just rolled up their sleeves and, stimulated by a sense of patriotism, compassion and duty, joined the legions of factory workers, farm workers, health care workers and the military services, sure in the knowledge that by doing this they were releasing a man to fight at the front:

> During the war full employment for women became the norm. The numbers in paid work rose by 555 percent to 7.5 million. This had an enormous impact not just on the economic but the social and political status of women. By 1917 women had replaced one in three men in the workforce; the biggest growth was in the munitions industry where almost a million women now worked. The Woolwich Arsenal at the outbreak of the war employed 14,000 men and no women but by 1918 there were 100,000 employees of whom half were women. These were a new sort of workplace, the first stage in the automated and mechanised warfare that characterised the war. Women were doing hard, dangerous, manual work that had previously been done by men – and doing it under military-style regimes[4].

The mass call to arms for fathers, brothers and sons was enabled, in large part, by the willingness exhibited by women to step into the breach, but it was by no means all

Introduction

unalloyed jingoism and endless bonhomie: factory and farm hours were extensive and exhausting; factory owners continued to exploit women as they had done so lucratively and comprehensively in and after the Industrial Revolution; farmers were sceptical and hostile; nursing matrons and sisters often used volunteers as skivvies and bullied and resented them; living conditions in hostels for nurses were frequently atrocious and unhealthy; and patients and fellow male workers could be physically and sexually abusive. Home-sickness was endemic; pay, if there was any, was often desultory and the gender pay gap yawned ever wide. Vera Brittain points to another concern for the woman away from home – often for the first time. Letters from home grew increasingly miserable with middle and upper class mothers in the safety and comfort of their drawing rooms bemoaning the absence of servants, the lack of afternoon tea visitors and the growing difficulties of obtaining half edible food. From France, VAD Brittain urges

> 'try to carry on without being too despondent and make other people do the same…for the great fear in the Army and all its appurtenances out here is not that it will ever give up itself, but that the civil population itself will fail us by losing heart – and so of course morale – just at the critical time'.

The servant crisis was, of course, a problem exclusive to the comfortable middle classes, but while most families were untroubled by this vanishing luxury, most of Brittain's colleagues were from the middle classes and so

> 'this despondency at home was certainly making many of us in France quite alarmed: because we were women we feared perpetually that, just as our work was reaching its climax, our families would need our youth and vitality for their own support'.

The summons to return home was by no means uncommon as Brittain herself was to discover, because 'the middle-aged generation, having irrevocably yielded up its sons, began to lean with increasing weight upon its daughters. Thus the desperate choice between incompatible claims…showed signs of afflicting us with new pertinacity'.

Worse, however, than all of this was the incipient stress, trauma, PTSD, that was insidiously installing itself in the minds of some war work women. It was not just the soldiers, sailors and airmen who were traumatised. If we can imagine what non-combatants might have seen and heard on a daily basis it is no surprise that doctors and surgeons, trained and volunteer nurses, stretcher bearers, ambulance drivers, orderlies and padres – were also assailed by combat trauma. The medical staff lived in constant fear of shelling, air raids and of contracting infectious diseases while ambulance drivers and stretcher bearers still went 'over the top', just for a different reason to the soldiers.

The horrors and carnage the women witnessed on a daily basis would have a lasting effect on many lives and attitudes. We cannot know how many women war workers suffered symptoms of what we now call post-traumatic stress disorder (PTSD). Like many of the men in their lives they mostly remained silent or dealt with it obliquely ; Brittain herself became a life-long pacifist and anti-war campaigner. One woman who did appreciate the potential impact of chronic fear and acute panic on a female workforce was Lady Katharine Parsons (1859 – 1933), a pioneering female engineer, whom we shall meet again later[5]. She pointed out that, apart from the anxiety caused in munitions workers working in close proximity to tons of high explosives, the threat from the throbbing Zeppelins unloading their own bombs from above added its own terror and adversely affected the psychological state of the munitionettes:

> Then there were the raids, sufficiently alarming to many people leading their ordinary lives in their well-screened houses, but when hundreds of workers were gathered within the brightly lighted shop…a highly nervous mentality was produced. Great judgement and careful handling were required on the part of those in charge of the workers, in order to repress and allay any symptoms of panic.

One of the many early papers published on the insidious condition that is PTSD in relation to the battlefield soldier was 'The Psycho-Pathology of the War Neuroses' delivered at the Malta Medical Conference on 9 April 1916, by M. D. Eder, BSc. Lond., and published in *The Lancet* of 12 August 1916. Eder begins

> From the combatant's point of view this has been described as industrial warfare; from the medical point of view it might be well characterised as nerve warfare, for an outstanding feature has been the large number of soldiers, both on our side and, so far as I can judge from the scanty references to the German literature that I have seen, on that of our enemies also, who have suffered from what are very properly called functional disorders, with or without injury or organic disease. Of such patients 110 have come under my own notice; a study of the material will be, I hope, not only a contribution to our knowledge of the psycho-neuroses but perhaps a help to an understanding of the psychology of the soldier.

For 'combatant' read also non-combatant; you didn't have to wield a rifle or a machine gun to qualify for this diagnosis. A scalpel, stretcher or a dressing would have done just as well; who is to say that the stretcher bearer's, nurse's or ambulance driver's gaze across the corpse strewn battlefield was any less traumatising or sickening than the view experienced by the infantryman, artillery man or machine gunner? Catherine Black, a one-time colleague of Harold Gillies, the maxillo-facial specialist at the Cambridge Military Hospital in Aldershot, was posted to France where she worked with rehabilitating soldiers suffering from shell shock, describing her experience as 'one of the saddest conditions of modern warfare'.

xviii

Introduction

Lindsey Fitzharris, in her *The Facemaker* (p. 134), tells us that 'at the beginning of hostilities, between three and four per cent of soldiers of all ranks were being evacuated from the front due to 'nervous and mental shock'. The term, apparently, comes from doctors' [erroneous] belief that the condition came from 'the concussive power of artillery barrages'.

That said, there was also much camaraderie; lasting friendships were forged and women were no doubt proud to be helping their country, they were buoyed up by their new-found independence, and relished the hitherto men-only skills they had mastered and the fact that they were now, for the first time, any man's equal in most areas of the workplace, on the farm, on the trams, in shipyards and steelworks, in the public services and military services.

The Munitions of War Act 1915

The Munitions of War Act of 1915 was an attempt to further control and restrict the working practices and behaviour of the thousands of women workers flooding into the munitions and small arms factories and other workplaces co-opted into war work. This Draconian act introduced tribunals at which fines were imposed for lateness, absenteeism and "skiving at work", which was defined as anything from smoking to toilet breaks or talking. Anyone thinking of moving on for better pay or benefits now had to produce a leaving certificate and any employer hiring job applicants without one would be fined. The Act also introduced "welfare supervisors" – female community police officers - whose job it was to enforce sobriety and moral standards on women. The officers haunted parks and were to be found skulking outside pubs and in alleyways. Unsurprisingly, 'they were hated and despised, ridiculed and resisted by women workers'.

Resistance to such prejudicial constraints was widespread and many women responded by joining trade unions. During the war union membership increased by 45 percent overall; for women it was 160 percent.

Women munitions workers got their own Act because they were by far the most numerous industrial sector and, for obvious reasons, their work was considered the most crucial to the war effort and to the winning of the war. Fatal disasters struck the canary girls; they often lived far away from home in purpose-built industrial communities such as Gretna and Barnbow in Leeds. The inevitable life-long, life-shortening occupational diseases contracted by munitions workers were but an additional evil to a hazardous occupation in an ever potentially perilous workplace.

But it was not just munitions with all its daily dangers; there was also opportunities in transport, health care and farm work to which women flocked in their many thousands. Women in both conflicts worked in factories that had been converted to war production - from marmalade to bullets, from chocolate to bomber aircraft - and, just as crucially, in government departments and military facilities, for example, Bletchley Park, the secret intercept establishment at Harrogate, the SOE and the Political Warfare Executive[6].

xix

PART ONE
WORLD WAR I

Chapter 1

Women at work During World War I – women as temporary men

This was a war not just of fighting, but of technological advances. All areas of industry, from aviation to food production, leapt ahead...On a social level, working Britain experienced change as well: with the men at war, it fell to the women of the country to keep the factories going, challenging preconceptions as they did.
– Anthony Burton, *The Workers' War:
British Industry and the First World War* (2014)

The much pedalled notion that the British woman suddenly began to engage in work outside the home with the declaration of war in August 1914 is a myth. My earlier book *Factory Girls: The Working Lives of Women and Children* (2022) shows that women had always been part of the workforce, in textiles, farming, education, the civil service, and the service industries. In 1914 there were something like five million women already in full time work, 1.6 million of them in domestic service. In addition, we have no real idea of how many were working from home and so were not included in these figures. In 1914 approximately 24% of the working age women in Leeds, for example, were already gainfully employed, mainly in domestic service jobs, as shop assistants, or doing work in small factories and workshops.

A woman's working life in industry at the start of the twentieth century was, for the most part decidedly grim: women were prey to the gender pay gap, they were discriminated against for the better jobs, they rose at an ungodly hour, toiled away at a working week that could be anything between 48 hours and 59 hours long, trudged home to their second job, which was the burden of keeping home and family together. Most women married around the age of 23 years, bore and raised up to six children – one at least of whom would die in infancy - lived in an often damp, insanitary and crowded house, sometimes suffered a drink-fuelled, abusive husband, brother or father; she could also expect to be made redundant on her wedding day (the marriage bar) and, to cap it all, could probably expect an early death at around age 50. The only upside to this squalid two-room life was, sometimes, the community spirit it fostered, dependable friendships, neighbourly trust and mutual help, and, despite it all, real happiness. This inviolable network of neighbours was on hand to look after the children when necessary, provide help with the onerous washing on a Monday and to offer freelance, well-intentioned but anecdotal medical care and advice. War work – despite its own serious issues – simply had to offer a better way of life, be it better pay, better hours sometimes, more respect from the outside world, more self-respect and a feeling that you were doing something worthwhile for your country[1].

Women's general lot was not helped by the marriage bar - teachers and civil servants, for example, only had their particular marriage bars abolished in 1944; also unhelpful was the patronising male view that the only reason why women elected to go out to work was for the 'pin money' they could earn to buy those nice little extra treats for themselves. Such a stereotypical, chauvinistic slur was deployed to force women back into the home in 1945. What the men of the day failed to acknowledge was that this apparently frivolous 'pin money' actually made an invaluable contribution to the family budget, allowing the family members to feed, heat and clothe themselves more satisfactorily than had often hitherto been the case.

It may come as some surprise to learn that the immediate impact of the declaration of World War I on British industry was "an abrupt and considerable curtailment of production." In August 1914, there was a great deal of *un*employment and short time working amongst both men and women. But most of those affected were in the industries which traditionally had been worked in by women: for example, only 34 percent of dressmakers were in work while in the boots and shoes industry the figure was 13 percent. Helen Fraser says 'luxury trades ceased to get orders; women journalists, women writers, women lecturers and women workers of every type were thrown out of work' (page 35). The Women's Factory Inspectorate concluded that the shock of it all was felt 'most intensely of all and for the longest of time by women'[2].

The British Empire mobilised something like 9 million men during the war: 900,000 were killed including 37,000 officers (which meant that all social strata were affected) and an estimated 1,693,262 were wounded, giving a casualty rate in the region of 29 percent including those categorised as missing. Britain and her empire could, in one sense, be said to have got off lightly when we consider that Russia, France and Germany all had casualty rates of between 64.9 (Germany) and 76 percent (Russia). In 1914 Britain had an army of 710,000 men complemented by the time of the armistice with an additional six million men who had been called up. In January 1916 conscription was introduced for men aged between 19 and 41 via the Military Service Act[3]. Previously, the Government had relied on voluntary enlistment, and latterly a kind of moral, conscience- driven conscription called the Derby Scheme[4]. It had now become apparent, though, that we were in it for the long haul and that we had to replace all those men donning a uniform to compensate for the jobs they were leaving behind. Conscription of women was the answer - no matter how unpalatable mobilising women was to many, in government and in the workplace amongst unions and employers. In short, the motivated and patriotic woman had a choice: she could be 'The Girl Behind the Man Behind the Gun' or else, if that did not appeal, the 'Girl Speeding the Plough'. The copywriters responsible for the ubiquitous National Service posters saw it as a simple decision: factory or field. By the end of the war the female population in factories had increased by 800,000; while the overall increase in female employment was nearer

1 million. Novice factory girls could find themselves working anywhere in the gamut of factory work from the unskilled 'hand picking bones in Fat Extraction Plants' work to becoming first class mechanics in engineering plants, small arms or munitions factories. The variety, the opportunities, were endless: women became chimney sweeps, road sweepers, bicycle messengers, park keepers, gardeners (some at Kew), funeral directors, bill posters, window cleaners, milk cart pushers, coal heavers and fire stokers in gas works.

Domestic Service

Before the war, the 1911 census reveals that in England and Wales there were 1,302,438 respondents toiling away in domestic service – the biggest occupational group of men or women in a single industry, including agriculture. Most were maids. As noted, the outbreak of war initially saw a steep rise in female unemployment, especially among women in service whose jobs were casualties of their middle-class lady employers' efforts to economise, as well as the lure of better paid work with fewer hours elsewhere. Moreover, working in service was not deemed particularly patriotic when other opportunities were starting to become available in traditional male bastions such as fitting shell fuses or filling grenades. From 1700 to 1911 about 12% of the female population of England and Wales were in service as cooks, nannies, cleaners and maids; by 1931 this had dropped to under 8%. The domestic service industry lost 40,000 women to competing sectors during the war. Half of the applicants for jobs on London buses in 1916 came from those formerly in domestic service.

And who can blame these women? Unremitting drudgery usually awaited the woman and girl in domestic service every morning when she woke up at dawn or before, to get the fires going downstairs followed by the daily, endless grind of cleaning, cooking, washing and the obligatory (even if feigned) obsequiousness to those upstairs. Servants could look forward to one day off a week and wages of 5s a week (equal to £13 today). And then there was the almost ritual abuse: physical, psychological, sexual. Women workers in the rag trade sweatshops also glimpsed a way out and went for it.

Interestingly, the resulting shortage of women in service occupations led to a sharp rise in the development and sales of labour saving devices such as vacuum cleaners, washing machines and refrigerators. Middle class women were having to roll their sleeves up and do their own chores and they, inexperienced in such skivvying as they were, needed all the help they could get.

Queen Mary's Needlework Guild

Moreover, widespread depression and gloom stalked the land, and this general antipathy was aroused further by the somewhat misguided formation, immediately after the outbreak of war on 14 August 1914, of Queen Mary's Needlework Guild, the aim of which was to supply socks and other woollens for the troops through the voluntary work of leisure class, middle class women[5]. Three hundred thousand pairs of socks were needed by 14 November and Queen Mary and Kitchener appealed to the women of Britain and the empire to knit them. Kitchener even gave his name to a stitch for reinforcing heel and toes in order to reduce military blisters. Pre-war the Army Ordnance Service routinely supplied the army with, among other items, 220,000 shirts and a million pairs of socks. Similar prodigious quantities were now required within the week – and demand could only rise as the war went on, and on. Knitting, apparently, was a classless occupation and knitting parties were organised in villages and towns the length and breadth of the country. The rich were especially productive: for example, Ettie Grenfell and her working parties at Taplow Court had knocked out 955 items by 11 December 1914. The country resounded to 'purl, plain, purl, plain' and the click of knitting needles could be heard on park benches, in trains, on trams and buses and in the front parlour. The less affluent women of Dundee contributed 6,000 pairs of socks in the same period.

All efforts were appreciated by troops and field nurses alike, for many of the trench-bound and trench-footed soldiers had been forced to wear the same socks for months on end, causing the sock to stick painfully to the skin, indeed to become 'moulded to the skin'. Not only did this impressive provision provide clean socks where socks did not exist – it also helped against frostbite and trench foot (which depleted a regiment's fighting strength) and kept soldiers relatively warm in poorly heated tented hospitals, ambulance trains and hospital ships; the boost to morale was inestimable.

Well-intended patriotism and benefits to morale and podiatric health apart, the 430 branches of Queen Mary's Guild met with vigorous opposition from the working women's organizations on the very reasonable grounds that the already serious levels of unemployment among women would be exacerbated by any national scheme to supplant paid workers with volunteers. Opposition also came from the newly formed War Emergency Workers' National Committee which emerged from a conference of labour bodies which met on 5 August 1914, "to consider the industrial and social position of the working classes as affected by the war.[6]"

Whatever, Helen Fraser tells us (p. 30) that within ten months the guild received 1,101,105 items – and that was only the articles sent direct to the Guild. Many, many more were dispatched directly to local regiments.

The Central Committee on Women's Employment

The executive committee included representatives from several well-known women's organisations; among these were Chair Mary Macarthur (Women's Trade Union League), Miss Margaret Bondfield (Women's Cooperative Guild), Dr. Marion Phillips (Women's Labour League), and Miss Susan Lawrence (London County Council).

On 17 August it was officially announced that the Queen Mary's Guild scheme had been modified in order to safeguard the interest of the women whose only asset was their labour power. The "Queen's Work for Women Fund" was established, and money was turned over to the Central Committee to provide work or assistance for women who were unemployed and destitute. The Central Committee was convened on 20 August 1914, by the Home Secretary "to consider, and from time to time report upon, schemes for the provision of work for women and girls unemployed on account of the war." Articles made in the resulting workrooms were distributed free, either through charitable organizations or directly through the local committees. Maternity outfits were distributed through maternity centres and schools for mothers; children's clothing was given to the school "Care Committees," and large parcels of clothing were distributed to Belgian refugees in England or on the continent, or were distributed among the destitute in the devastated regions of France.

An order contracted by Queen Mary to the Central Committee for 75,000 woolen body belts formed part of the Queen's gift to the troops. The Committee was able, through this order, to assist the carpet trade, which was greatly depressed on the outbreak of the war. The yarn for the belts was obtained from firms previously engaged in producing carpet yarn, and the actual production of the belts provided employment for a considerable number of women in Kidderminster, Belfast, and elsewhere.

As noted, in 1914 unemployment was more severe among women than among men for a number of reasons, such as the fact that the cotton trade, the biggest of the women's industries, suffered more than any other industry in Britain from the first shock of the war. So-called "luxury trades" country-wide but particularly in London, were especially depressed as a result of the "panic economy" that accompanied the outbreak of the war - these were, of course, "women's trades." Employment dried up in dressmaking, millinery, blouse making, and similar trades while droves of women clerks, domestic servants, charwomen, actresses, typists, manicurists, and other "toilet-specialty" employees were suddenly thrown out of work. Working women were more adversely affected by the dislocation of trade than working men because, obviously, the military offered immediate alternative employment to men. Interestingly, the reduction in the number of working men employed outside the military between July 1914 and October 1914, was 10.7 percent, almost the same percentage of working men known to have joined the army and naval forces.

Substitution

Nevertheless, within a year the nation's economy started to bounce back, including the very industries which had been blighted with redundancies and lay-offs. Women were now in short supply as the demand for labour in the textile factories, principally for uniforms, increased. Substitution, as it was called, where women

Women at work During World War I – women as temporary men

replaced men, started in summer 1915 and gathered pace beyond January 1916, fuelled by the conscription of men.

In July 1914, 3,224,600 women were working; in 1918 that figure had risen to 4,808,000. Their proportion of the workforce in 1914 was 24%; in 1918 it was 37% of a much increased total workforce. Throughout the war the number of women employed in industry grew by over 1.5 million with over 700,000 replacing men in substitute jobs. In the metal and engineering trades the increase of women workers grew from 9.4 to 24.6 percent. In chemicals (including explosives) the growth was 20.1 to 39.0 percent; munitions saw a huge rise from 2.6 percent to 46.7 percent. Patriotism dictated that normal safety regulations and limited working hours were relaxed or suspended while the Factory Acts were largely paused. Longer hours, shift work, Sunday working and curtailed meal breaks became the norm – all the things that had been fought for for the past few decades.

Women were accordingly disproportionately affected by this new occupational austerity: Sylvia Pankhurst later described their parlous situation (*The Home Front,* 1932) while the government set up a commission to investigate the effects of this recent normalisation of working practices and how it impinged on health, fatigue, performance and productivity in women-filled munitions factories and workshops. Seebohm Rowntree (1871 – 1954), using statistics supplied by the Factory Inspectorate, analysed data on nearly 200,000 women working in 1,396 factories. The findings were not good: Rowntree classified 31 percent as having acceptable conditions, 49 percent second class and 20 percent third class. Meal rooms, washing and first aid facilities, rest rooms and 'suitable supervision' were all found wanting[7].

In 1917 the Labour Department of the Ministry of Munitions staged an exhibition of photographs of women at work. This was reviewed by *Building News,* the trusted organ of the construction industry, under the title 'Women as Constructors', revealing the astonishment of men at the sight of women doing physically demanding and skilful building jobs, doing *their* (the men's) jobs and doing them well:

> ... women architects, even before the war, we knew, but that women bricklayers, carpenters, woodworking machine operators, and, indeed, workers in almost every branch of the building trades, would have attained in a couple of years to a skill unsurpassed by men...was a development which few would have predicted.
> - *Building News and Engineering Journal*, 28 March 1917, 268

Women, though, enjoyed an historical reputation in the building trades. Bruce's *Handbook to Newcastle-on-Tyne* (1863) tells how 'At the beginning of the century [1800] and for more than ten years afterwards, all the bricklayers' labourers were women. They boldly ascended the highest buildings, carrying bricks and mortar upon their heads'. This was preceded by an indignant footnote in Mackenzie's 1827 history of the town which was concerned with the decadence of women builders:

'The singular practice of engaging women as labourers to bricklayers and slaters impresses strangers with an unfavourable and erroneous idea of the delicacy and humanity of the inhabitants. As the gentlemen seem not have sufficient gallantry to reform this abuse, we hope that ladies will exert themselves successfully in abolishing a custom so disgraceful to the town, and in providing employments more suitable and becoming for those poor girls than that of mounting high ladders, and crawling over the tops of houses'.[8]

Ministry of Labour figures reveal that the numbers of insured female workers in the building trade between 1914 and 1918 increased from 7,000 to 31,400 (PRO, CAB 21/1527).

A similar Damascene flash occurred in the munitions industry (discussed at length in the next chapter) when Lady Parsons in *The Engineer* described the extensive skills exhibited by women in all areas of their work and condemned those male engineers who insisted on the opinion that

'women are only capable of doing repetition work on foolproof machines. Many women developed great mechanical skill and a real love of their work. In the case of a firm repairing guns, two girls dealt with guns varying from a 13in. naval gun weighing 50 tons to the 8lb. tank gun. They could design, repair and calculate the factor of safety of a damaged gun. Others were taught in one day to work a 12%-inch lathe. This was an industry built up during the war'.

Parsons claimed that it proved conclusively that women were able to work on almost every known operation in engineering. Women, after all, were shown to be capable of working from drawings and plans without instruction just as well as any man.

Misogyny in the workplace

But the baying opposition, the sniping and male insecurity continued to some extent. One factory in Castleton, Lancashire had to resort to sacking men who refused to show women how to work machinery. The men, however, went to a tribunal which found in their favour and fined the company £35 with 25 guineas costs. A woman tool fitter was endlessly harassed by male colleagues who nailed up her drawer and poured oil into it through a crack. We applaud an engineering works woman who 'was sacked: there was a man who chewed tobacco and kept spitting in my pocket and I hit him'. When at Edinburgh Castle, a 50 year old highly respected and accomplished Scottish suffragist and surgeon, Elsie Inglis, offered the Army her invaluable services to the RAMC at the Front she was impolitely and, euphemistically no doubt, told by the War Office representative in Edinburgh,

'Dear lady, go home and sit still, no petticoats here'. The British Red Cross was similarly indisposed to allowing women anywhere near any front line.

Elsie Inglis and the Scottish Women's Hospitals Units (SWH)

Despite, or perhaps because of, this inane response Elsie was undeterred and established the highly effective and successful Scottish Women's Hospitals Units (SWH) in 1914 in which thousands of women, united in their desire to get things done and to help save lives, served in Corsica, France, Malta, Romania, Russia, Salonika and Serbia. They provided much-needed nurses, doctors, ambulance drivers, cooks and orderlies. By the end of World War I fourteen medical units had been outfitted. Some came out shell shocked, living with what we now know as post traumatic stress disorder (PTSD), some died in action. All manner of work was done, not least on the often forgotten Eastern Fronts where the wounded were brought in from the battlefields; and cess pits containing months' old putrefying bodies and body parts were cleared. Elsie Inglis was an inspirational leader of women and she and her colleagues saved many a man both physically and psychologically. The good work the SWH did was priceless. Wounded and dying troops benefitted by the thousands, and so do we thanks to the copious letters and memoirs they have left, providing a peerless record of a unique movement in women's history. *The War Worker* showcased their achievements and their patriotism[9].

Clerical workers

In the early days of the war, office workers began to feel that it was somehow more patriotic working in a factory – particularly a munitions factory – than in a typing pool; this led to an exodus of clerical staff resulting in men for the first time typing their own letters or writing them out longhand. Again, who can blame the women? Small arms and munitions work seemed more interesting - it certainly made a bigger and more tangible contribution to the war effort and was, although certainly more hazardous, much better paid. According to a Chief Woman Inspector of the Board of Trade Labour Exchange (who should know) 'Women love substitution jobs: there is a patriotic glamour about replacing men which is not to be found in the normal pre-war occupations of women'. The exodus from the typing pool was, as we shall see, reversed with the introduction of the commercial typewriter.

The Women's Social and Political Union (WSPU)

That Inspector was right: women in general were anxious to help: in July 1915, Emmeline Pankhurst's WSPU backed and orchestrated 30,000 women who marched in London demanding the right to work. The WSPU had agreed to pause campaigning for votes for women for the duration of the war while suffragettes who had been jailed for their protests and often force-fed, were released. The hope was that women would patriotically work towards peace while supporting the war effort. The benefit for women would be that by demonstrating they could do traditional men's work competently this would strengthen their case for winning the elusive vote.

The Women's Emergency Corps (WEC)

Suffragists Decima Moore and Eveline Haverfield established the WEC to help the forces, though without the support from the pacifists within the WSPU. The aim of the *Women's Emergency Corps* was to train women doctors and nurses; motorcycle and motor car messengers joined the *WEC Motor Department* for which they had their own *Women's Motor Manual*. Formed two days after the declaration of war the WEC worked closely with a number of like-minded societies; they included the *Soldiers' and Sailors' Families Association, the National Union of Women Workers, the Young Women's Christian Association War Clubs, the Women's League of Service* and *Schools for Mothers*, and the *Children's Care Committees*. Their *Kitchen Department* served up 28, 378 square meals in four months and 1,065 pounds of plum puddings for Christmas 1914. With the *National Guild of Housecraft* they gave lessons in domestic work to unemployed girls. Their *Interpreting Department* was the first to assist Belgian refugees while an army of interpreters met arrivals at stations and docks to advise on hotel accommodation, boarding houses and lodgings. They ran lessons in elementary French and German in fifty or so centres for soldiers in training.

The Corps later evolved into the *Women's Volunteer Reserve*[10]. Adelaide Anderson and Frances Durham, two of the first women senior civil servants, had already been working for a decade to improve the working woman's lot and opportunities in a man's world; they continued this in the *Women's War Work Sub-Committee* established in April 1917 in conjunction with the Imperial War Museum to produce a photographic record of women in all types of work, collect ephemera and written accounts – most of the work had been considered inappropriate for women. The resulting photographs and ephemera provide an invaluable document of social and women's history in Britain. The chief photographers were Horace Nicholls and G.P. Lewis.

The Woman's War Register

Nevertheless, although the employment situation was greatly improved by the spring of 1915, there were thousands of unemployed women still impatiently queuing up at the Labour Exchanges. The government issued an appeal urging all women who were "prepared, if needed, to accept paid work of any kind - industrial, agricultural, clerical, and so on - to enter themselves upon the Register of Women for War Service." "The object," it was said, "is to find out what reserve force of women's labour, trained or untrained, can be available if required." The public information messages were unequivocal, urging women to 'Do your Bit – Replace a Man for the Front'. This ill fated Women's War Register, despite the opposition by men, attracted 33,000 applicants within two weeks but although 110,714 women had registered by the middle of September, work had been found for only 5,511 (five percent) of them. Byzantine bureaucracy was the major impediment. As Helen Fraser said, 'you do not solve any problem by registers. You solve it by getting the workers and work together' (page 37). A frustrated and angry Emmeline Pankhurst weighed in in June 1915, making a point about patriotism that must have stung the government:

> 'Imagine what women are thinking when they find in Germany half a million women today are engaged in making ammunition – while 70,000 odd women who registered themselves at Easter at one single invitation of the Board of Trade are only being utilised to the number of 2,000'.

The whole thing turned into a farce, arousing much opposition among the various labour groups, not least the *War Emergency Workers' National Committee* "who believed it to be a thinly disguised attempt to recruit low-paid labour". Some good did come of it, though: the Ministry of Munitions was established in late 1915 to resolve the severe shortage of munitions. Again, women were the answer and their employment was encouraged in 'controlled establishments' which fell outside the remit of the unions and their restrictive practices. There were, however, consequences: the exodus from the mills to better paid munitions factories caused a corresponding shortage of female workers in textiles and an unwelcome reduction in output which was so desperate in places that one Lancashire textile manufacturer appealed for the school leaving age to be lowered to twelve.

Over half a million women started new jobs in munitions factories between July 1915 and July 1916: as well as with the textile industry, disenchantment with domestic service was, as noted, another source of recruits. *The Domestic News* had seen it coming, observing that 'it was not all patriotism that prompted them [to leave], rather a desire to escape a condition of employment that was distasteful to them...on account of what may be termed the bondage of domestic service'.

The cloud of national depression gradually lifted as industry adapted itself to the new demands and a shortage of labour rather than unemployment soon became the chief matter of public concern. Pankhurst was still up against an adamantine wall of opposition in October 1915 when she described pervasive opposition and prejudice as 'almost intolerable in times of peace, but which is something like treachery and traitorism in time of war'. What progress there was was always on the understanding that any changes were temporary and that things would seamlessly revert to type when the war ended.

Women in transport

There was a critical need for increasing outputs of coal and steel as well as for managing the efficiency of the rail network for goods traffic and the movement and mobilisation of troops. The National Union of Railwaymen's particular agreement, however, was predicated on the understanding that the employment of women was 'an emergency provision...and would not prejudice in any way any undertaking given by the companies to re-employment of men...on the conclusion of the war'. The travelling public was initially critical too with complaints that having women announcing arrivals and departures was 'unfeminine', and the less said about women wearing trousers the better ! Nevertheless, as we shall see, things did change and women took on jobs cleaning trains inside and out, plate laying, track maintenance, even graduating to jobs as porters, guards and station masters. Trams and buses were also staffed by women - with female conductors, cleaners, clippies and drivers; vans, particularly those transporting the mail, were driven by women – undeterred even by the onerous operation of the crank handle to get the vehicle going. By the end of the war there were 4,000 or so female bus workers. Coal wagons at collieries and steamrollers did not escape the female touch either. Women worked as navvies too, digging roads and tunnels and building bridges, metaphorically as well as actually.

After the initial employment doldrums there was obviously a revival in the industries in which the allied governments were placing contracts for the outfitting of armies with munitions and materiel, especially the leather, tailoring, metal trades, chemicals and explosives and food trades as well as the hosiery, and the woollen and worsted industries. Having helped secure the jobs, the work of the suffragists and suffragettes turned to the intractable task of procuring equal pay for women – projected in part through the pages of *The Women's Dreadnought*. One munitions worker in Croydon wrote to the paper stating how new employees were paid 8s a week as opposed to the norm of 12s 6d with a raise condescendingly promised 'when they knew their work'. Take off the 3d insurance and 5d unemployment contributions and there was precious little left on which to keep a home and family running. Jameson's of Poplar, a government contractor, was named and shamed for paying sweated rates of pay: 'Strange patriotism this, that allows the Government contractors who are making money out of this war to sweat the women workers in this disgraceful fashion'.

Industrial adaptability and rapid conversion proved to be the key. In February 1915, *The Labour Gazette* had reported numerous examples of the kind of readjustments that were constantly being made. Thus we know that the employees of corset factories in Bath and Portsmouth, who had been thrown out of work at the beginning of the war, were now employed in making army knapsacks. From Walsall we learn that the lighter and less skilled branches of the leather industry had absorbed dressmakers and other unemployed tradeswomen. From the East Midlands a continued depression in the lace industry was reported, but it was hoped that a new industry for the manufacture of tapes, braids, etc., for which lace workers were well adapted, would begin soon. In the tackle-making trade in Redditch, girls from the hook departments were being occupied with the production of hosiery machine needles.

'A Report on the Replacement of Men by Women in Industry'

After a year of war an illuminating situation report in 'A Report on the Replacement of Men by Women in Industry' made to the British Association for the Advancement of Science identified with some impatience three prominent features of the prevailing labour market: the serious shortage of skilled work people; the considerable extension of women's employment; and the limited extent to which women had replaced men at work. It went on to emphasize that valuable time had been lost through the popular belief and misguided optimism that 'the war would be 'over by (last) Christmas'.

The report illuminated that the trades in which the extension of women's employment had been most marked were engineering, explosives, leather work, tailoring, meat-preserving, grain-milling, basket-(shell) manufacturing, elastic webbing, scientific-instrument making, brush making, electrical engineering, canvas sack- and net-making, leather-tanning, rubber work, hosiery, hardware, wire drawing, tobacco, boot and shoe trade, shirt making, wool and worsted and the silk and jute trade. It appeared, however, that only a small proportion of the extra women employed in these trades were actually doing men's work. The fact that fewer men and many more women were employed had led to the assumption that women were replacing men, but the report showed that this was actually happening only "in special instances and to a limited degree." Actually, the war had to a large extent created an increased demand for goods in industries where a larger proportion of women than men were normally employed anyway, pre-war. For example, army clothing was of the kind made "in the medium branches of the trade in which female labour normally predominates. This part of the trade has drawn women and girls from its other branches and from its fringe of casual labour as well as from other trades in which there is a surplus of female labour."

The publication of the report appears to have galvanised the longed-for replacement of men by women in occupations not customarily entered by women before the war. Although this got the work that needed doing done, it was not without its short and long-term problems and created a huge dilemma: the women were largely unskilled and inexperienced so by 1916 skills training centres were being set up to rectify this – no bad thing for women in general. At the same time, though, there arose the vexed question as to what happens to these women, and indeed the men that they were replacing, when the war finally ends (in victory)? Before the war the men had usually endured years in low paid apprenticeships and as journeymen to get to where they were when they suspended their careers and exchanged tools for weapons before leaving for the various fronts. On the other hand, employers now found themselves with a surplus of cheap labour because they could pay women less: for example, a male lather operator was paid 10 ¾ d per hour while his female counterpart had to make do with 5 ¼ d.

The 1919 Restoration of Pre War Trade Practices Act

Any uncertainty as to what to do or to what may happen was eliminated when the solution was embodied in the 1919 Restoration of Pre War Trade Practices Act which enforced the return to pre-war conditions so that most of the 3.5 million men demobilised from the armed forces walked straight back into their former jobs. The women, on the other hand, were obliged to walk straight back into their homes and resume their pre-war occupations as wives and mothers – their role as temporary men over. The Act caused over 25 percent of working women to return from factories to domestic service when they were dismissed to make way for returning soldiers, whilst others established societies to support women to stay in the careers they had entered during the war. The Act gave employers up to two months to return to pre-war practices and then required them to be maintained for at least a year.

For reasons of patriotism, some employers had been keen to see their men enlist anyway, promising that their jobs would be held open for them on their return. In Leeds, Hepworths even contributed £2 towards kit and gave 5s a week to dependents while staff were away. Less philanthropic were Chadwick Brothers, textile manufacturers of Hunslet, who threatened with dismissal any worker aged between eighteen and thirty-five who had not tried to enlist by 4 September. Those who did enlist did so with a promise of their job back on return and 10s per week for dependents while they were serving. Leeds Corporation was particularly generous, and persuasive: jobs were secure, and for non-manual workers, half of salary was paid while away. Manual workers got 5s per week for dependents while the wives of married men received 5s per week plus 2s per week extra for every child under fifteen. By August 1914 the Corporation had paid out £34,484.

Meanwhile the War Office kept up the pressure on industry with its September 1916 book *Women and War Work* by Helen Fraser, published because it was believed that more awareness of the success which had been achieved by women in nearly all branches of men's work was most desirable and would lead to the mid-war release to the colours of large numbers of men who had hitherto been considered indispensable in their war work and detained at home.

Clerical work and the commercial typewriter

Indeed, as we have seen, for many women the war has been described as "a genuinely liberating experience" that made them feel useful in a time of crisis and which also gave them the freedoms and the wages which only men had enjoyed

Women at work During World War I – women as temporary men

so far. One of the beneficiaries of this liberation was clerical work which hitherto was a bastion of male dominance and control: men clerks would painstakingly write letters longhand and then copy them out into the company letter book. Then an office revolution hit with the arrival of the commercial typewriter in 1874, a machine which could write 'almost as fast as by hand' – and when the revolutionary shift key was incorporated in 1878 the already liberated typist knew no bounds. Significantly, though, it was soon discovered that women were also actually able to type competently and so they percolated into the clerical workspace, limited only by the inferior standards of literacy traditionally bestowed on women by the comparatively deficient education they received. Approximately 1,600,000 women joined the clerical workforce between 1914 and 1918, of which 200,000 were in government departments and 500,000 worked as clerical staff in private business, public transport, and the Post Office – between 1914 and 1916, 35,000 women joined the Post Office making sure letters and postcards from soldiers at the front reached their families and friends.

Helen Fraser (p.p. 38-39) sums up this brave new clerical and professional world:

> In professional work today women are everywhere. There are 198,000 women in Government Departments, 83,000 of these new since the war. They are doing typing, shorthand, and secretarial work, organizing and executive work. They are in the Censor's office in large numbers and doing important work at the Census of Production. There are 146,000 on Local Government work...They are replacing men chemists in works, doing research, working at dental mechanics, are tracing plans.

This quiet revolution was not confined to the office or the school desk. As Fraser says, women were infiltrating everywhere:

> They are driving motor cars in large numbers. Our Prime Minister has a woman chauffeur. They are driving delivery vans and bringing us our goods, our bread and our milk. They carry a great part of our mail and trudge through villages and cities with it. They drive our mail vans, and I know two daughters of a peer who drive mail vans in London. I know other women who never did any work in their lives who for three years have worked in factories, taking the same work, the same holidays, the same pay as the other girls. Women are gardeners, elevator attendants, commissionaires and conductors on our buses and trams, and in provincial towns drive many of the electric trams.
>
> In the railways they are booking clerks, carriage and engine cleaners and greasers, and carriage repairers, cooks and waiters in dining cars, platform, parcel and goods porters, telegraphists and

ticket collectors and inspectors, and labourers and wagon sheet repairers. They work in quarries, are coal workers, clean ships, are park-keepers and cinema operators. They are commercial travellers in large numbers. They are in banks to a great extent and are now taking banking examinations.

Factories, especially the dangerous explosives and munitions factories, were employing up to 950,000 women by Armistice Day. Germany, by the way, was not far behind with 700,000 women in their munitions factories. All of a sudden British women were also doing the heavy lifting: building ships, unloading coal, stoking furnaces and shifting high explosive shells. This all resulted in the increase in the proportion of women in total employment from 24 percent in July 1914 to 37 percent by November 1918.

So female job opportunities and mobility increased hugely with many women abandoning domestic service and textile mills for factory work, much to the dismay of many a middle-class woman who, as we have seen, found herself having to get the fire going, do the dusting or washing up herself, or else delegated it to her reluctant and, no doubt, resentful daughters.

Dilution

It took World War I and those initial severe labour shortages to galvanise a real threat to male exclusivity in many trades, industries and professions. Employers were initially reluctant to hire women and the trade unions were implacably opposed. To lift their barriers to entry they insisted that Lloyd George, Minister for Munitions add a provision in March 1915 that women were allowed to do only parts of the skilled jobs usually done by men; thus semi-skilled men were promoted to skilled jobs and women taken into semi-skilled work. This ensured that women remained in subordinate positions and could not earn a fully skilled wage, even though the TUC disingenuously claimed to have supported equal pay since the 1890s. The unions remained fearful that this dilution, in addition to the lower levels of pay women earned, would lead to fewer jobs for their male members when they came home from the front. *The Factory Times* magazine in 1916 pronounced "We must get women back into the home as soon as possible. That they ever left is one of the evil results of the war!"

Despite the barriers to entry, the doing down of women and their allocated tasks, the imposition of minimised skill levels and male stubbornness, it did not take very long for women to rise above it all and to attract widespread publicity that praised the alacrity with which they learned new skills, their diligence, dexterity, productivity and the high quality of their work.

Field Marshall Haig, Commander in Chief of the British Armies in France, was never a supporter of women's labour and insisted that women be employed as dilutees, proposing a ration of 200 women to substitute for 134 men as clerks and in domestic service. Haig feared that women were a deleterious influence on the exclusive male world of which he was part along with the rest of the British Army, suggesting, for example, that women's employment in Base Depots would result in 'the likelihood of sex difficulty' and the disruption of the army's work in the depots. It was decided that women would, wherever possible, be segregated so as to preserve the connection between soldiering and masculinity. Women working in a war situation were also criticised by the troops themselves in the findings of a Commissioner's Report by the Ministry of Labour investigating the WAAC in March 1918 in the light of accusations that the women were seen as 'mannish', unfeminine and sexual predators preying on Tommy Atkins and were affecting recruitment to the WAACs. It turned out that these slurs originated from soldiers' letters home in which they exhibited ' jealousy and hostility towards the WAAC 'because they had been dislodged from non-combatant tasks' by the women.

Ironically it took a tragedy in which nine WAACs perished in a bombing raid at Abbeville for the discrimination and vilification to calm down and, as reported in *The Times* of June 1 1918, allowing the corps to show that women had earned their 'right o khaki'. The WAACs had been renamed the Queen Mary's Army Auxiliary Corps (QMAAC) that April. Again, ironically, as the sight of uniformed women became more commonplace back home, those not in uniform attracted scorn for their apparent lack of patriotism, just as their male colleagues had earlier in the war.

The concomitant increase in female trade union membership from only 357,000 in 1914 to over a million by 1918 represented an increase in the number of unionised women of 160 percent. This compares with an increase in the union membership of men of only 44 percent. The war forced unions to deal head on with the vexatious issue of women's work and its remuneration. For example, female shop workers were being paid around half as much as men doing equivalent work while teachers earned less than 80 percent of a man's salary.

As Gail Braybon points out in *Out of the Cage: Women's Experiences in Two World Wars* (1987), only women welders, tutored by the Women's Service Bureau, managed to form a skilled, unionised group though this offered no guarantee that they would retain their jobs post war. Joanna Burke adds that while by 1918 around 1 million women were members of female trade unions, their wages did not significantly grow (*Women and Employment on the Home Front During World War One*, BBC) due to dilution.

But it was not just in industry that the women of the nation stepped up and substituted. As Jennifer Gould points out in her *Women's Corps*, 'The outbreak of war prompted the formation of numerous women's voluntary organisations, and a number of women worked to extend women's role, but it was the continuing manpower crisis which, in 1916, persuaded defence ministers and others seriously to consider forming corps of women to substitute for men in the Army'.

The recommendations of both the Manpower Distribution Board and a military report advocating substitution of women in certain jobs, together with the desire of senior War Office staff to gain control over women's voluntary groups working for the Army, combined to secure the formation early in 1917 of the first of the three women's military corps, *the Women's Army Auxiliary Corps*. This was followed soon after by *the Women's Royal Naval Service* and the *Women's Royal Air Force*. Inevitably there were the usual 'rumours of immorality in the corps, and the manner in which a lack of formal status created difficulties for the women in command'.

In the first year of the war, a war which incidentally was not over, of course, by Christmas (nor by the following three Christmases) 382,000 women joined the nation's workforce followed by an additional 563,000 in the second year. Women may be forgiven for thinking they were there to stay.

Chapter 2

Women in the services

Elisabeth Shipton, in her *Female Tommies* (20014) tells us how, when war was declared, women formed long queues at local labour exchanges or at women's recruiting huts to volunteer for whatever roles were available to help the war effort[1]. New organisations such as the Women's Emergency Corps leapt into action to co-ordinate employment and Voluntary Aid Detachment (VAD) staff set up training programmes for new volunteers. From the myopic view of the British chiefs of staff, nursing was the only appropriate role for women in the military – indeed, over the course of the war, 19,000 women served with distinction as nurses and between 70,000-100,000 as VADs. But women were to do so much more.

In 1916, the Department of National Service deliberated as to whether to call up men in their fifties to free up yet more soldiers for front-line service. Shipton adds that a small but determined number of women established their own privately funded medical organisations such as the *Scottish Women's Hospital,* as we have seen, and the *Women's Hospital Corps,* and, 'not to be denied, made their own way overseas. In 1915 the VAD introduced general members who would undertake non-medical work, such as cooking, cleaning and administrative roles'. Along with groups like the *First Aid Nursing Yeomanry (FANY)*, these women proved they could operate in a war zone under duress despite the angry opposition of the War Office[2].

However, it was soon realised this would not raise the numbers needed. The misogyny suffered by Dr. Elsie Inglis when she offered her services to the Royal Army Medical Corps as mentioned above is probably the most famous example, and is covered in detail below.

The Women's Army Auxiliary Corps (WAAC)

The Women's Army Auxiliary Corps (WAAC) was established in December 1916 with Dr Mona Chalmers Watson as its first Chief Controller. We are told by the Imperial War Museum's *The Vital Role of Women in the First World War* 'that Its formation was largely due to a War Office investigation which showed that a large number of non-combatant tasks were being performed by soldiers in France. It was clear that women could do many of these jobs, potentially freeing up 12,000 men for service in the front line'.

Things changed completely in 1916 when Britain faced a major manpower shortage due not least to the carnage at the battle of the Somme. With recruitment in decline, Britain brought in conscription, but it was still not enough: the thought of women carrying out basic military tasks was beginning to sound credible. A review was launched and on 16 January 1917 Lt Gen HM Lawson released his report, supporting women's services in order to release men for front-line duty, in other words, substitution. After two and half years of internal conflict, dilatoriness and procrastination, speed and urgency were now of the essence. There was no more time to waste and four weeks later Mona Chalmers Watson was appointed Chief Controller with Helen Gwynne-Vaughan as the Overseas Chief Controller. Gwynne-Vaughan later remembers that she was adamant that they should be the Women's Army Auxiliary Corps (WAAC) as opposed to 'Women's Corps' as she, understandably, did not want to be called 'Chief W.C.'

The first unit of fourteen cooks and waitresses arrived on the Western Front on 31 March 1917 in the officers' club at Abbeville with more following in the next few weeks, posted to various bases. In due course roles were expanded to include clerks, drivers, mechanics, telephonists, telegraphers and typists. Eventually, 9,000 women served with the unit in France.

Helen Fraser (p. 82) adds:

> For France, no woman under twenty or over forty is eligible. After volunteering, they are chosen by Selection Boards and medically examined. They receive a grant for their uniforms. The workers wear a khaki coat-frock – a very sensible garment – brown shoes and soft hat and a great coat. At the end of a year they get a £5 bonus on renewing their contracts, and they get a fortnight's leave in a year.

Unsurprisingly, the uniform was not popular – is it ever? – but most recruits accepted that 'their feminine ideas on dress were now of no account'. Nevertheless, the idea of breast pockets was rejected as they 'emphasised the female form'; the skirts were considered most daringly short as they were twelve inches off the ground'. More seriously, though, according to Helen Gwynn-Vaughan, 'the women provided their own underclothes, and, while these were often excellent and usually neat and appropriate, instances occurred when they were in rags or hardly existed at all'. She had seen that women from poorer backgrounds wore the very minimum of underclothes – for them knickers were an upmarket item.

The organisation of the WAAC reflected the military model: their officers (called Controllers and Administrators rather than Commissioned Officers, titles jealously protected) messed separately from the other ranks. The WAAC equivalent of an NCO was a Forewoman, the private a Worker. The women were largely employed on unglamorous tasks on the lines of communication: cooking and catering, storekeeping, clerical work, telephony and administration, printing, motor vehicle maintenance. A large detachment of WAACs worked for the American Expeditionary Force and was an independent body under their own Chief Controller [www.longtrail.co.uk/army/regiments-and corps].

Florence Leach was the controller of the cooks. In 1918, women doctors (attached to the QMAAC) were first posted to France. One such was Dr Phoebe Chapple, who was awarded the Military Medal for tending the wounded regardless of her own safety during an air raid on a WAAC camp near Abbeville in May 1918. In all, five military medals were awarded to members of the QMAAC, all for brave conduct during air raids or shelling in rear areas.

A total of 17,000 members of the corps served overseas, although never more than 9,000 at one time. In April 1918, nearly 10,000 members employed on Royal Flying Corps air stations, both at home and in France, transferred to the Women's Royal Air Force on the formation of the Royal Air Force.

We know from the National Army Museum (https://www.nam.ac.uk/explore/queen-marys-army-auxiliary-corps) that Margaret Caswell served in the Women's Legion before being transferred to the WAAC in 1917. Given the rank of worker, Caswell was sent to France to work as a waitress at an officers' club at Abbeville Camp. On the night of 29-30 May 1918, German aircraft attacked QMAAC Camp 1 at Abbeville. 'One of the bombs hit the protection trench, killing Caswell and eight of her colleagues, and wounding seven others. Overall in the war, 81 women of the QMAAC were killed, and five were awarded the Military Medal for their services'.

The corps was eventually disbanded in 1921. Many former QMAACs returned to the colours, joining the newly formed Auxiliary Territorial Service (ATS) during the Second World War.

The Women's Signallers Corps

Their Commandant-in-Chief was Mrs. E.J. Parker – Lord Kitchener's sister. The corps believed women should be trained in every branch of signalling so that men could be released by women taking over signalling work at fixed stations. Women, therefore, learned semaphore, and Morse, telegraphy, wireless, whistle, lamp and heliograph. They were also taught map reading.

The Hush Waacs

'There are only about a dozen of them; they come from the Censor's Office and between them have a thorough knowledge of all modern languages. They decode signalled and written messages, script of every kind' (Fraser p. 85).

The Women's Royal Naval Service (WRNS) was formed in November 1917, with 3,000 women. According to *The Vital Role of Women in the First World War* 'This doubled in size with 'Wrens' working in over 100 different roles. The Women's Royal Air Force (WRAF) was born on 1 April 1918 with the Royal Air Force. Members of both the WAAC and WRNS transferred to the new service, which grew to 32,000, serving at home and in Germany and France. They undertook mechanical and technical roles as well as cooking, driving and administration'. By 1918 over 57,000 women had served in the QMAAC (9,000 of which were overseas), 5,500 in the WRNS and 9,000 in the WRAF.

The Women's Royal Naval Service (WRNS)[3]

For almost as long as there has been a Royal Navy women have played their part, initially as laundry workers in naval hospitals or else they inveigled their way onto ships of the line by masquerading as men. In 1854 the intrepid Mrs Eliza Mackenzie led a squad of six nurses to the Navy Base Hospital at Therapia near Constantinople during the Crimean War.

Nevertheless, the Royal Navy was still hesitant about taking women on board until an 1883 report highlighted the lamentable provision of personnel ashore led to the creation of the *Naval Nursing Service* with six nursing sisters posted to Chatham and five to Plymouth. The Second Boer War (1899-1902) gave nurses working on hospital ships an opportunity to excel and to show their mettle; Queen Alexandra was so impressed she became President of the Nursing Staff, leading to the creation of *Queen Alexandra's Imperial Military Nursing Service (QAIMNS)* and the *Queen Alexandra's Royal Naval Nursing Service (QARNNS)*. In 1901 things moved up a level when a *QARNNS* Reserve unit of trained nurses was established to expedite their movement from posts in civilian hospitals. This was the state of play in 1914 when the QARNNS personnel were the only women serving in the Royal Navy, and so it remained until 1919 when there were still only 81 *QARNNS* nurses backed up by over 200 reservists. These, with units from Voluntary Aid Detachments under the Admiralty Medical Department, did sterling work at fifteen naval hospitals and, more perilously, aboard nine hospital ships. HMHS *Britannic*, sister ship to the ill-fated RMS *Titanic,* was sunk off the Greek island of Kea in 1916 with the loss of 30 lives; one survivor was Red Cross Stewardess Violet Jessop, a *Titanic* survivor four years earlier.

The Women's Royal Naval Service (WRNS or Wrens) was the women's branch of the United Kingdom's Royal Navy. First formed in 1917 with Dame Katharine Furze as Director (equivalent in rank to Rear Admiral), it was disbanded in 1919, then revived in 1939 at the beginning of World War II, remaining active until integrated into the Royal Navy in 1993. WRNS included wireless telegraphists, radar plotters, weapons analysts, range assessors, electricians and air mechanics. And then there were the sail-makers, painters, cleaners, wood turners, fitters, cooks, bakers, motorcycle and motor car drivers, porters, garage workers, telephonists and clerks. At Immingham they adjusted naval gyroscopes and drew maps and at Battersea Experimental Workshops they drew up designs for all manner of new military machines and guns. Some made wire submarine nets, polished torpedoes and primed depth charges. They listened in on wirelesses in listening stations, they coded and they decoded performing the same watches as the men and worked

Women in the services

night shifts. They telephoned firing orders during Zeppelin and Gotha raids; they decoded the signals notifying the surrender of the German fleet in November 1918 in Granton Naval base in Edinburgh. Forty-nine officers and 22 ratings were awarded medals. Those qualified to be officers were to apply to the Professional Women's Register in Westminster.

Most Wrens were UK based but others were posted to Genoa, Malta and Gibraltar. Wrens would substitute in the Royal Navy, the Royal Marines, Royal Naval Reserve, Royal Naval Volunteer Reserve, Royal Naval Division UK and Royal Naval Air Service – all things Naval once done by men, except manning a warship.

On 10 October 1918, nineteen-year-old Josephine Carr from Cork, a Wren Clerk shorthand typist became the first Wren to die on active service, when her ship, the Holyhead bound mail steamer *RMS Leinster* was torpedoed by *UB 123* just outside Dublin Bay. The ship sank in eight minutes with the loss of 500 lives. Two other Wrens survived.

By the end of the war the WRNS had 5,492 members, 438 of them officers. In addition, about 2,000 members of the WRAF had previously served with the WRNS supporting the Royal Naval Air Service and were transferred on the creation of the Royal Air Force.

The Women's Royal Air Force (WRAF)[4]

The Women's Royal Air Force was the women's branch of the Royal Air Force. Like the WRNS it had two lives: the first from April 1918 to 1920 when it enjoyed a total strength of 32,000, and the second from 1949 to 1994. The target strength had been around 90,000; figures are unreliable until 1 August 1918 when the strength was 15,433, with approximately 5,000 recruits and 10,000 who transferred from the WAAC and the WRNS. This first incarnation never exceeded 25,000.

How did the WRAF come about? During World War I, members of the Women's Royal Naval Service (WRNS) and the Women's Army Auxiliary Corps (WAAC) worked on air stations operated by the Royal Flying Corps (RFC) and the Royal Naval Air Service (RNAS). When it was decided to merge the RFC and RNAS to form the Royal Air Force (RAF), there was much concern about the loss of their specialised and industrious female workforce. The requirement for a separate women's air service gave birth to the WRAF on 1 April 1918. Personnel from the WAAC and WRNS were allowed to choose to transfer to the new service: over 9,000 decided to join. Civilian enrollment amplified WRAF numbers. They were posted to RAF bases, first in Britain and then later in 1919 to France and Germany.

Depots were opened in 1918 at Handsworth College, in Glasgow, at RAF Flowerdown, RAF Spitalgate near Grantham, and at York. In the 1950s the WRAF Depot and WRAF Officer Cadet Training Unit were opened at RAF Hawkinge in Kent. In April 1920 the WRAF was disbanded. In only two years, 32,000 WRAFs had proved a major asset to the RAF and paved the way for all future air service women.

An exhibition at the RAF Museum [https://www.rafmuseum.org.uk/research/online-exhibitions/women-of-the-air-force/womens-royal-air-force-wraf-1918-1920/] tells us:

> The work of the WRAF was divided into four basic trades: Clerks and Store women, Household, Technical and Non-Technical. Initially little training was given with wages based on existing experience and skills. The majority of women were employed as clerks, Members of the Household Section with shorthand typists the most highly paid of all airwomen. Women allocated to the Household section worked the longest hours, doing back-breaking work for the lowest pay. The Technical section covered a wide range of trades, most highly skilled, including tinsmiths, fitters and welders.

By 1920 over 50 trades were open to women including tailoring, photography, catering, pigeon keeping and driving. The work of these women obviously released men for combat and gave further proof that women could do just as well as any man in the workplace.

The minimum age for joining the WRAF was eighteen and came with a complex selection process. As with men aspiring to join the army, stringent health checks often meant the exclusion of many candidates from poorer backgrounds and polluted cities. Those middle and upper class educated candidates were enrolled as officers; the other ranks were known as 'Members' - the backbone of the service. WRAFs fell into two categories: 'Immobiles' who lived at home and were attached to their local station and 'Mobiles' who lived in quarters on or near their workplace and could be transferred elsewhere if required.

Conduct was strictly monitored and regulated with the WRAF constitution and rules laid-out in an official booklet: the *Standing Orders* listed a ban on smoking on duty and in the street, as well as uniform requirements and a complaints procedure. The high standards set by the WRAF led them to being regarded as the most professional and disciplined of all the women's services.

24 March 1919 saw the first group of WRAFs land in France to begin their overseas service. Later that year a contingent was posted to Germany. https://www.rafmuseum.org.uk/research/online-exhibitions/women-of-the-air-force/womens-royal-air-force-wraf-1918-1920/ reveals that 'Their task was to assist the army of occupation and to replace men demobilised from the forces. Based in Cologne, they were employed as domestics, clerks, telephonists, nurses and drivers and became known as the 'Ladies of the Rhine'. Dedicated and diligent, they also helped raise RAF morale by staging sports days and dances'.

On 1 February 1949, the World War I incarnation was resurrected when the Women's Auxiliary Air Force, which had been founded in 1939, was re-established as the Women's Royal Air Force. The WRAF and the RAF grew ever closer over the following decades, with increasing numbers of trades opening up to women; the two services formally merged in 1994, marking the full assimilation of women into the British forces and the end of the Women's Royal Air Force.

Chapter 3

Women nurses, physiotherapists & doctors

It is the men and women who died on active military service or were seriously injured during World War I who invariably and rightly attract the most publicity, most column space in newspapers and by far the most mentions on the internet. Their names really do 'Liveth for Evermore' which is good, because that is exactly what we all want.

However, as Sue Light pointed out in her blogpost http://greatwarnurses. blogspot.com/ *Dead Nurses*, most of those who served their country did not die but returned home again to either get on with the rest of their lives as best they could, or to suffer from the long term physical and psychological effects of war. Most women served on the Home Front, shielded to a large extent from the perils of the front line, except that is the myriad munitions workers who worked under hazardous and sometimes lethal conditions 'and who history has chosen to sideline more than any other group of women'.

Sue Light goes on to tell us how 'If you include nurses working in the military wards of civil hospitals the total figure for nursing staff engaged in caring for military personnel during wartime is likely to have totalled more than 150,000'.

Countless books have been published since 1918 in which the authors endeavour to record the lives of nurses and related workers in World War I. One that fulfils this objective admirably is Lyn MacDonald's *The Roses of No Man's Land* (1980): towards the end of her 360 pages, in the closing chapter entitled 'The Aftermath', she compiles for us some 'unchallangeable statistics' which leave us with as stark a picture of the human wreckage left by the war as we are ever likely to get. Apart from the horror that the statistics invoke *per se* we can also get from these statistics a graphic picture of the gruesome workload which the nurses, physiotherapists, doctors and surgeons (and orderlies, ambulance drivers, stretcher bearers and burial details) were challenged with on an often daily basis. She achieves this with a detailed examination of the disability pensions still being paid out in 1938 some twenty years after the Armistice to men 'wholly or partially disabled as a result of their war service'. Here are her findings:

- 8,000 pensions being paid to men with one or both legs amputated
- 3,600 to men with one or both arms amputated
- 90,000 to men with withered or useless limbs
- 2,000 to men rendered totally blind

- 8,000 to men partially blinded
- 11,000 to men permanently deafened by explosions
- 15,000 to men with severe head injuries which their chronic debilitating pain or diminished mental capacity precluded any chance of working again
- 25,000 paid out to men with neurasthenia, shell shock, social anxiety disorder or PTSD
- 2,800 with epilepsy
- In addition, in 1938 3,200 men were sill incarcerated in mental sylums and
- 7,000 were disabled with inoperable hernias
- 2,200 incapacitated with frostbite
- 41,000 were suffering the long-term effects of gassing, mainly bronchitis and tuberculosis
- 38,000 were stricken by heart disease due to the fear, stress and strain of battle
- 28,000 crippled with rheumatism after months and years of trench life
- And 32,000 unclassified severe war wounds

At some stage of their invalidity every one of these victims had to be nursed, diagnosed and rehabilitated; physiotherapy may have been applied and many operations carried out. Of course, it does not include the many tens of thousands of injured who did not make it to the Armistice and pension application stage and so are not included in the statistics even though they would all have been nursed at some stage. MacDonald hints that this was a best case scenario: the Ministry of Pensions was not known for its 'softheartedness'. One injury can provoke other unrelated but equally debilitating sequelae over time but it is unlikely that any of these were ever compensated. In February 1980 pensions were still being paid out to 27,000 disabled men who fought for King and country some 60 years before.

It is with this tragic human traffic in mind that we examine the different agencies and organisations involved in the care of the wounded soldier, be it on one of the many Fronts, behind the lines, on the ambulance ships and trains, in the ambulances and in the hospitals and rehabilitation units back in the UK.

War Hospital Supply Depots

Where did all those bandages come from? Who supplied the nightshirts for soldiers in hospital? Where did we get the mountains of laundry for all the beds? Who made the crutches? War Hospital Supply Depots are a big part of the answer. They were organised by charitable individuals and staffed by civilian volunteers, mainly women engaged in sewing and stitching the required materials. Without them there would have been nothing like enough dressings nor clothing for the patients in the many hospitals and rehabilitation centres up and down the country. The supply depot network was founded in August 1915, with the object of supplying the Military Hospitals of Britain and its Allies, free of cost, with surgical dressings and other requisites for the treatment and care of patients. There were more than 2,700 War Hospital Supply Depots and Work Parties throughout the United Kingdom and overseas.

Retailers too did their bit to maintain morale and keep us safe on the home front. Turner & Co in Sunderland had a wonderful product line including Sleeping Helmets and Pyjama Suits. But it was the Chemico Body Shield ('the greatest invention of the age') which was the must - have buy. This provided discerning purchasers with the assurance that it 'will stop Revolver Bullets at six paces, Flying Shrapnel, Bayonet, Sword and Lance Thrust'. The protection against lance thrusts must have been what tipped it for any indecisive shoppers.

The Almeric Paget Military Massage Corps (APMMC)

A little known, and therefore underestimated, element of Britain's medical forces in World War I that played a crucial role in the all-important rehabilitation of wounded soldiers. Massage and remedial gymnastics were the forerunners of today's physiotherapy - there was an official training scheme which led to the certificate of the Incorporated Society of Trained Masseuses. It was mostly taken up by women who had no previous nurse training, and was seen as a rather more respectable way to earn a living for a middle-class young woman.

The Almeric Paget Massage Corps first saw the light of day in August 1914 when a prescient couple, Mr and Mrs Almeric Paget, funded 50 fully trained masseuses to be posted to the principal Military Hospitals in the UK. The service was such a success that the staff numbers were soon increased: Mr. and Mrs. Paget then supplied 120 masseuses free of cost to the Government.

According to the National Archives, https://www.nationalarchives.gov.uk/womeninuniform/almeric_paget_intro.htm, the work was obviously intense, starting at 9am with a 30 minute lunch break and a 10 minute tea break at 2.15. Each masseuse would see 30-40 patients per day and provide treatments that included massage, hydrotherapy, electrotherapy and "... stimulating muscles with the 'Bristow coil' or subjecting a limb to interrupted galvanism, ironization or a Schee bath, diathermy or radiant heat".

In November 1914, the Pagets were approached by the War Office and asked to open a centre in London where officers and men could receive Massage and Electrical Treatment and thus relieve the Out-Patient Departments of the London Military Hospitals. 55 Portland Place was lent for this purpose by Lady Alexander Paget (moved later to 2 Cambridge Gate) and a full suite of electrical equipment was installed. Throughout the war an average of 200 patients per day benefited from the services provided by this clinic.

Sir Alfred Keogh, Director-General Army Medical Service, inspected the clinic in March 1915 and the service subsequently became the model for all the massage and electrical departments in convalescent hospitals and command depots throughout the UK. A grant to fund the expansion was also provided and the first convalescent camp opened at Eastbourne with over 3,000 patients, 500 of whom were massage patients.

Eligibility requirements for enrolment in the Corps were two years at Physical Training College, or a Certificate from the Incorporated Society of Trained Masseuses, or six months of satisfactory and appropriate work experience. The word "military" was added to the corps' title in December 1916 and in January 1919 APMMC became known as the Military Massage Service by Army Council Instruction.

https://www.greatwarforum.org/topic/175814-almeric-paget-military-massage-corps/ tintin1689 A user on the Great War Forum adds that:

> 'Each Convalescent Camp had a Massage Institute where massage, physical exercise, muscle extension, heat treatment, vibrational treatment and electrical and chemical treatment were administered. Thirty-two masseuses would treat 25 patients each per day, attending to four patients each simultaneously. The most common treatments were bathing, massage and special exercises for trench foot, electric shock treatment and Swedish exercise for functional paralysis resulting from shell shock and daily exercise for those recovering from gassing. Corps members also changed dressings. It must be remembered that these were the days before penicillin, and septic wounds were a grave problem. The Corps conducted experiments with electric currents, it being believed the bacteria might gravitate to the positive pole'.

Until early 1917 members of the corps were only required to serve in the UK, but from then on service overseas was an option. Fifty-six masseuses served in France and Italy between January 1917 and May 1919. In total 3,388 women and men served in the APMMC, peaking at 2,000 in 1919. There were over 2,000 actually at work on the day the Armistice was signed.

Queen Alexandra's Imperial Military Nursing Service (QAIMNS)

March 1902 saw the birth of the QAIMNS as part of the reforms of the army and Indian nursing services at the end of the Second Boer War; the new unit replaced the existing *Army Nursing Service* and *Princess Christian's Army Nursing Service Reserve* to form one military nursing service for the army in the United Kingdom, India and the colonies. Contemporaneous to this a new Advisory Board for Army Medical Services was instituted.

Stipulations for entry were of their time: they included British parentage, a fitting social status and age between 25 and 35. Pay scales were Matron-in-Chief £250, rising to £300; principal matron, £150, rising to £180; matron, £70, rising to £120; sister, £37 10s. rising to £40, and nurse, £30, rising to £35 per annum. If a serving nurse of QAIMNS reached the age of 50 she would become entitled to a service pension. The pension would depend on length of service and a year spent in a "tropical climate" would be counted double.

The demanding (for the time) personal requirements and the relatively few hospitals which met the training standards led to the QAIMNS being challenged to recruit the numbers it required. By August 1914 there were fewer than 300 full-time members deployed at home and overseas. The numbers did not greatly change during the war, with most recruits being taken into its reserve.

Queen Alexandra's Imperial Military Nursing Service Reserve (QAIMNSR)

Belatedly established in 1908, the QAIMNSR had a target at establishment of 500 members but like the permanent service it always fell short. By August 1914 it had fewer than 200 members. A recruit would agree to serve on reserve for three years and would be paid a £5 per annum retainer. The War-time recruitment offer proved to be a winner: a one-year contract was on the table and it attracted over 2,000 in the last months of 1914 and more than 12,000 by war's end.

In any event the main body and the reserve were able to send six parties to Belgium and France by 20 August 1914 (Fraser, *Women and War Work* p. 22).

Queen Alexandra's Royal Naval Nursing Service (QARNNS)

As we have noted, nursing and the navy go back as far as 1744; the uniformed Naval Nursing Service was established in 1884 and staffed by trained nurses. These nurses served on shore, initially at Haslar, Chatham and Plymouth to provide a professional organisation that reflected the developments taking place in civilian hospitals and within the Army Nursing Service.

By 1919 there were eighty-one members of the regular service, assisted by just over 200 Reserve nurses employed during wartime, providing care at fifteen naval hospitals and on nine hospital ships. It was not until World War II that the regular establishment increased substantially.

Princess Christian's Army Nursing Service Reserve (PCANSR)

Although this organisation was subsumed into the QAIMNS when it was established, over 300 of its former members, many with experience honed in the Boer War, were still on its reserve in 1914. Some of them were mobilised for service with the QAIMNSR but until they formally registered with the latter they remained members of the PCANSR.

Civil Hospital Reserve Nurses

Although Queen Alexandra's Imperial Military Nursing Service had its own reserve of nurses, formed in 1908, it was, as noted, never able to attract enough members of the right calibre. In the summer of 1909 a new initiative by the War Office brought into being the Civil Hospital Reserve, a group of trained nurses from throughout the United Kingdom vetted and recommended by their civil hospital matrons and each one willing to mobilise with the military nursing services in case of any future war. Although no known register of CHR members survives, individual service records usually indicate if a woman was mobilised as part of the Civil Hospital Reserve, and gives her hospital of origin. These nurses wore the uniform of QAIMNS Reserve, initially without a service badge, and as the war progressed the majority signed new contracts and transferred to the QAIMNS Reserve itself.

The Women's Reserve Ambulance Corps (WRAC, also known as the Green Cross Corps)

The Women's Reserve Ambulance Corps was a volunteer aid organisation established in 1915[1]. Its members worked to direct people at stations, transport hospital patients and help generally during German bombing raids. The corps sent personnel to the Dardanelles during the Gallipoli campaign and arranged the first all-female ambulance convoy to the British Army on the Western Front. The corps became a founding member of the *Women's Army Auxiliary Corps* in 1917 and continued until September 1919.

The Corps developed from Evelina Haverfield's proposal to raise a *Women's Volunteer Rifle Corps* in August 1914. The WRAC emerged in 1915 and in the beginning its activities were restricted to London. The unit was funded through donations and subscriptions from the public.

Women served at London's Victoria Station to provide directions to lost persons and assistance to those who were in need of overnight accommodation; this included large numbers of servicemen departing for the front and those returning wounded or on leave. At one point it was providing assistance to 16,000 service personnel a month.

The unit was first on the scene of the first major Zeppelin raid on London in September 1915, helping to treat the wounded. They assisted the police in subsequent bombing raids, tending to the injured and dying, retrieving corpses and clearing the streets. In 1916 they sent the first all-female ambulance convoy to the British Army on the Western Front in France.

Women nurses, physiotherapists & doctors

A branch of the corps was later established in Bournemouth and was known as the "Bournemouth Battalion". It comprised three officers and 45 other ranks and, from March 1916, was equipped with a Sunbeam motor ambulance. The battalion ferried patients from the local station to various hospitals and also acted as ward orderlies, cleaners and canteen workers.

Typically, the corps received mixed reports in the press. In 1916 the *Illustrated War News* stated that "of all the societies and organisations ... that the present conflict has called into being, none is doing better or more useful work than the Women's Reserve Ambulance". However misogyny was never far away: it was criticised elsewhere for "encroaching too closely on male territory" and its members were accused of making use of the opportunity presented by the war to "have the time of their lives".

Women drivers

Women behind the wheel in the service of their country has been seen as a powerful stand-out symbol of the general emancipation enjoyed by women due to their adoption of hitherto masculine roles; indeed, as Julia Pattinson says, it can be seen

'as an aspect of female war service that did not fit within the discourse of nurturing and care, roles traditionally attributed to women. The pot-holed roads of France present a useful terrain – both literal and contextual – in which to theorise the female ambulance driver-mechanic as a symbol of gender modernity.

In her *Women of War* Pattinson examines the motor car as a symbol of modern femininity using the censored accounts of FANYs' letters home, reports published in the Corps's magazine and newspaper articles, the embellished tales of daring told during the war to publicise and promote the unit's activities, and retrospective accounts captured in print and on tape, in order to reveal both the thoroughly modern pleasures and the perils of driving and car maintenance. She considers media attitudes toward the female driver and the establishment opposition that they slowly eroded. While the war enabled 'new configurations of female masculinity, providing a space where women could play with their gender identities, protected by their class background'.

The Hackett-Lowther Ambulance Unit

The Hackett-Lowther all-female Ambulance Unit was established in 1917 by Norah Desmond Hackett and May Toupie Lowther. Having acquired vehicles and recruited women they set off for France. The unit could boast 20 cars and 25 to 30 women drivers; it operated close to the front lines of battles in Compiègne, and was attached to the 2nd Army Corps of the French Third Army. Lowther was awarded the Croix de Guerre in July 1918. As well as all that she was the London president of the Relief for Belgian prisoners in Germany committee. She returned to London in August 1919 after two-and-a-half years in France

It seems possible that several members of the unit enjoyed relationships with other women – a supposition only relevant when we consider that this unit, and in particular the experiences of Toupie Lowther, inspired Radcylffe Hall to write her famous lesbian novel *'The Well of Loneliness'*.

Midwives

Life, of course, went on during the war and babies continued to be born with and without the help of midwives. *The Midwives Chronicle: The Heritage Blog of the Royal College of Midwives* tells us that the birth rate during the war years was also much lower than in previous years. According to the ONS, there were 879,096 births in 1914, dropping slightly to 814,614 in 1915, 785,520 in 1916, and 668,346 in 1917, 662,661 in 1918 and 692,438 in 1919 as soldier and sailor mortality and the absence of men started to impact.

The Midwives Chronicle blog reveals that many midwives joined the VAD during the war, but many also stayed on in midwifery. Obstetricians (usually male) got to keep their professional status and income as they were still allowed to intervene in all but the absolutely normal deliveries. Midwifery examinations were expensive at up to £50 and the three month training away from home meant rent; Latin, of course, was still used in medical terminology, so many poorer girls or those not educated in the elite schools had little chance of entering the profession.

As with midwifery, the work of the district nurse did not abate just because there was a war raging[3]. In 1914 local authorities employed 600 health visitors; by 1918 there were 2,577. The number of child welfare centres rose from 350 in 1914 to 578 by 1918 – a triumph for health visiting, neonatal medicine and preventative medicine.

Theatre nurses

One of the many roles discharged by nurses in the field was what today we call theatre nursing, which involved attending and assisting at major life-saving operations involving trauma surgery, amputations and facial reconstruction.

> 'Wound care too was paramount. Multiple wounds, large wounds and very infected wounds had to be dealt with carefully and with new and varied antiseptic treatments. A typical military nurse would have had to use impregnated dressings, understand the actions of the different antiseptics which they poured and irrigated through

wounds. They used a very complex technique called the Carrel-Dakin wound irrigation technique, using Dakin's solution, (sodium hypochloride) in a glass bottle. This involved running the irrigation solution through rubber tubes into the deepest part of the wounds to treat them and clean them out'.

https://www.independentnurse.co.uk/professional-article/nursing-in-the-first-world-war/64504.

One of the few good things to have come out of the war was the formal registration of nurses. At the start of the war, nursing was unregulated, meaning that more or less anybody could call themselves a nurse (or a midwife), and many women, as we can see, offered their services in this unofficial manner. The year 1919 saw a major change when the nurses' register was established.

Maxillofacial Surgery

In World War I facial injuries requiring major reconstruction proliferated: men were shot in the face, peering over their trenches, they had their jaws blown away by shell blasts and shrapnel, and they had their faces kicked in by horses. Lindsey Fitzharris, author of *The Facemaker: One Surgeon's Battle to Mend the Disfigured Soldiers of World War I* (2022) reveals that

> 'Plastic surgery flourished during the and was eventually ushered into the modern era by men like Harold Gillies… Gillies went back to Britain and petitioned to open his own specialty facial reconstruction unit at the Cambridge Military Hospital in Aldershot, and that's how it all began. Eventually he was so overwhelmed by the number of men needing his help that in 1917 he opened the Queen's Hospital, which later became Queen Mary's Hospital, in Sidcup – a hospital dedicated to facial reconstruction.'

Gillies 'brought in artists, photographers, radiographers and mask makers, building a wonderful creative team who all worked towards rebuilding a soldier's face'. Invaluable nursing care apart, women also contributed with the mask making.

> The masks were non-surgical solutions that were created by artists like the sculptor Anna Coleman Ladd [1878 – 1939]… And they're exquisite – when you look at them, it looks almost like a human face. But you have to remember that they are still unmovable. If you were sitting in front of someone wearing one of these masks, it could be a bit unsettling because the masks were expressionless; they couldn't operate like a face. They were also very uncomfortable to wear, they were fragile, they didn't age with the patient'.

Voluntary Aid Detachments (VADs)

At the end of the Boer War, with unusual prescience, the War Office was concerned that should Britain be embroiled in another war, the medical and nursing services would not be able to cope: the peacetime medical care needs of a standing army were comparatively small and specific, and to find thousands of trained and experienced personnel at very short notice, without the expense of maintaining them in peacetime, was an almost intractable problem. R. B. Haldane's new Territorial scheme of 1907 solved some of those problems, and opened up new possibilities of co-operation between voluntary agencies and the Army: on 16 August 1909 the War Office issued Lord Keogh's 'Scheme for the Organisation of Voluntary Aid in England and Wales,' which set up both male and female Voluntary Aid Detachments to plug certain gaps in the Territorial medical services, with a similar scheme for Scotland following in December of that year.

The Voluntary Aid Detachment was a unit of volunteer civilians providing nursing care for military personnel in the United Kingdom and various other countries in the British Empire. The VAD emerged from a fusion between the British Red Cross and Order of St John of Jerusalem to support the Territorial Medical Services. VADs were inextricably enmeshed in the war effort, but they were never military nurses; they were not under the control of the military, unlike the Queen Alexandra's Royal Army Nursing Corps, the Princess Mary's Royal Air Force Nursing Service, and the Queen Alexandra's Royal Naval Nursing Service. Initially, the detachments were intended for home service only, to staff auxiliary hospitals and rest stations. Later, VAD nurses worked in field hospitals on the edges of the battlefield, and in longer-term places of recuperation back in the UK. The female detachments usually comprised a Commandant, a Medical Officer, a Quartermaster, and twenty-two women, two of whom were trained nurses.

Why were VADs largely middle class women? A working class woman had a number of choices as to how she might serve her country: munitions or other factory work, Land Army or health care. Her middle class counterpart, however, was prevented from taking on paid work, by what Henriette Donner in her 1997 paper, 'Under the Cross' refers to as 'Bourgeois notions of respectability'.

The Joint War Organisation (JWO)

In August 1914, the British Red Cross and the Order of St John proposed a Joint War Organisation (JWO) to work with common aims, reduce duplication of effort and coordinate fundraising; resources were pooled under the protective emblem of the Red Cross; an agreement was concluded on 24 October 1914. They were joined by the St Andrew's Ambulance Association in Scotland. The JWO was the main point of contact with the increasingly overstretched Royal Army Medical Corps (RAMC). It was run from Devonshire House in Piccadilly, loaned for the war by the Duke and Duchess of Devonshire.

In the early days of the war PoW's would receive food packages from their respective governments; however this was soon blocked and along with other charitable organisations, the JWO, under the banner of the International Red Cross, stepped in to send a parcel every two weeks to each prisoner. The total cost of parcels in World War I was £5,145,458-16s–9d.

The Central Prisoner of War Committee of the Red Cross and Order of St John initiated a monthly journal, *The British Prisoner of War* beginning in January 1918, to help the families and friends of British and Commonwealth prisoners of war. The JWO was disbanded in 1919.

As volunteers, VADs worked without pay, so volunteers were mainly middle class or upper class patriotic British women, well educated and with a sense of purpose. By the summer of 1914 there were over 2,500 Voluntary Aid Detachments in Britain with 74,000 VAD members, two-thirds of which were women and girls; within four years the number had grown to 4,000 VADs and 125,000 volunteers.

Detachments usually met at least once a month, with many meeting as often as every week, and women had to work towards gaining certificates in 'Home Nursing and First Aid' within twelve months of joining. With this they learned to bandage, to apply simple dressings, and the basics of invalid cookery and hygiene. Some were seconded to go into local hospitals for a few hours each week to observe ward work, and, due to the low number of men being recruited, women could also gain experience in stretcher duties, the transport of the sick and wounded and general improvisation.

http://www.scarletfinders.co.uk/181.html Scarlet Finders tells how:

> 'Red Cross and Auxiliary hospitals sprung up rapidly in church halls, public buildings and private houses, accommodating anything from ten patients to more than a hundred…much of the basic work was the responsibility of the VADs – they cleaned, scrubbed and dusted, set trays, cooked breakfasts; they lit fires and boiled up coppers full of washing. They also helped to dress, undress and wash the men – which was of course a big step for young women who may never have been alone and un-chaperoned with a man before, other than perhaps their brothers'.

But it was not all plain sailing with the VADs. Initially, the Red Cross was not keen to allow civilian women a role in overseas hospitals: as noted, most volunteers were of the middle and upper classes and unaccustomed to hard work, indeed any work in many cases, and the rigours of hospital discipline. To the military authorities VADs at the front line were *verboten*. Officially, VADs were recorded as being assigned to one hospital, but over time they also worked - often unofficially and sporadically - at a number of hospitals locally, with a view to providing continuity of care to some patients after hospital transfers.

By 1916 the military hospitals in the UK were employing about 8,000 trained nurses with about 126,000 beds, and there were 4,000 nurses abroad with 93,000 beds. By 1918 there were about 80,000 VAD members: all told 12,000 nurses were working in the military hospitals and 60,000 unpaid volunteers were active in auxiliary hospitals of various kinds. During the four years of war 38,000 VADs worked in hospitals and served as ambulance drivers and cooks. VADs served near the Western Front and in Malta and Mesopotamia, Gallipoli and later the eastern front.

Paradoxically, there was tension between volunteer and professional when some volunteers showed disrespect towards the paid nurses.

We get a vivid but honest picture of this discord through the four volumes of diaries left to us by Edith Elizabeth Appleton O.B.E. R.R.C. As Dick Robinson, Edie's great nephew, said in 2012 on his web page quoting many of her entries, 'Edie takes a generally good view of the VADs – with a few notable, and sometimes very amusing, exceptions'[1]. [http://www.edithappleton.co.uk/VADs/voluntary_ aid_detachment.asp]. Here are a few sample entries:

January 30th 1916
Hardly slept at all today. Nurses are the most inconsiderate wretches under the sun – they tramped about slammed doors and pulled plugs to distraction, then the orphans were let loose to kick tins and play and the paper man blew his horn, toot tooting and yelling "Petit Parisien". Now at 1:30 a.m., I feel I shall bust if I don't say what is truly unkind: that the V.A.D. who sits in this room will drive me to drink – she talks tracts, gives tracts and is bulging with saintly and innocent holiness till I could shriek … 10 a.m. Poor little V.A.D. It was horrid of me to feel irritated at her – she is such a good conscientious little soul.

June 28th 1918.
A sad tragedy happened at 5 yesterday morning. A mental patient, a lady driver, managed to dodge her special attendant and flung herself over the cliff. Her body was soon picked up quite smashed in every part. She evidently meant to do it as she had left letters for people telling them so. It is said she had a similar attack a few years ago and her father insisted on her coming out to France to work - he thought the complete change and occupation would cure her. I think myself, if he knew her tendency, it was wrong at any time to allow her to be in charge of helpless men.

The deployment of VADs was sometimes problematic: they did not always fit into military hospitals' protocols and order. They obviously lacked the advanced skill and discipline of trained professional nurses and were often critical of the nursing profession. However, relations improved as the war dragged on: VAD members heightened their skills and efficiency while trained nurses became more accepting of the VADs' efforts and contributions. VAD Hospitals, 1,786 of them, were also opened in most large towns in Britain. Many VADS were decorated for distinguished service. Though membership was not limited to women, the vast majority of volunteers were women. By the end of the war in 1918, of the 126,000 that had served 243 were killed (for example, Edith Munro a nurse who died in East London in 1916), 364 decorated and 1,005 mentioned in dispatches; they no doubt paved the way for a greater inclusion of women in both military and medical professions for generations to come.

"Working parties" operated in most towns to collect clothing, make bandages, splints and the like. A network of "'Central Work Rooms'" was established in 1915 to organise these working parties and standardise the items being created which were then gathered at "Work Depots".

Other activities included: rest stations at railway stations; fundraising – over £21 million was raised; a missing and wounded service; air raid duty; libraries; patient transport; providing grants such as to Hammersmith Hospital to help rehabilitation. Red Cross collecting boxes were moved from National to Regional VAD control, with local VADs keeping 20% of the funds collected, 80% going for national use.

However, at the end of the war, it was agreed by the leaders of the nursing profession that untrained VADs should not be allowed onto the newly established register of nurses.

Well known VADs include:

Enid Bagnold, author of the novel *National Velvet,* on which the 1944 film with Elizabeth Taylor was based. Her account of her experiences are related in her memoir *A Diary Without Dates* published in 1918.

Vera Brittain, in *Testament of Youth,* recounting her experiences during World War I; the following is an extract describing the horrors of her daily routine in France:

> "I am a Sister VAD, and orderly all in one. Quite apart from the nursing, I have stoked the fire all night, done two or three rounds of bed pans, and kept the kettles going and prepared feeds on exceedingly black Beatrice oil stoves and refilled them from the steam kettles utterly wallowing in paraffin all the time. I feel as if I had been dragged through the gutter. Possibly acute surgical is the heaviest type of work there is, I think, more wearing than anything else on earth. You are kept on the go the whole time but in the end there seems to be nothing definite to show for it - except that one or two are still alive that might otherwise have been dead... Gazing half hypnotized at the disheveled beds, the stretchers on the floor, the scattered boots and piles of muddy clothing, the brown blankets turned black from smashed limbs bound to splints by filthy bloodstained bandages. Beneath each stinking wad of sodden wool and gauze an obscene horror waited for me and all the equipment that I had for attacking it in this ex-medical ward was one pair of forceps standing in a potted meat glass half full of methylated spirit."

Florence Farmborough was born in Steeple Claydon, Buckinghamshire, on 15 April 1887. She was named after Florence Nightingale, who lived nearby. Home educated by a governess before attending St. Thorolds in London, Florence moved to Russia in 1908 where she worked as an English teacher. When World War I started, Farmborough immediately offered her services as a nursing sister at the hospital established by Princess Golitsin in Moscow. Later she accompanied Russian troops in Poland, Austria and Romania. Florence was posted to Podgaytsy Hospital in Russia and leaves us with this disturbing account of a novel surgical procedure:

> "I was surprised and not a little perturbed when I saw that tiny bags, containing pure salt, are sometimes deposited into the open wound and bandaged tightly into place. It is probably a new method; I wonder if it has been tried out on the Allied Front. These bags of salt - small though they are - must inflict excruciating pain; no wonder the soldiers kick and yell; the salt must burn fiercely into the lacerated flesh. It is certainly a purifier, but surely a very harsh one! At an operation, performed by the lady-doctor, at which I was called upon to help, the man had a large open wound in his left thigh. All went well until two tiny bags of salt was placed within it, and then the uproar began. I thought the man's cries would lift the roof off; even the lady doctor looked discomforted. 'Silly fellow,' she ejaculated. 'It's only a momentary pain. Foolish fellow! He doesn't know what is good for him.'".

Mary Borden was an American who worked in the Allied hospital she set up in Dunkirk[2]. She later wrote about it in her autobiography, *The Forbidden Zone* (1929) from which the extract below is derived. Mary soon had to learn about death and the dying as she took on massive responsibility for the survival or otherwise of her patients:

> "It was my business to sort out the wounded as they were brought in from the ambulances and to keep them from dying before they got to the operating rooms: it was my business to sort out the nearly dying from the dying. I was there to sort them out and tell how fast life was ebbing in them. Life was leaking away from all of them; but with some there was no hurry, with others it was a case of minutes. It was my business to create a counter-wave of life, to create the flow against the ebb. If a man were slipping quickly, being sucked down rapidly, I sent runners to the operating rooms. There were six operating rooms on either side of my hut. Medical students in white coats hurried back and forth along the covered corridors between us. It was my business to know which of the wounded could wait and which could not. I had to decide for myself. There was no one to

tell me. If I made any mistakes, some would die on their stretchers on the floor under my eyes who need not have died. I didn't worry. I didn't think. I was too busy, too absorbed in what I was doing. I had to judge from what was written on their tickets and from the way they looked and they way they felt to my hand. My hand could tell of itself one kind of cold from another. My hands could instantly tell the difference between the cold of the harsh bitter night and the stealthy cold of death."

Agatha Christie briefly details her VAD experiences in her posthumously published autobiography. Some women went to the Western Front as letter writers for soldiers who were either too ill to write their own letters, or illiterate. *May Bradford*, the wife of John Rose Bradford, Physician to the British Expeditionary Force, later recalled how she educated men on the treatment of women:

"To one man I said, 'Shall I begin the letter with my dear wife?' He quietly answered: 'That sounds fine, but she'll be wondering I never said that before.' ... One day a youth was brought in with both eyes shot away. After all his messages to his wife and children had been written down, he put up his hand to try and find mine. 'Sister', he said, 'is it a fine day, and are the birds singing?' I pictured it all to him. 'Well,' he answered, 'I have much to live for still.'

E. M. Delafield is the author of the *Diary of a Provincial Lady* series and some 30 other novels; her experiences working at the Exeter VAD Hospital provided her with material for one of her most popular novels, *The War Workers*, published in 1918.

Others included *Dame Rachel Crowdy*, English nurse who was Chief of the Department of Opium Traffic and Social Issues Section of the League of Nations from 1919 to 1931; *Amelia Earhart*, American aviation pioneer; Hattie Jacques, English comedy actress; *Naomi Mitchison*, Scottish writer; *Olivia Robertson*, British author and co-founder of the Fellowship of Isis; *Sophia Duleep Singh*, suffragette; and *Freya Stark*, explorer and travel writer.[3]

The Women's National Service League

Three weeks before the Germans took the city on 9 October 1914, Mrs St. Clair Stobart Corps established a Hospital in the Summer Concert Hall on the Rue de Harmonie, Antwerp. The Women's National Service League were there too and were among the last to cross the bridge and escape before the Germans blew it up.

Women's Hospital Corps[4]

On the outbreak of war in August 1914 women, as we have seen, were just as eager as men 'to do their bit', but female doctors who volunteered their services to the War Office were most often rebuffed out of hand. The facts are that although more than 1,000 women had qualified in medicine since Elizabeth Garrett Anderson became the first woman trained in Britain to join the Medical Register in 1865, nearly 50 years on they were still restricted to treating women and children and so were effectively barred from jobs in general hospitals, and from working behind the front lines.

A very early war time voluntary group calling themselves the Women's Hospital Corps (WHC) formed in September 1914 and, under the leadership of former militant suffragists Drs Flora Murray and Louisa Garrett Anderson (Elizabeth's daughter), swerved round the bureaucracy and systemic sexism of the British government by going directly to the French Embassy with their offer to run a military hospital in Wimereux, France. Their plan was eagerly accepted, despite having previously been rejected by the War Office, and they were granted work permits to travel to France. Within two weeks, Murray and Anderson recruited enough medically trained women to staff an entire hospital: nurses, orderlies, and clerks. The women made uniforms and raised funds for the necessary supplies and established military hospitals for the French Army in Paris and Wimereux, as they had proposed. Wendy Moore tells how

> Rallying friends and comrades from the suffragette movement, the pair raised £2,000 for medical equipment, recruited a team of fellow doctors, nurses and orderlies and kitted them out in military-style uniform. Then, on 15 September, they set off from Victoria Station for Paris with their unit of 14 women and four male nurses'[5].

Moore goes on to tell how, on arriving in Paris, the doctors were given a luxury hotel, the Hôtel Claridge, as their military hospital. However, the hotel was completely new and had never opened with the result that it had no lighting, heating or hot water; apparently, even the plaster on its walls was still damp. However, in less than 48 hours the two intrepid women had turned the dining rooms into wards and set up 100 camp beds. The ladies' cloakroom was converted into an operating theatre, with a fish kettle for a sterilising unit, while the grill room became a mortuary. That very evening 50 wounded men arrived on stretchers and the surgical team worked through the night.

Formidable as it all sounds, Murray, a physician and anaesthetist, and Anderson, a surgeon, had no prior experience of battlefield trauma or emergency surgery and they had never operated on men. But, as Moore points out, the scale and complexity of the trauma they encountered, with the majority of their patients experiencing gangrene, were new to all surgeons – novel or experienced, male or female. 'The shell injuries are dreadful & the men come to us worn out after days in the trenches', Anderson told her mother. 'The cases come to us very septic & the wounds are terrible.'

Two months later the Women's Hospital Corps opened a second hospital in a small hotel in Wimereux (between Boulogne-sur-mer on the Côte d'Opale and Calais), which they rapidly converted into a 60-bed unit. It was the first women-run medical unit sanctioned by the army.

Endell Street Hospital

Early in 1915 Murray and Anderson were summoned to the War Office, where Sir Alfred Keogh, head of the Royal Army Medical Corps (RAMC), invited them to run a major military hospital in central London. After closing their units in France, they set about the task with alacrity. The War Office gave them the former St Giles Union Workhouse on Endell Street in Covent Garden, which they transformed into a 573-bed hospital staffed entirely by women, mainly suffragettes, from chief surgeon to orderlies. The hospital also employed women as drivers, dentists, pathologists, and surgeons. One such surgeon was Mrs Lilian Marie Wemyss Grant who worked at Endell Street as an Assistant Surgeon before going as Medical Officer in 1918 to HM Factory, Gretna (Britain's largest cordite factory). Most of the hospital equipment came from the existing military hospital in Wimereux.

'In March, the women were given a five-storey former workhouse in Endell Street, Covent Garden, filled with debris and broken furniture. Electric lighting, lifts and cooking facilities had to be installed and everywhere cleared, deep cleaned and painted. It was 'indescribable chaos', wrote Flora Murray. Yet despite the support of the army's top doctor, they still met with hostility and obstruction from the War Office. When they arrived to inspect the site, they were greeted by an RAMC colonel who blurted: 'Good God! Women!' After weeks of dilatory progress, Murray and Anderson insisted on taking charge of conversion works themselves. They recruited 180 staff, including 14 doctors, 29 trained nurses and more than 80 orderlies – all women – while the RAMC supplied 20 men (later reduced to six).

The Endell Street hospital was officially established as a RAMC hospital under the War Office in May 1915 by Murray and Anderson. While working under the War Office, the women doctors received the pay and benefits of commissioned officer grades from lieutenant to lieutenant colonel, but they had no rank and could not order men around.

By early May Endell Street Military Hospital had 17 wards, an operating theatre and an X-ray room, as well as a theatre and a library with 5,000 books. The women's experience in France told them that psychological trauma meant that their patients were 'more wounded in their minds than in their bodies', Murray and Anderson ensured the wards were homely and cheerful, with bright bedding and fresh flowers. The bleak exercise yard was turned into a tranquil green oasis. Flowers, bright colours, and proper lighting – all of which contrasted with the typical drabness of military hospitals – were testament to the women's all-important inclination to take into consideration the patients' psychological health as well as their physical injuries. The first wounded arrived on 12 May, two weeks earlier than expected.

The hospital adopted the motto, "Deeds not words", which was, of course, also the motto of the WSPU.

Librarians and entertainment officers visited with the patients to raise morale. Gardeners helped in the courtyard and staff without any family or friends at the hospital spent time with lonely patients.

A number of auxiliary Voluntary Aid Detachment hospitals with a total of 150 beds were attached to the Endell Street hospital. When the pressure was really on, when billeting of convalescent men was allowed, the number of registered patients was as high as 800. Endell Street Hospital cared for some 26,000 patients during the five years it was operational. On average the women surgeons performed some twenty operations per day during that time. Sometimes as many as 80 injured soldiers would arrive each night.

Of the 26,000 patients who passed through the wards of Endell Street Military Hospital, the vast majority were British with a significant number from the Dominions and Colonies. There were 2,207 Canadians, 2,000 Australian and New Zealand patients, including those wounded in the Gallipoli campaign who began arriving in August 1915. In addition there were 200 US troops; a few Russian, Greek, Japanese, and French wounded were patients at the hospital. A small ward for service women was opened late in the hospital's life and satellite hospitals included Dollis Hill House Auxiliary Hospital which opened in 1916.

Endell Street stayed open throughout the war, treating those 26,000 patients. Moore concludes by telling how 'the hospital 'manned by women' was hailed a triumph by the press and described by its patients as the 'best' in London. Its doctors performed more than 7,000 major operations and pioneered medical advances in trauma surgery. When the war ended Endell Street stayed open for a further year, treating the victims of the influenza pandemic. It finally closed its doors in late 1919'.

'A key feminist organization of the First War, the WHC has largely been forgotten, partly because of its relatively small size and partly because of its anomalous status as a female-run hospital under the direct patronage of the War Office.'(Jennian F. Geddes).

Scottish Women's Hospitals for Foreign Services[6]

Founded by the extraordinary Dr Elsie Maud Inglis, who was a suffragette and one of Britain's earliest qualified female medical doctors. Her idea was for the Scottish Suffrage Societies to fund and staff a medical hospital as part of a wider suffrage effort from the Scottish Federation of the National Union of Women's Suffrage Societies and funded by private donations, fundraising of local societies, the National Union of Women's Suffrage Societies and the American Red Cross. As we know, the British military authorities (in)famously told her to "Go home and sit still". Not to be deterred by such oafish arrogance, Inglis just got on with it. By the end of August 1914 they had raised more than £5,000; like the Women's Hospital

Corps the Scottish Women's Hospitals offered opportunities for medical women who were denied entry into the Royal Army Medical Corps.

The National Union of Women's Suffrage Societies sent nurses to Russia, under the name of the Millicent Fawcett Units, after its president. They opened a maternity unit in Petrograd: ' a veritable haven of helpfulness to the distressed refugee mothers (Fraser, p 26). Next, the unit established a Children's Hospital for Infectious Diseases at Kazan on the Volga fighting diphtheria and scarlet fever: 'they succeeded in saving most of the children, who would certainly have died in their miserable homes'. That summer they took over a small doctorless hospital at Stara Chilnce treating refugees and peasants. A holiday home was opened in Suida to take convalescents from the Petrograd Maternity Hospital. Finally they opened an Infectious Disease hospital for soldiers and peasants in Volhnia, some 60 miles behind the front line in Galicia.

The first Scottish Women's Hospital was staffed, equipped and established at Calais to support the Belgian Army in November 1914. In December 1914, Vicomtesse de la Panouse, wife of the French military attaché to the French embassy in London helped the group fill another location at the ancient Royaumont Abbey with 200 beds, after which it became known as Scottish Women's Hospital at Royaumont, officially called Hôpital Auxiliaire 301. By December a second hospital was based there. It remained operational throughout the war and treated French wounded under the direction of the French Red Cross. Further hospitals were opened at Troyes (Château de Chanteloup, Sainte-Savine) and Villers-Cotterets along with the popular and supportive canteens at Creil, Soissons and Crepy-en-Valois.

Also in December, a hospital team led by Dr Eleanor Soltau was dispatched to Serbia. Other units quickly followed them and Serbia soon had four hospitals working night and day. The conditions in Serbia were dire. The Serbian army had a mere 300 doctors to serve more than half a million men, and in addition to the numerous battle casualties the hospital had to deal with a typhus epidemic that tore through the military and civilian populations. Serbia had fought a successful military campaign against the invading Austrians but the battling had brought the nation almost to its knees. Both soldiers and civilians were half starved and exhausted and in those conditions diseases thrived and hundreds of thousands perished. Four SWH staff, Louisa Jordan, Madge Fraser, Augusta Minshull and Bessie Sutherland died during the epidemicic; Jordan and Fraser are buried in Niš Commonwealth Military Cemetery. By the winter of 1915 Serbia could hold out no longer. The Austrians had been reinforced by German and Bulgarian forces who invaded again, and the Serbs were forced to retreat into Albania.

From December 1914 to November 1915 the hospital was based in Kragujevac.

In April 1915, Dr Inglis was in charge of unit based in Serbia. Within seven months of mobilising, the SWH were attending 1,000 beds with 250 staff which included 19 female doctors working with each of the Allied armies, except the British.

The SWH staff had a choice: stay and be taken prisoner (and worse), or go with the retreating army into Albania. In the end some stayed and some went. Elsie Inglis, Evelina Haverfield, Alice Hutchison, Helen MacDougall and others were taken prisoner and were eventually repatriated to Britain. The others joined the Serbian army and government in its retreat and suffered the indescribable horrors that involved, sharing in the hardships endured by the Serbian army. The SWH went on to set up a convalescent hospital in Corsica in December 1915 to help displaced Serb women and children.

About the same time, the mobile hospital at Troyes in France was ordered to pack up and was attached to a division of the French army and dispatched to Salonika in Greece as part of a belated move by the allies to provide practical assistance to the beleaguered Serbs. The hospital (known as the Girton & Newnham Unit after the Cambridge University women's colleges which funded it) was established in a disused silkworm factory in the border town of Gevgelia, though it soon had to be relocated to Salonika when threatened by the rapid Bulgarian advance. Much of the work at Salonika was spent fighting malaria. It was joined there in August 1916 by the Ostrovo Unit or the American Unit 90 miles north–west of Salonika at Lake Ostrovo (now Lake Vegoritida in Greece), and supported the Serbian Army's retreat into its homeland. A Transport Column was also despatched to Ostrovo - this was a motor ambulance unit which allowed SWH to collect casualties quickly rather than wait for casualties to be brought to them, and included volunteer women motor ambulance drivers like Elsie Cameron Corbett.

Dr Inglis was taken prisoner of war and repatriated. She immediately moved with another unit to Russia. Evacuated home after the revolution there, she died in Newcastle on the day after her return in November 1917. The NHS Louisa Jordan Hospital in Glasgow is named after one of the SWH nurses who died in Serbia.

By 1918 there were fourteen SWH units, across mainland France and Corsica, Malta, Romania, Russia, Salonika and Serbia. Over 1,000 women from various backgrounds and many different countries served with the SWH. Only medical professionals such as doctors, nurses, laboratory technicians and radiographers received a salary and expenses; while non-medical staff such as orderlies, administrators, drivers, cooks and others were not paid at all and were in fact expected to pay their own way. Why did they join? For some women it was one of the few opportunities open to women to help the war effort; others saw it as a rare chance for adventure and freedom in a world that up till then offered women very few life chances; and all shared, with varying degrees, the desire to improve the lot of women both universally and generally. Over £500,000 was raised to fund the organisation and during the war hundreds of thousands of patients' lives were saved, all nursed and helped by the SWH.

Dr Helena Rosa Wright (17 September 1887 – 21 March 1982)

Elsie Inglis was by no means the only gifted woman medical practitioner who struggled to be recognised as the asset she so clearly was by the authorities.

Dr Helena Rosa Wright was a pioneer and hugely influential figure in birth control and family planning both in Britain and internationally. She was a renowned educator and an avid campaigner for government funded family planning services. She was the author of several books and training guides on birth control, sex education and sex therapy.

From 1908 she attended the London Royal Free Hospital School of Medicine for Women in Bloomsbury, London winning a MRCS (Eng.) and LRCP (Lond.) in 1914 and MB, BS (Lond.) in 1915. Later that year she started work in the outpatients department of Hampstead General Hospital in Camden Town, later transferring to the main hospital in Haverstock Hill as house surgeon. However, having been reported to the police due to her foreign name (her maiden name was Loewenfeld, after her father, a Silesian refugee) she had to resign her job at the hospital in May 1915. After a short break she took up an appointment as a house surgeon at the Hospital for Sick Children, Great Ormond Street. Meanwhile, she was active in the Student Christian Movement and was a member of the London Inter-Faculty Christian Union and had declared herself a pacifist. Her beliefs prevented her from joining the Royal Army Medical Corps but she worked as a civilian junior surgeon under military supervision at the Bethnal Green Hospital. With her husband she spent five years as a missionary in China, where in October 1921 she fulfilled her ambition by taking up the position of associate professor of gynaecology at the Shandong Christian University.

Before the 1907 Territorial and Reserve Forces Act, Britain had no national medical or nursing service devoted to the care of the volunteer army, the Reservists. The regular army had been supported by the Army Medical Service, together with Queen Alexandra's Imperial Military Nursing Service, which employed fewer than 300 nurses to provide nursing care in military hospitals at home and abroad. The Act made provision for both medical and nursing support to be available to the volunteers for the first time. Lord Haldane initiated the *Territorial Force Nursing Service* in March 1908, when he invited twelve women to form a Territorial Nursing Council; six were society ladies, including his sister Elizabeth, and the other six were eminent London matrons. The new Matron-in-Chief of the service was Sidney Browne, who had retired from a similar position in QAIMNS in 1906, and the group met for the first time at the War Office on 16 June 1908 to discuss the steps to be taken to form a nursing service for the Territorial Force.

The Territorial Force Nursing Service (TFNS)

At the start of the war, the provision for territorial force hospitals in towns and cities in the UK was 23, each with accommodation for 520 patients and a staff of 91 trained nurses. To qualify for appointment as a sister or staff nurse in the TFNS, the stipulation was for candidates to be over 23 years of age and must have completed three years training in a recognised hospital or infirmary. However, at the time women rarely began their nurse training before the age of 23 so the actual average age at joining was much higher.

To make matters worse, there was a chronic shortage of fully trained nurses, and, bizarrely, until about 1910 some members of the Army Nursing Board were implacably opposed to recruiting from the staff of civilian hospitals in peacetime. Nevertheless, in July 1908 the TFNS was inaugurated, draft proposals were published, and the enrolment of staff for the 23 hospitals was set in motion. By March 1909 all four Scottish hospitals and 11 in England were up to establishment, and only London had made no early move to staff its hospitals but after a crucial meeting on March 15th 1909, the 400 nurses required were quickly recruited.

The nurses who joined the TFNS would get neither pay nor special training during peacetime in return for their selfless commitment. On 1 January each year they were required to commit themselves further and declare their intention to serve on, while continuing in their second jobs in civilian hospitals and private homes: it was taken for granted that the high quality of their training, and their continued employment within the nursing profession would easily qualify them for military nursing without further training. They each received a silver service badge, though, but other items of uniform which were not compulsory during peacetime were bought at their own expense.

http://www.scarletfinders.co.uk/92.htmlScarlet Finders tells how in 1913 the TFNS was given permission for its members to volunteer for overseas service if not required for duty at home; this was termed the "Imperial Service Obligation", and at the outbreak of war there were 2,117 members of the service ready for mobilisation. They could also serve overseas under the British Red Cross or other organisations approved by the Foreign Office. No hospital could have more than twelve members who had agreed to these conditions. Of the more than 8,100 members who served in World War I, some 2,280 did serve overseas.

Most members, though, spent their wartime service in the United Kingdom, not only in the 23 territorial hospitals, but also in hundreds of auxiliary units throughout the British Isles. Soon they were also employed in the eighteen territorial hospitals abroad, and alongside their QAIMNS colleagues in military hospitals and casualty clearing stations in France, Belgium, Malta, Salonika, Gibraltar, Egypt, Mesopotamia and East Africa.

Of the 23 UK territorial force hospitals, nineteen were open and receiving casualties by the end of August 1914, with the other four opening by the end of September. The website www.scarletfinders.co.uk tell us that 'The number of nurses in every field of the profession increased rapidly during the first six months of war, and continued to rise throughout the next four years. Although traditionally, military nurses were required to be either single or widowed with no dependents, during wartime the extreme shortage of trained nurses meant that married women were welcomed into the TFNS, and if a serving nurse wished to marry, permission was normally granted for her to remain in the service. However, in 1920 all married women were required to resign, and the service reverted to single women only: what was expedient in war was not deemed appropriate for peacetime nursing'.

Women nurses, physiotherapists & doctors

The figures for the actual number of women who served as trained members of the TFNS varies with different sources; for example, the figure given by Ian Hay is 7,117, of whom 2,280 served overseas, while Elizabeth Haldane gives a figure of 8,140 women who were part of the wartime TFNS, with the same number (2,280) serving abroad[7]. In October 1918, just before the Armistice, there were 3,095 trained nurses of the service in military hospitals in the United Kingdom, with 1,964 in overseas stations.

The First Aid Nursing Yeomanry (Princess Royal's Volunteer Corps) (FANY (PRVC))

My idea was that each member of this Corps would receive, in addition to a thorough training in First Aid, a drilling in cavalry movements, signalling and camp work, so that nurses could ride onto the battlefield to attend to the wounded who might otherwise have been left to a slow death."

– Captain Edward Baker 1910

An all-female registered charity was formed in 1907 and was active in the seemingly incompatible activities of both nursing and undercover intelligence work during the World Wars. Its members wore a military-style uniform, but it was not part of the Regular Army or Army Reserve; officer members were not eligible for Sandhurst, nor did they hold a commission.

FANY was formed as the First Aid Nursing Yeomanry in 1907 as a first aid link between the field hospitals and the front lines, and got its 'yeomanry' name as its members were originally mounted on horseback. FANY was started in 1909 by Edward Baker, and was re-organized with its aim directly laid down in 1910 by Mrs. McDougall (then Miss Ashley Smith). When first founded the women enrolled wore scarlet tunics with white braid facings, and navy blue skirts with white braid round the hem. They had lessons in side-saddle riding and elementary instruction in stretcher drill and bandaging. The Membership was over one hundred in August 1909, but in January 1910 it had crashed to seven or eight active members. In February 1910 astride-riding was made compulsory, and drills were held once a week, with alternate drills in stretcher work and horsemanship.

REPORT ON THE WORK AND ORGANIZATION OF THE FIRST AID NURSING YEOMANRY, TO 1ST NOVEMBER 1917, Imperial War Museum, Women's Work Collection:

A training regime was established: the objective of the Corps was to assist the Royal Army Medical Corps by providing mounted detachments with horse ambulance wagons, to take over wounded at Clearing Hospitals or Dressing Stations and convoy them to Base Hospitals or to the nearest railhead. For this work members were trained to move, feed and tend patients in a skilled manner, and to prepare sheds, tents or any available buildings as temporary hospitals. The training was carried out under R.A.M.C. instructions and trained nurses and members received a thorough grounding in stretcher drill, moving patients, improvising and applying splints, and in bandaging and cooking.

Baker, a veteran of the Sudan Campaign and the Second Boer War, saw the need to improve the way wounded soldiers were removed from the battlefield and transported to a field hospital; he knew that an individual rider could get to a wounded soldier faster than a horse-drawn ambulance. Baker also knew that speed saved lives. The first contingent included his daughter, Katy.

Each woman was trained not only in first aid but signalling and drilling in cavalry manoeuvres. There were further stipulations: a 5'3" minimum height bar, 17-35 age window, joining up for twelve months and attending drills as required. The enrolment fee was 10/- for ordinary members; Riding School and Headquarters 6/- per month. Members must be prepared to turn out for active service at 24hrs notice unless they have joined for Home service only. Add to that the disappointment that the British high command would not countenance the deployment of women on the front line.

All did not go smoothly at first; the website continues:

In 1910 a discontented group, led by Mabel St Clair Stobart, broke away from the FANY to form the *Women's Sick and Wounded Convoy*. Flora Sandes, who was later to be the first female member of the Serbian Army, was one of these. In 1912 the WS&W Convoy went to Serbia in the 1st Balkan War. Baker soon after disappeared from the scene, and the Corps came under the control of two determined and distinguished women, Lilian Franklin and Grace Ashley-Smith. They transformed the FANY, acquiring a horse-drawn ambulance; replacing the elaborate uniform with more practical khaki; introducing astride riding (and divided skirts); making the all-important contacts within the British military that were to prove vital to their success in 1914. Although often subjected to scorn and hostility from the wider general public, they succeeded in gaining support from the Brigade of Guards, the Royal Army Medical Corps (RAMC) and the Surrey Yeomanry, all of whom helped to train them at their annual camps.

As noted, the original uniform gradually became more practical and less flamboyant, including, importantly, a divided skirt to allow public riding astride their horses.

When their offer to assist as front line paramedics was refused by the War Office Mrs. McDougall crossed to Antwerp early in September 1914 to offer the services of the Corps to the Belgian Army who asked her to work at the Belgian Field Hospital, and later to go out as interpreter with a motor ambulance from the

Antwerp Red Cross to bring in wounded from the English Naval Division. The Belgian Red Cross of Antwerp first offered a Convalescent Home in Avenue Marie Thérèse, and later commissioned Mrs. McDougall to staff a hospital of 300 beds in the Rue des Retranchments with FANY. The bombardment prevented this.

Not to be deterred, a party of six FANYs, including Lieutenants Franklin and McDougall, plus three trained nurses and two male orderlies, crossed over to Calais on October 27 with a few cases of bandages and hospital stores to drive ambulances for the Belgians and the French. They were soon followed by a privately funded motor ambulance. The Belgian Army welcomed them: their first deployment was in an Antwerp hospital, and for the next two years the FANYs were busy driving ambulances, opening a hospital and two convalescent homes and setting up a casualty clearing station near the Front.

There were hundreds of Belgian wounded from the Yser, arriving in Calais and just dumped on the docks getting little care and exposed to the elements. General Clooten, who commanded the Belgian troops, at once arranged with the Belgian Surgeon-General that the FANY should take over two dilapidated convent schools full of wounded on the Rue de la Rivière opposite Notre Dame in Paris and called Lamarck Military Hospital. Other members came over to help get it up and running; bedding was sent by other friends at home. They turned the ruined schools into a 100-bedded hospital, and nursed typhoid cases and wounded alike. There were many difficulties, and no means of obtaining beds or sheets or basins. The staff themselves slept in a box-room and in billets in the town. Gradually the FANY collected their funds (£12), dressings, beds and various comforts.

More wounded soldiers continued to pour in even before it was fully equipped and supplied. In November 1914 the two 'Women of Pervyse', Mairi Chisholm and Elsie Knocker (later Baroness de T'Serclaes) drove their motor ambulance through the ruins of Pervyse in west Flanders and set up a first aid post and soup kitchen, the Pervyse Post de Secours Anglais, the first of many during the war. They had to leave Pervyse when the front moved. Knocker and Chisholm returned to Pervyse when the front moved again and remained there until March 1918 when both suffered from the effects of a gas attack[7].

Rachel Hosie, *British 'angels' who braved WW1 trenches* (2014) - tells us that:

> The two women set up their first aid post in autumn 1914. Their run-down cellar house, Le Poste de Secours Anglais, as it became known, was just metres away from the Belgian frontline... The two women lived in treacherous conditions. They had to move twice because houses were destroyed, they had no running water, no bathroom and only basic food like tinned tomatoes and sardines...As well as their medical work, Mairi and Elsie were a constant presence on the frontline, often handing out hot cocoa and soup to the grateful Belgian soldiers.

When General Clooten asked Mrs McDougall to go down and report on the conditions prevailing at the Camp du Ruchard, the new camp for Belgian convalescents, she found the conditions there atrocious: the men were badly housed and living in mud.

There were about 700 convalescents, many of whom were epileptic or insane. Tea, chocolate and coffee were sold at 5 centimes, or one halfpenny the cup, and cake for 10 centimes each. Chocolate, soap and biscuits were sold also. English lessons were arranged for, and newspapers, magazines and writing paper were distributed. A piano was hired from Tours, and a gramophone, bagatelle-boards and games of all kinds were provided. A trained nurse was paid by the F.A.N.Y. to nurse the consumptives, of whom there were several hundred, and to supervise the distribution of Benger's food and other additions to the hospital rations...In 1916 a cinematograph was added and proved a great success. This was purchased chiefly with a large sum sent form the citizens of Aberdeen for the F.A.N.Y. work. Miss Crockett and Miss Walker have now gone with the insane and epileptics to the new hospitals at Soligny-la-Trappe to carry on their work of devotion.

Around May 1915 the FANY became a unit of the Anglo-French Hospitals Committee of the British Red Cross Society. The website describes how:

'The wartime *FANY Gazettes* recount the primitive conditions in which they cheerfully lived and worked; Zeppelin bombing raids; supply trips to the Front; evacuating the wounded under fire; facing death and disease with equanimity; battles with bureaucracy. One describes how in the second chlorine gas attack in May 1915, they doused their sanitary towels in eau de cologne and held them over the faces of the British soldiers, because the men didn't have respirators in that early stage of the war.

In July 1915 Mrs McDougall asked the War Office in London to consider the employment of women drivers of the FANY for driving motor ambulances at any British base, thus freeing the men drivers for work further up the line. The retort was a 'curt negative' – 'It was not considered practical to employ women to drive for the British wounded in France.' However, on reflection, and after swallowing a large slice of humble pie, on 1 January 1916, the haughty War Office sanctioned the FANY to provide the first sixteen women to drive officially for the British Army, with the establishment of an ambulance section at Calais, replacing BRCS drivers. Their role was to transport the dead and dying from clearing stations to hospitals and hospital ships and the transport of all British sick and wounded in and around Calais – about 80,000 cases were carried during the first year. It increased from sixteen to thirty-six drivers and followed by the establishment of several convoys for the French Army, stationed in the southern sector of the Front, near Verdun.

Women nurses, physiotherapists & doctors

In 1915 a convoy had formed at the Hôpital le Passage in Calais, which became known as the Belgian Convoy. The FANYs were enrolled into the Belgian Army. In 1916, they took on the role of mechanics fixing their own motor ambulances and other vehicles; they set up regimental aid posts, motor kitchens and even a mobile bath vehicle which provided the luxury of a hot bath to 40 men per hour and a chance to get their clothes disinfected.

By the Armistice, the Corps had won numerous decorations for bravery, including seventeen Military Medals, one Legion d'Honneur, 27 Croix de Guerre and 11 Mentions in Despatches. Although a number of FANYs were injured while serving in France, there was only one fatality: Evelyn Fidgeon Shaw CdeG died while serving with the French and was buried by them with full military honours in Sézanne, in the Marne department and Grand Est region in north-eastern France[8]. The *Corps Gazette* mentions how one girl, Pat Waddell, lost a leg when hit by a train while driving an ambulance, yet returned to duty a few months later with an artificial leg.

The website, concludes this wonderful history:

In January 1918 a second British convoy was formed at St Omer. It was a joint FANY/VAD unit and for bravery under fire on 18th May 1918 became the most decorated women's unit of the war, 16 Military Medals and 3 Croix de Guerre[9].

The website concludes

In January 1918 a group of FANYs was sent to drive for the Michelham Convalescent Home in the south of France. They served there until 1919.

According to www.fany.org.uk.history 'In 1916, the FANY started to work officially for the French Army through the Société de Secours aux Blessés Militaires (SSBM). They agreed to take over a small hospital at Port a Binson, near Rheims, the FANY to supply drivers and nursing staff which required a vigorous whirl of fundraising. It was operational until January 1918. Further ambulance convoys were based at Amiens, Châlons-sur-Marne, Bar le Duc, Chateau-Thierry, Epernay, and Sézanne.'

The website continues: 'In September 1918 what was to become known as The Last Convoy left London. It arrived in Nancy just after the Armistice where the FANYs transported the thousands of returning refugees. FANYs from other convoys were variously assigned to duty in Strasbourg, Compiègne, Brussels, and Cologne[10].'

The Coffin Jump installation which can be seen at the Yorkshire Sculpture Park was inspired by the work of the FANY during the First World War.

Special Military Probationers

Special Military Probationers were women who had negligible formal training as nurses; they served more or less under the same conditions of service as Voluntary Aid Detachments and did similar work. However, they were recruited and employed by the War Office, and had no connection with the Joint War Committee of the British Red Cross Society and St. John of Jerusalem.

The British Women's Hospital, Richmond

According to a local website: In 1915 the Star & Garter hotel was purchased by the Auctioneers and Estate Agents' Institute for presentation to Queen Mary, as Patron of the British Red Cross Society, for use as a hospital for paralysed and permanently disabled soldiers and managed by the British Red Cross. It began life as such in January 1916, but the hotel building was soon found to be too small and generally unsuitable for its new role. It was finally demolished, in 1919, to make way for the present building – the Royal Star and Garter Home for Disabled Sailors, Soldiers and Airmen -which was opened in July 1924 by George V and Queen Mary. The home was principally paid for by the women of the British Empire, who adopted it as their war memorial.

The Munro Ambulance Corps

The Munro Ambulance Corps was initiated in August 1914 by Hector Munro (aka "Saki" (1870 - 1916) as a kind of flying ambulance service. He was one of the directors of the Medico-Psychological Clinic in London. The aim was to transport wounded troops from the battlefield to hospitals in Flanders under the auspices of the Belgian Red Cross. The corps comprised five women and five men, a few doctors, and two ambulances when it left for Belgium on 25 September heading for Ghent.

According to *The Great War in Stereoviews* -

> Despite the presence of gas lamps, the gas supply had ceased, resulting in night time operations by candlelight.
> The ambulance personnel made a number of hair-raising trips under fire to pick up wounded. The stereoviews of the ambulance corps at Furnes do not convey a sense of danger, but one of an ambulance riddled with shrapnel holes makes that point.

Women's Sick and Wounded Convoy Corps (WSWCC)[11]

The Women's Sick and Wounded Convoy Corps (WSWCC) was a British all women's medical organization established in 1910 by Mabel St Clair Stobart. Most of the early members came from the First Aid Nursing Yeomanry whom Stobart took with her after her falling out with the FANYs organisation: she had issues with the funding of the organisation and thought that it was not doing enough to champion women within the military. At the beginning there were fifty women. The training regime was a combination of traditional medical training, basic military skills such as signalling, and horse riding.

The WSWCC was organised into service companies under strict military orders. It was claimed that in case of war, a well-trained body of women could take to the field within twenty-four hours' notice, fully uniformed and equipped for hospital work. Riding, camp and hospital cooking, bicycling, home nursing, laundry work, signalling, and stretcher drill were all part of the training. Riding drills were held monthly. Particular attention was paid to the preparation of simple meals tailored for the sick and wounded. The training in every department was thorough and very modern for its time.

When Mabel St Clair Stobart went to further her cause, he said 'there was not work fitted for women in the sphere of war'. Stobart ignored him and sailed for Belgium where she set up a hospital for French and Belgian casualties under the Belgian Red Cross.

Mabel Annie St Clair Stobart (née Boulton; 1862 –1954) was a British suffragist and aid-worker. She and her all-women medical units served in the Balkan Wars between the Ottoman Empire and former territories of Bulgaria, Greece, Montenegro, and Serbia in October 1912. The British Red Cross Society (BRCS) had sent a team to the war zone, but purposely did not send any women, as the society deemed the conditions "quite unsuitable for women." Stobart thought otherwise and when she arrived in Sofia she received a positive response from the head of the Bulgarian Red Cross, but permission from the head of the military medical division was still required. Rather than hang about waiting for him, Stobart set off to the front to see him. After delivering an impassioned speech about the merits of British women, Stobart was granted permission for her unit to come and be "...near the front as possible".

Stobart cabled the news to the unit in England, with the result that three women doctors, six fully trained nurses, and four trained helpers, along with three cooks, set off for Sofia and were dispatched to the front lines near Kırklareli. The unit spent five weeks in the country, treating the wounded and sick until the armistice was signed in May 1913.

In August 1914 she and her team travelled to Belgium where they were arrested as spies, surrounded by soldiers who were ordered to cock rifles, fix bayonets, and shoot if they so much as moved or talked to each other. An hour later they were marched to a hotel, their luggage was searched revealing incriminating maps and a camera; they themselves were strip searched, before being led to the railway station at 5 p.m. escorted by eighteen members of the Garde Civique and six criminals, and loaded onto a dirty coal truck, which travelled till around 7 p.m., arriving in Tongres. Eventually, after a circuitous journey via Aachen, the unit was released and returned to London.

Later, Stobart was involved in Serbia where a typhus epidemic was ravaging the country causing the death of around 150,000 people including about half of Serbia's doctors. Stobart, along with several other medical units from the Red Cross, headed to the affected area. With the exception of a few men, all of the Serbian Relief Fund unit No. 3 were women.

The medical division of the Royal Serbian Army, in late September 1915, asked Stobart to run a frontline field hospital. Along with some doctors and nurses, sixty soldiers would be under her command. Appropriately for this position, she was given the rank of Major, which made her the first known woman to attain the rank of major in the world. The unit was named the First Serbian-English Field Hospital.

The war was not going well for Serbia in the autumn of 1915: Bulgaria had joined the war on the side of Serbia's enemies. During the retreat through neutral Albania well-over 250,000 soldiers died or were missing with no estimate on the number of civilian deaths. Stobart arrived at the front with her unit just before the start of the retreat and suffered little loss.

Ambulance trains and ambulance train nurses

One marvellous production which rolled out of York Carriage Works was the ambulance train made from existing carriage rolling stock; it comprised sixteen carriages and was known as '*Continental Ambulance Train Number 37*'. It was 890 feet 8 inches long and weighed 465 tons when loaded, without a locomotive. The pacifist Friends Ambulance Unit was originally founded as the 'Anglo-Belgian Ambulance Unit' by a group of Quakers at the start of the war in 1914. The unit went on to be composed of both Quakers and conscientious objectors as a way to make a contribution to alleviating the suffering of the wounded and operating under the banner of the British Red Cross. The trains were used to evacuate large numbers of injured soldiers, and over 1,000 men belonging to The Friends Ambulance Unit were sent to France and Belgium during the course of the war for this purpose.

Painted khaki, the train bore the Geneva Red Cross painted on the window panels and frames on each of the carriages on both sides.

Overall, the Ambulance Car could carry between 445 and 659 patients and staff, depending on how it was configured. Obviously, good ventilation, light and infection control were paramount; there were electric fans everywhere with extra ones for gassed patients. To promote hygiene, round corners were used and the toilets, wash rooms and treatment room all had concrete floors. The kitchen was floored with lead while other areas were covered in linoleum. A smooth ride was essential for the injured: to that end the train had bolster, side bearing and auxiliary springs on the four wheeled bogies which ran on 'patent cushioned wheels'.

In the early days of the war the first British ambulance trains were rudimentary, to say the least, consisting of French goods wagons with straw strewn on the floor. By August 1914 things started to improve when the Royal Army Medical Corps (RAMC) was given three locomotives, some goods wagons and carriages. These were converted and divided into three 'trains' comprising wards, surgical dressing rooms and dispensaries and were designated British Ambulance Trains 1, 2 and 3 respectively. During 1915 they carried 461,844 patients.

RAMC conversions continued up to train number 11. It was decided that a number of 'standard' trains should be built to War Office specifications by various British railway companies. In November 1914, the first specially built medical train

Women nurses, physiotherapists & doctors

was sent out from the UK designated number 12. No train was assigned number 13; the last to arrive in France was number 43. The movement of the injured from the trains soon became highly efficient: Boulogne was the main port for embarkation for the wounded and it is recorded that on one occasion it took only nineteen minutes to detrain 123 casualties. The main disembarkation points in the UK were Dover and Southampton. Over the course of the war, Dover dealt with 1,260,506 casualties, unloaded 4,076 boats and loaded 7, 781 ambulance trains. The patients were then sent by one of the twenty 'home standard' ambulance trains, or by an emergency ambulance train, to a receiving station, where they were transferred to road vehicles, usually by volunteer first aiders, which took them to their destination hospital.

York's *Number 37* was one of forty-two British Ambulance Trains pressed into service overseas, mainly on the Western Front but three were also deployed in Italy and one in Egypt. A further twenty-two saw action in the UK while the American Expeditionary Force used nineteen more conversions, including one being built in York, identical to *Number 37*, which was still unfinished when the armistice was signed. Before it left for the front, in 1917 *Number 37* was used for an exhibition which was attended by 36,404 people touring the train and raising £1,802, 5s for the Red Cross[12].

The tragedy and pathos of the circumstances surrounding the work on the ambulance trains is admirably captured by Phillip Gibbs of the *Daily Chronicle* after seeing an ambulance train near the village of Choques filling up with men suffering all manner of trauma. The first to board were thousands of "lightly wounded", he said, who "crowded the carriages, leaned out of the windows with their bandaged heads and arms, shouting at friends they saw in the other crowds. The spirit of victory, and of lucky escape, uplifted these lads...And now they were going home to bonny Scotland, with a wound that would take some time to heal". Next were stretcher cases "from which no laughter came". One young Londoner "was so smashed about the face", reported Gibbs, "that only his eyes were uncovered between the bandages, and they were glazed with the first film of death". Another young soldier "had his jaw blown clean away. A splendid boy of the Black Watch, was but a living trunk", he said, "both his arms and legs were shattered and would be one of those who go about in boxes on wheels". A group of blinded men, "were led to the train by wounded comrades, 'groping', very quiet, thinking of a life of darkness ahead of them..."

We get an equally harrowing picture of the practical difficulties of working on an ambulance train from the *Anonymous Diary of a Nursing Sister on the Western Front*:

> "October 25 couldn't write last night: the only thing was to try and forget it all. It has been an absolute hell of a journey – there is no other word for it. ...They were bleeding faster than we could cope with it; and the agony of getting them off the stretchers on to the top bunks is a thing to forget. A train of cattle trucks came in from Rouen with all the wounded as they were picked up without a spot

of dressing on any of their wounds, which were septic and full of straw and dirt. The matron, a medical officer, and some of them got hold of some dressings and went round doing what they could in the time, and others fed them. Then the [censored] – got their Amiens wounded into cattle trucks on mattresses, with Convent pillows, and has a twenty hours' journey with them in frightful smells and dirt ... they'd been travelling already for two days."

The Friends Ambulance Unit was disbanded from 1919 but hospital trains continued to be used in World War II and up until the end of the Cold War in 1991.

Canteens

Just as important from a morale-boosting and sustenance point of view was the provision of refreshments to the fighting troops in the form of canteens. The problem in 1914 was that there were none, apart from the *Canteen and Mess Society* which was a shambolic organisation tasked with setting up the *Expeditionary Forces Canteens (EFC)* as part of the Army Service Corps, which it did by early 1915 with one Ford motor car to serve between nearly half a million men. Huts were erected near the front lines serving ginger beer, coffee, tea, chocolate and cigarettes. Canteen staff doubled up as stretcher bearers. Further back rest houses and clubs were built with facilities which included laundries, clubs and mineral water vendors. Many of the staff were recruited from the WAACs, but only after they had passed an examination which included baffling, hilarious questions like:

What change, in English silver, would you give to a customer who spent 4.80 francs and tendered a Canadian one dollar note?

and

What quantities of the following articles are required to make an eight gallon urn of tea, and how many cups should it realise? a) Tea b) Sugar c) Milk

Some regiments set up their own canteens; for example, the men of the 6th Black Watch converted a dug-out into a cafe, which became a 'great draw' with three thousand eggs sold in its first week. Along with the YMCA, Catholic Women's League and Church Army, independent efforts like 'Miss Barbour's canteen' sprang up behind the lines, as mentioned in the the *Globe* newspaper, which reported: 'Miss Barbour has given of her means to make the fighting men happy. No praise can be too high for the work she is doing.' Further north in Boulogne, socialite Lady Angela Forbes unfolded a trestle table every night on the railway station platform to serve soldiers with tea and cake.

Soda fountain kiosks supplied from Egypt on camels sprang up in the Palestinian desert; an ice factory was established for the troops fighting around Salonika. In France the WAACS set up a printing press and ran off a magazine and canteen menus which included one in Urdu for the Indian soldiers. In Mesopotamia the canteen was on a steamboat which called in at Basra to collect uniforms for British army nurses made in the tailoring shop there. In December 1920, after the war had ended, the British

Women nurses, physiotherapists & doctors

Government established NAAFI by combining the Expeditionary Force Canteens (EFC) and the Navy and Army Canteen Board (NACB) to run the recreational establishments needed by the Armed Forces, and to sell goods to servicemen and their families. All in all, it would be a major source of employment for women in the interwar years and beyond, with them making up over half of the NAAFI workforce.

While the troops were being catered for, it seems that women were once again being left out in the cold and a pamphlet titled 'May we have huts too?' was published by the Young Women's Christian Association to launch their "National Appeal for £183,000 to provide clubs, huts and hostels for the army of 1,421,000 girl and women war workers". One of these war workers wrote:

> I have just returned from France, and I can say, without hesitation, there is no more urgent need at the moment than the provision of some club for these splendid women during their off duty time. The Y.W.C.A. Huts are not a luxury, they are an absolute necessity.

These clubs were intended to provide a

> "happy wholesome environment... with rest, recreational, and educational facilities, and social friendship, where girls may associate with their men friends under proper supervision". The leaflet includes comment on the effects of the war on women, including the suggestion that "girls are passing through a great transitionary period, and woman is either being made or marred by these new conditions"[13].

Combat Stress – the charity

This invaluable charitable organisation was set up in July 1919 soon after the Armistice with its first "recuperative home" opening on Putney Hill in 1920; its previous name was the *Ex-Servicemen's Welfare Society.* Currently, Combat Stress is supporting over 5,900 veterans aged from 19 to 97. Their treatment and support services are always free of charge. The website explains how:

Combat Stress is the leading service provider in the care of Veterans' mental health. We are able to deliver specialist, trauma-focused treatment and support to Ex-Service men and women whose problems are chronic, complex and long term. We also provide help and advice to their families. The founders of Combat Stress saw how thousands of servicemen from the First World War with severe mental health problems received little or no sympathy. Many men were suffering from shell-shock and were sent to mental war hospitals. Combat Stress changed attitudes to mental health. The charity's founders believed that veterans could be helped to cope with their mental health problems through a rehabilitation programme. In 1919 Combat Stress started occupational therapy including basket weaving[14].

Combat stress reaction, PTSD, shellshock, lunacy

Today, the condition we most usually associate with combat stress is post traumatic stress disorder (PTSD); it is no exaggeration to suppose that this has probably been a factor to some extent or another in the mental health of many veterans in every conflict there has ever been in history. The only problem is that, until recently, it has been rarely diagnosed and therefore more rarely treated.

But how many of the servicemen who have seen an episode of intense combat ever return to 'normal' life? The impact of disability through lost limbs and other physical trauma is life-changing and lifelong; it impacts not just the veteran but also the veteran's family and carers, changing their lives forever. But then there is also the psychological trauma: it may look as though the transition back to normality has been made with no ill effect but no one can know what is really going on in the mind and memory of many a returning soldier, sailor or airman. All former combatants feel some degree of fear or anxiety when in action; often in the field it resolves into aggressive, adrenalin-fuelled reaction - flight or fight - but extended periods of fear and anxiety can later elide into long term PTSD – post traumatic stress disorder or combat stress reaction. Call it what you will.

The significance of PTSD for this book, as already noted above, is that nurses and other medical workers behind the front lines, either in the rear or back in the UK, were themselves exposed to PTSD, albeit more surreptitiously than is usually the case for their combatant colleagues. Surgeons, doctors, nurses, orderlies, stretcher bearers, all witnessed close-up the atrocious, sickening injuries inflicted on the soldiery of all sides; all smelt the putrefying flesh and watched the gangrene or the gas slowly consuming their patients. Any number of combat soldiers, and other frontline personnel including medical and nursing staff, returning home from World War I may have suffered greatly but often silently from the horrors they had witnessed. Others still will have been emotionally and spiritually devastated after witnessing man's extreme cruelty to man.

In 1915, members of the British Army had been given the rather insensitive and less than compassionate order that:

Shell-shock and shell concussion cases should have the letter 'W' prefixed to the report of the casualty, if it were due to the enemy; in that case the patient would be entitled to rank as 'wounded' and to wear on his arm a 'wound stripe'. If, however, the man's breakdown did not follow a shell explosion, it was not thought to be 'due to the enemy', and he was to [be] labelled 'shell-shock' or 'S' (for sickness) and was not entitled to a wound stripe or a pension.

In World War I, shell shock (a label discouraged by the authorities) was not considered to be a psychiatric illness resulting from injury to the nerves during combat. The terrors of trench warfare translated into about 10% of the fighting soldiers being killed (compared to 4.5% during World War II) and the total proportion of troops who were killed or wounded was about 57%. As we have seen, whether a person with shell-shock was considered "wounded" or "sick" depended on the circumstances. When faced with a minority of soldiers mentally breaking

Women nurses, physiotherapists & doctors

down, there was a groundless suspicion that the problem lay in the character of the individual soldier, not because of what he experienced during the war. The fallacy that 'nerves' was just an excuse for 'funkiness' or cowardice prevailed.

In August 1916, Charles Myers was made Consulting Psychologist to the Army. He stressed that it was necessary to create special neurological centres near the front line using treatment based on the following PIE principles which were in place for the "not yet diagnosed nervous" (NYDN) cases:

- Proximity – treat the casualties close to the front and within sound of the fighting.
- Immediacy – treat them without delay and not wait until the wounded were all dealt with.
- Expectancy – ensure that everyone had the expectation of their return to the front after a rest and replenishment.

"But, because of the Adjutant-General's distrust of doctors, no patient could receive that specialist attention until Form AF 3436 had been sent off to the man's unit and filled in by his commanding officer." This pointless bureaucracy of course created significant delays, but it erroneously demonstrated that between 4-10% of shell-shock W cases were 'commotional' (due to physical causes), and the rest were 'emotional'. This put an end to shell-shock being notifiable as a valid disease, and it was abolished in September 1918. The 1916 Lunacy Act was the single statutory provision under which in 'appropriate circumstances' traumatised veterans could be locked up in asylums[15]. Moreover, once the special Neuroasthenic Centres were up and running, the associated research relating to causes of shellshock and the patients' backgrounds ensured that the British Medical Association had its own shock when, in the words of Lynn MacDonald (*Roses of No Man's Land* p. 231), they were struck by the exceedingly high incidence of breakdowns among the very men, who through training and a high degree of discipline, ought to have been able, in their view to withstand the stresses of battle and bombardment – the regular soldiers of the pre-war army...this gave lie to the theory, held by some, that discipline would prevent 'nerves', as well as cure them'. Others preferred to believe that it usually affected recruits from poorer backgrounds or from 'broken families' due to the death of one or both parents – as evidenced by gaps in the pay books where next-of-kin should be entered or entries indicating n.of k. as sibling, distant relative or even an orphanage – many believed that such 'instability of background' led to 'instability of character'.

In any event the symptoms were many and varied and ranged, according to MacDonald, from 'total paralysis and deaf-mutism to curvature of the spine! from violent hysteria to the type of debilitating nervous weakness, which many years later, would be known as 'battle fatigue'. Dodging bullets, shells, bombs and bayonets was exhausting work. To some extent, before the military authorities took over with their own brand of therapy, the nurse, VAD, doctor and surgeon had to deal with these cases.

In 1919 things got worse for the neurasthenic when the 1919 Mental Treatment Amendment Act ordained that 'all ex-servicemen confined in mental war hospitals under martial law, should be committed without right of appeal to asylums operated by the Ministry of Pensions'.

Obviously, this deterred many families from seeking help; it also exposed the fact that money was an issue here with 65,000 veterans claiming disability pensions for neurasthenia, 9,000 of whom remained hospitalised. The June 1922 Report of the War Office Committee of Inquiry into 'Shell Shock' tried in vain to right the wrongs[16]. What the committee did expose was the continuing scepticism, one example of which was the testimony that 'any soldier above the rank of corporal seemed possessed of too much dignity to become 'hysterical". So, shell shock, PTSD – whatever you want to call it – was believed by some to only affect the common soldier and not senior NCOs or officers and gentlemen. Astonishing, even in those times. As Claire Hilton says in the preface to her book, *Civilians, Lunacy and the First World War:*

> Asylum patients were low priority on the scale of social welfare, regarded as a burden on the economy and unable to contribute to the war effort. Standards of care and treatment fell, discharge rates plummeted, and death rates due to infectious diseases escalated far in excess of those in the community.

During the war, 306 British soldiers were executed for cowardice; many of whom were victims of shell shock. Eighty-eight years later on 7 November 2006, the Government of the United Kingdom gave all 306 a posthumous conditional pardon. The Shot at Dawn Memorial at the National Memorial Arboretum in Staffordshire commemorates these men.

One contemporary who had a special interest in combat stress, or neurasthenia as she called it, was writer Dorothy L. Sayers (1893 – 1957)[17]. Shell shock makes its debut with Lord Peter Wimsey in her first book *Whose Body?* The follow up, *Clouds of Witness*, exposes more shell shock. Her real life experience of the condition manifested in her relationship with her husband, 'Mac' Fleming who was gassed and presumably one of the two relatives she refers to in 1915 as having had a 'breakdown'; the press got hold of neurasthenia, mentioning it 367 times that year and then constantly until 1918 with demobilisation bringing more and more cases. It is, though, with *The Unpleasantness at the Bellona Club* (1928) that we get the most graphic account of a wife living with neurasthenia through the character of George Fentiman. The novel is set in the Bellona Club, a fictional London club for war veterans, named after the Roman goddess of war.

Chapter 4

Women working on the land: farms, forage & forests

The victory or defeat in this great War may be brought about in the cornfields and potato lands of Great Britain – President of the Board of Agriculture, 1916

Women's Land Army (WLA)[1]

"Come out of the towns and on to the downs, where a girl gets brown and strong; with swinging pace and morning face she does her work to song." – The Land Army Song

Women gardeners

Normally in society, only lower class women worked in gardens, employed as weeders and other menial, unskilled, poorly paid and often back-breaking, boring work. A breakthrough came when the Royal Botanic Gardens at Kew first employed female gardeners in 1896 - all of whom had qualified at the Horticultural College for Women in Swanley, Kent. Swanley was originally founded in 1889 as a men only college. However, by 1894 most of its students were women and in 1903 it became a women-only college; by 1918, Swanley was also offering its first courses in garden design. Indeed, the end of the 19th century witnessed an upsurge in interest in agriculture from educated women which led to the establishment by Daisy Greville, Countess of Warwick, of Studley College exclusively for women, and the Glynde School for Lady Gardeners. These compensated in part for the fact that places for women in the established agricultural and horticultural colleges were few and far between. Greville, in the Christmas 1897 edition of *The Land Magazine*, published a training regime scheme for women in the lighter branches of agriculture and gardening, primarily to create suitable forms of employment for middle-class women. She believed that "dairy work, market gardening, poultry-farming, bee-keeping, fruit growing, horticulture, [and the] grading, packing and marketing of produce, would appeal to many women of education…".

By 1910, there were seven colleges for aspiring women gardeners – mostly from the professional classes as the tuition and boarding fees, ranging between £60-100, were well beyond the means of the lower classes. In 1914, male gardeners at Kew and from gardens all across Britain left to join the Forces and women stepped in as Kew began to employ trained female gardeners from horticultural colleges and private gardening schools.

The enlightened Curator of the gardens at Kew, William Watson, rebuffed the predictable opposition to women gardeners: "the gaps must be filled or the gardens will cease to be." Watson further defended women gardeners, and those employed at Kew in particular, writing that "their enthusiasm, industry and efficiency are equal to those of the average young man. They work the same hours, and are paid the same wages as the men who have been engaged to keep the places of those who have enlisted."

These small, selective steps forward in the role of women in gardening were to prove invaluable when the need came for allotments and public spaces to be cultivated for the production of vegetables and fruits in wartime.

By December 1919, only six women gardeners remained at Kew, all of whom worked in the Flower Department. By the end of March 1922, the employment of women gardeners at Kew ended until the outbreak of World War II.

Britain's lack of preparedness in 1914

In 1915 a main plank of Germany's strategy to secure victory lay in starving Britain into surrender through a submarine blockade; Britain simply had to become much more self-sufficient in food. In 1914 Britain produced just 35% of the food it ate. Britain, with a predominantly urban population of 36 million, imported around 50% of the country's requirements, so when Germany successfully mounted counter naval blockades in 1915, the nation faced a cataclysmic problem. Prodigious quantities of grain used to come in from North America; mutton and lamb from New Zealand and Australia; beef from Argentina. The 13 April edition of *Farmer and Stock-Breeder* reported increases in imports of bacon, eggs, barley, oats, maize, and potatoes – of which over two million hundredweight used to be imported from Germany. Between 1846 and 1914 the total acreage of corn grown had shrunk by 25 per cent. Then in 1917, the harvest failed and Britain was left with just three weeks worth of food reserves. The prospect of famine and malnutrition loomed[2].

How did the WLA come about? The organisation had existed since 1899; in February 1916 it sent a deputation to meet the forward-looking Lord Selborne at the Ministry of Agriculture who agreed to fund a *Women's National Land Service Corps (WNLSC)* with a grant of £150. Smallholding advocate Louise Wilkins was to lead the new organisation which was to focus on recruiting women for emergency war work. They were tasked with boosting recruitment and providing propaganda about the good cause of women of all classes undertaking agricultural work. The new members of the organisation were not to become agricultural workers as such but to organise others in villages, for example, to do this work. This was the *Corps of Village Forewomen:* 'It is essential that women of the right type should be recruited at once…women who have knowledge of village life and country conditions. Selborne seemed to be the only man around who saw the writing on the wall. Prime Minister Asquith and the President of the Board of Trade, Walter Runciman, were still wedded to the 1903 Royal Commission on Agriculture which found that 'the country's dependence on imported food was not significant, and that there was little risk of a cessation of supplies'. Government intervention was not deemed necessary and it announced 'that it did not feel justified in giving farmers financial inducements to increase cereal acreage[3]. It was not until December 1916 that the Ministry of Food was set up.

By the end of 1916 the *Women's Farm and Garden Union* had recruited 2,000 volunteers, but they estimated that 40,000 were required. At the Women's National Land Service Corps's suggestion a Land Army was formed. The WNLSC continued to deal with recruitment and the network assisted in the launch of a "Land Army" - by April 2017 they had over 500 replies and 88 joined the new Land Army, where they became group leaders and supervisors.

The Government urged women to sign up to the WLA, which offered cheap female labour to farmers who traditionally were highly reluctant to employ women. Helen Fraser (p. 62) reports that 'the farmers were stiff to move in some cases and especially disliked the idea of having to train the women. "They weren't going to run after women all day – they had too much to do to go messing round with girls!' Women were something of a last resort as the first choice – soldiers - had other calls on their time and were often not always the experienced land workers they claimed to be. The second choice – prisoners of war - were equally unsuitable because the authorities foolishly did not feed them enough to endure an arduous 12 hour day. Whatever, over a quarter of a million women volunteers flocked to help.

In time the Land Army would take on 23,000 workers, who took the place of the 100,000 workers lost to the forces. The women were paid 18 shillings a week which could be increased to 20 shillings (one pound) if they were considered efficient.

January 1918 saw the publication of the first issue of *The Landswoman*, the official monthly magazine of the Women's Land Army and the Women's Institutes. Women who worked for the WLA were popularly known as Land Girls or Land Lassies.

Agnes Greatorex from Cardiff left her life in domestic service for the very different world of Green Farm in Ely, Cardiff. 'As part of the BBC's *All Our Lives* series in 1994 she went back to re-live the day she swapped the front parlour for the milking parlour. She said: "We had to get up at five in the morning for milking, and then we'd have to take it up to Glan Ely hospital. After that - especially during the winter - we'd have to muck-out the cow sheds. Then we might get half an hour for breakfast'. "I'd be out there picking up stones from the field or cutting hay, and I'd be as happy as a lark…When I became a Land Girl I thought that's it, I'm independent," she said[4].

WLA was not part of the army or even under the control of the War Office – it was funded and controlled by the Board of Agriculture and Fisheries – but, as an organised body supporting the war effort, it deserves its place in any consideration of the female fighting forces. In 1916 Meriel Talbot became director of the Women's Branch of the Board which was staffed entirely by women.

When the 250,000 women volunteers joined up they were given little more than some basic kit and orders to work hard: they were issued with shoes with leather gaiters to protect their trousers, broad hats and a badge, and for indoor jobs, heavy cotton coats. There were extras on offer: from boots at 25s to sou'westers at 2s. The recruitment posters though promised much more: 'God speed the plough and the woman who drives it'. WLA eventually employed 113,000 women; female labour then made up some one-third of all labour on the land, the remainder being a mix of enemy prisoners, Army Service Corps, infantry labour units and agricultural workers outside military age.

In February 1917, Germany intensified its submarine warfare which made matters much worse. Their campaign still hinged on starving Britain into surrender and, within a month, nearly 500,000 tonnes of Allied merchant shipping languished on the floors of various seas and oceans, along with their precious cargoes.

As stated above there was a lot of resistance to these women doing so-called men's work: here is an example of the sexism and misogyny characteristic of the day: a *London Telegraph* article published in May 1916 reported[5],

> 'At the Ryedale Agricultural Club, held at Helmsley [near York], yesterday, Mr. Hebron said he could not get women workers for love or money. Women labour on the land was a farce. They were simply out on spooning expeditions, trying to catch husbands. (Laughter.) Women's place was at home.'

A website reveals that some with conservative values were outraged by the Land Girls' uniform, viewing their trousers as disgraceful cross-dressing. In response, the government issued posters that celebrated the land women's patriotic efforts and feminized the new roles in an attempt to change public attitudes and allay concerns over the masculinisation of women. The bible of women's land working, the *Land Army Handbook,* was unequivocal: 'You are doing a man's work and so you're dressed rather like a man, but remember, just because you wear a smock and breeches, you should take care to act like a British girl who expects chivalry and respect from everyone she meets'. The self-appointed spokeswomen for the middle classes seemed rather more concerned that these land ladies did not ruin their hands: one pointed out an article in her old school magazine which bossily ran: 'You haven't got to ruin your hands, one good nail brush, one cake of soap, a pair of nail scissors, and a pot of Vaseline – I need not tell you how to use them - and the soldiers are sacrificing far more than their hands, aren't they'.

Those wanting to sign up for the Women's Land Army had to be over 20 years of age, and were required to submit references, complete paperwork that demonstrated their education and literacy, attend an interview, and pass a physical examination. If accepted, each Land Army Girl signed a six-month or one-year contract, agreeing to be sent anywhere in the country that she was needed. She was typically paid between 20 – 25 shillings a week, and charged 17 shillings/week for room and board. Not much change there then. *The Women's Land Army Handbook* required each recruit to pledge that she would "behave quietly," "secure eight hours' rest each night," "avoid entering the bar of a public house," "not smoke in public," and "never wear the uniform after work without her overall, nor walk about with her hands in her breeches pockets."

Girls were issued with a knee-length tunic or overall (that could be no more than 14 inches above the ground), breeches, a hat, coat, boots, and leather leggings. After thirty days of service, she was issued a green armband to denote her patriotic service, to which was added a stripe for every six months of work. Land Girls also received a LAAS (Land Army Agriculture Service) badge after two months and were eligible to earn good service ribbons and distinguished service bars.

Formal training was scarce and offered piecemeal, but Land Army recruits were encouraged to send for leaflets on such topics as the construction of pigsties, advice to beginners in bee-keeping, thatching, potato growing, cleanliness in the dairy, and ringworm in cattle. They worked nine to ten hours a day in all kinds of British weather, often six days a week, at wages significantly below those of women who were "doing their bit" in munitions or clerical work.

County War Agricultural Committees organised food economy lectures with the stalwart support of the Women's Institute who helped spread the word about pickling vegetables, bottling fruit; special economy recipes filled women's magazines, books and newspapers. In 1918 Dame Meriel Talbot could report that 12,637 Land Army members had been distributed as follows: 5,734 milkers, 293 tractor drivers, 3,791 field workers, 635 carters, 260 ploughwomen, 84 thatchers, 21 shepherds.

Notable members included the archaeologist Lily Chitty, one of the "pioneers in the mapping of archaeological data" who worked on the land in Shropshire; and the botanist Ethel Thomas (1876–1944) best known for her work on double fertilisation in flowering plants and as the first Briton to publish on the topic.

Dame Emilie Rose Macaulay, DBE (1881–1958) was an English writer, most noted for her award-winning novel *The Towers of Trebizond*. During World War I Macaulay also worked in the British Propaganda Department, after some time as a nurse and later as a civil servant in the War Office.

Women's Defence Relief Corps

Founded by Mrs Dawson Scott in September 1914, the corps was supported by the Board of Agriculture for a while, though it would be eclipsed by the more successful Women's Land Army. It also had a "semi-military" section that trained women in marksmanship and military drill for home defence purposes.

It expanded to two divisions: the civil section which focused on the original aim of women's employment and a "Semi-Military or good-citizen section". The latter division was a paramilitary unit of women who wanted to "defend not only herself, but also those dear to her". The semi-military section was set up after women were refused training by the official home defence units. The section drilled along military lines and trained women in marching, scouting and marksmanship.

The corps mobilised to carry out agricultural work in spring 1915 and would go on to play a key role in putting farmers in touch with casual female labour. The corps advertised the available posts as suitable vacation work for women and stipulated a minimum wage of 18 shillings per week. By 1916, the corps was sending out work teams totalling 465 women who focused on light agricultural work such as fruit picking, hop harvesting and hay making. By the end of 1916 the number of women in the corps had increased to 2,000.

The Women's Agricultural and Horticultural International Union (WAHIU)

The WAHIU was established in 1899 after a group of women who had attended the International Conference of Women Workers in London in July 1899 decided that they would like to stay in touch. Initially the society had 22 members, producing their first leaflet in 1900. The name was changed to The Women's Farm and Garden Union in 1910, and to the Women's Farm and Garden Association in 1921.

Women's Farm and Garden Union

The Times of 24 May 1916 reported on the annual meeting of the little known Women's Farm and Garden Union at Chelsea Hospital, London. According to the paper, the Union had a membership of about 500, the majority being women working their own land. The Museum of English Rural Life at Reading University reveals how in the following year the Women's Farm and Garden Union was taken over by the Board of Agriculture, and was subsumed into the Women's Land Army.

National Political League (NPL)

Formed in 1911, its main aim was to further social and political reforms on a non-party basis. Soon after the outbreak of war it established the Land Council and helped professional middle-class women (and men – especially disabled soldiers and sailors) to find suitable work on the land and to further other social reforms. Since the outbreak of war, 2,000 women had registered with the NPL.

The Women's National Land Service Corps (WNLSC)

The forerunner of today's *Working For Gardeners Association* was created in 1899; it has had various names including the *Women's Farm and Garden Society (WFGS)* and the *Women's Farm and Garden Union (WFGU)*. Its original objective was to improve the employment opportunities for women working on the land. During World War I, it created the Women's National Land Service Corps (WNLSC) in 1916 and by the end of the year, it had recruited 2,000 volunteers, mostly middle-class women from urban districts; the aim was that these women would be shining examples for rural women in local villages to emulate. They sought to recruit the 'right type of women' who 'would create a favourable impression on the farming community'. Candidates from outside London were interviewed by members of the Head Mistresses' Association. The WNLSC wanted 'young, strong, healthy, educated women fond of animals and outdoor life'.

Women's Forage Corps (WFC)

It could be said that in World War I the British army ran not on its stomach but on horse power; the prodigious demand for forage was incessant. While motorised transport gradually replaced the horse as the war progressed, equines nevertheless remained a primary mode of transport not least because four synchronised strong legs could negotiate the cloying mud better than any four wheels: when war broke out in 1914 the British army possessed only 25,000 horses; in 1917 the army had over 800,000 horses on active service.

Horses, not humans, were the first to be affected by rationing. A shortage of equines loomed in May 1917 so it was ordained that it was illegal to feed a horse on oats or grain without a licence while the Food Controller was drawing up a scale of rations. Nothing was allowed for horses who were kept for pleasure.

Lucy Betteridge-Dyson, in her November 2020 *Women and Horses in the First World War* tells us how 'With good access to the international horse market, the British Government spent approximately £67.5 million on horses and mules throughout the war and made it a priority to ensure that they were well cared for and returned to service where possible'. The British Army had over 70 veterinary hospitals across the Western Front, treating some 2.5 million horses of which 2 million were returned to duty. The success of the Army Veterinary Corps was reflected in the low average mortality rate for horses in the British Army of just 14%, which was a vast improvement on previous figures from the Boer War.

After an interview to confirm a base level of fitness and 'a good constitution', Women's Forage Corps recruits could choose between working in either agricultural, forage or timber-cutting sections.

The units of Women's Forage Corps (WFC) or Forage Corps (FC) were based at army camps and depots in the United Kingdom; working in gangs of six, its women assisted with hay-making, forage, checking bales on arrival at railway stations and supervising loading, stable work, driving horse carts, chaffing, wire-stretching, making and mending sacks and tarpaulin sheets. It also included Section Clerks for the related clerical work. Six Forage Department Companies were formed in

England, one in Scotland and one in Ireland. As trench warfare proliferated, local stocks of hay were quickly exhausted and supplies had to be sent from the UK.

It was largely drawn from women in service but also included some women of independent means with their own horses. They landed roles at the smaller depots such as those at Russley Park in Wiltshire, which became known as the Ladies Remount Depot. Russley was a convalescence depot for up to around 100 horses, mostly officers' chargers. These were fine horses which had been wounded or became ill at the front, and their time at Russley was spent in rehabilitation to prepare them for a return to service. Women working at Russley were specifically chosen for their knowledge of horses. From 6 January 1916 the depot received 365 horses and issued 308.

As Lucy Betteridge-Dyson says 'many animals perished during the conflict. 1917 on the Western Front proved to be the most dangerous time and place to be a horse in the World War I (excluding the East African Campaign which presented unique challenges) with over a quarter of animals seeing service killed or missing'.

Members earned an average of 26 to 30 shillings a week by 1919, drawing army rations and sometimes with a caravan (for messing rather than accommodation) and cook assigned to their gang. Their uniform consisted of gaiters, haversack, dark green breeches, hats and jerseys, khaki overcoat, overalls and black boots, with brass shoulder insignia of the initials "FC". Higher ranks wore a khaki tunic and shirt, shoulder rank badges, shoulder "FC" insignia and a brass badge showing "FC" within the eight-pointed star of the Royal Army Service Corps.

The WFC numbered 8,000 by 1917, though this had fallen to about 6,000 by 1919.

Women's Forestry Corps (also WFC)

In 1914 there were no records or statistics relating to timber reserves in Britain; the best we had was Ordnance Survey maps showing three million acres of woodland, although we did know that we imported eighty percent of our hardwood and ninety-five percent of softwood and that this, like foodstuffs, was at risk from German submarines.

The Women's Forestry Corps came under the aegis of the Timber Supply Department of the Board of Trade. Also known as *The Women's Timber Service,* it maintained a supply of wood for industrial and paper production at home and also for construction in all theatres of war. Trenches, of course, were shored up by timber, as were mines with pit props. Gun butts, cannon wheels, army bases, PoW camps, aircraft, telegraph poles, railway sleepers and shipbuilding all demanded wood. We know that the WFC recruited 200 women in Scotland – many worked alongside the women of the Canadian Forestry Corps who had been drafted in to help with the ratcheting up of home production in 1916. In 1917 the Timber Supplies Department was set up with graduate foresters running 182 sawmills. Many of the new timber girls were taken on by private estates; for example eleven

Women working on the land: farms, forage & forests

'ladyworkers' went to the Blair Atholl estate in March 1917. Lord Tullibardine reported that 'when they were not squabbling, they work well.'

Of course the work was more than just wielding an axe and sawing; about 370 women passed through the measurers' training camp at Wendover in Buckinghamshire (with a five percent drop-out); this involved felling and marking and was skilled work. Women recruits for this were largely teachers and senior bank clerks; many became fore(wo)men in charge of gangs of twenty or so. Cutters formed the largest category and within a month of joining they were competently felling trees.

It was by no means easy for the women on a number of levels. Volunteers often had to improvise outfits and trousers to make working outdoors feasible as well as finding suitable tools and equipment. Despite this the vital work that was done was picked up by national and local press who began to challenge the more stereotyped views of what women could and could not do. The trousers were an issue; young lumberjills (as they came to be known) reported feeling very self conscious as they faced the mockery of men who had never seen a woman wearing trousers before.

Of the 2,000 Women's Forestry Corps in 1918, 350 were measurers and forewomen and 1,500 loggers. By the armistice they had assessed, stripped and processed over 450,000 acres of woodland leaving British forests severely depleted with half the best timber felled. In 1919 the Acland Committee recommended a programme of afforestation and increasing the home production of timber. The Forestery Act was passed and, portentously, the Forestry Commission came into being to safeguard what was left in case of another war.

Flax

The University of Leeds undertook valuable research to minimise the debilitating effects of war on food supply and land use, not least in the cultivation of flax, the training of women and ex-servicemen who volunteered for farm work, and the support given to local allotments and training centres throughout Yorkshire.

Flax was a vital material in the manufacture of the aeroplane; consequently it emerged as a crucial weapon of war. Fibres from the flax plant were used to make linen which was stretched and treated with chemicals to construct the wings of aircraft.

Chapter 5

Other women's wartime organisations

The Women's Volunteer Reserve (WVR)

This organisation was established in December 1914 and was given impetus by the German fleet's shelling of Hartlepool, West Hartlepool, Whitby and Scarborough, and the deaths of civilians and destruction it caused. The WVR developed out of the earlier *Women's Emergency Corps* on the initiative of Decima Moore and the Hon. Evelina Haverfield – a militant and influential suffragette – who seized the opportunity provided by the crisis to carve out a role for women. The WVR was soon joined by many women from the more comfortable classes and was in the early days an unlikely mix of feminists and women who would not normally have associated with such 'dangerous types'. The women were trained to be signallers, despatch riders, telegraphists and drivers, as well as engaging in the more traditional roles of first aid and nursing.

The recruits were organised on military lines and expected to practice Swedish drill, fencing, study Morse code and semaphore, and practice on the rifle range[1]. They became involved in several ventures, not least of which was in providing a uniformed group called *the Lady Instructors Signals Company*, who trained Aldershot army recruits in signalling until 1918. However, the work was largely of a domestic, fund-raising nature. The WVR was rather expensive to join – recruits had to pay for their own khaki uniform which included a felt hat and was, at more than £2, well out of the reach of the average woman. The WVR had an influence in the establishment of the Women's Legion, which had a more widespread appeal.

Women's Auxiliary Force (WAF)

Launched in 1915 by Misses Walthall and Sparshott, the WAF was a uniformed voluntary organisation for part-time workers; WAFs worked in canteens and provided social clubs; they also worked on the land and in hospitals.

An organisation named the *Women's Agricultural Auxiliary Corps* also existed, but it is not known whether this was the same or part of the WAF or was entirely separate.

The Women's Legion (WL)

Launched in July 1915 by Edith Vane-Tempest-Stewart, the Marchioness of Londonderry, the Women's Legion became the largest organisation that could claim to be entirely voluntary. Although it was not formally under Government control or part of the army, its members adopted a military-style organisation and uniform. The WL volunteers became involved in a wide range of work, including agriculture, gardening, canteen work, cookery and motor transport. More than 40,000 women joined its forces. The success of the WL was a factor in influencing the Government on how to organise female labour in the latter half of the war. In February 1917 all 7,000 Women's Legion cooks and waitresses were transferred into the Women's Army Auxiliary Corps.

The A Street Near You website gives brief details of seven WL fatalities during the war; the youngest 18, the oldest 39.

Volunteer Motor Mobilisation Corps (VMMC)

One of a number of voluntary organisations which made their motor cars available to ferry disabled soldiers from ports and convoy trains from stations to hospitals, convalescent homes, rehabilitation centres and their homes. They were also on hand to take convalescent soldiers (mainly limbless) on days out, drives to the seaside, 'airings and entertainment' and the like. For example, their *Motor Squadron* was conveying an average of 12,654 casualties per annum. Overall, the VMMC benefitted over 100,000 convalescent soldiers at over 60 London hospitals from November 1914 (6,425 from St Bartholomew's alone).

Cars, of course, were still something of a rarity in 1914 and many of what there was would have been driven by men, but we do know that a number of lifts were provided by women owners and drivers. Other such organisations included *the London Volunteer Rifles* and the *National Motor Volunteers*. The latter had 30 Corps in fourteen counties using about 2,000 vehicles. Some Corps purchased motor ambulances and trailer ambulances at their own expense. The *National Motor Volunteers* were particularly active during air raids where they had hundreds of cars instantly available, conveying warnings, transporting casualties and evacuation work. It is estimated that the *NMV* alone covered over three million miles during the war.

The psychological and social impact on women

It was not just in the workplace that women were taken for granted or regarded as lower grade workers by unions and some employers. As we have seen, it is often forgotten that women were just as likely as combatant men to be the victims, often life-long victims, of war. From a largely male perspective, along with inanimate buildings and other infrastructure they make up much of war's societal collateral damage. Women are often left to pick up the pieces during and after war, sometimes literally. Women wait anxiously at home, always expecting the worst of bad news; for women, more often than not, their war is not over when the actual war ends. Where there is loss of husband, father, son or brother they are left to grieve and mourn and frequently to struggle on with their lives, often bringing up young fatherless children, often living desperately day to day without the male wage. Where the father-husband-serviceman comes home wounded or disabled to his land fit for heroes, the women may well have to spend their new lives as unpaid carers working without state support, tending limbless or otherwise traumatised ex-servicemen, coping with all the grinding physical and psychological issues long-term disabling injury brings. To some extent it has always been that way in war despite the worthy but empty promises that next time we will get it right; to some extent it still is the same today, as the aftermath of recent conflicts so clearly shows.

Teaching and academia

Despite it all, World War I did present employment and opportunities in the UK for long term career advancement for some, usually middle class and aristocratic, women. Teaching experience was easier to come by as was postgraduate research work in university cities: 'The woman teacher has invaded that stronghold of man in England, the Boys' High and Grammar Schools, and is doing good work there' (Fraser p. 39). Nevertheless, the career-routes for educated women were, unsurprisingly, more limited than those for men. Burman, *Gendering decryption*, p. 51 tells us that some ten years after the end of the war

> 'The vast majority (between half and three-quarters) of all female graduates in the 1930s became teachers. Continuing with academia was difficult, due to lack of funding, positions and the constant segregation and discrimination of women in the universities. Women often resigned when getting married, and the universities showed exceptional skill at making life difficult for those who did not. There are instances of women not being granted leave to give birth, on account of the fact that a man would never ask for leave for such a thing'.

Human biology was clearly not one of the strong points enjoyed by the composer of such nonsense. To a small degree, some women with scientific backgrounds suddenly found themselves unexpectedly in demand and were employed in medical and scientific laboratories and in engineering, particularly in munitions and explosives research. However, as Burman concludes:

Frequently, women were not allowed to use the laboratories, probably in order to make the courses impossible for women. At University College, London, one female student was barred from the chemistry course as women would be "scarred for life and have their clothes burnt off them as the men threw chemicals around", a statement combining fears of impropriety with stereotypes of male childishness and alleged female susceptibility to hysterics. At Cambridge, a similar prohibition was solved by Newnham College building their own laboratory, which was open to all female students. Not just practical reasons were given to exclude women from the sciences. In the case of mathematics, it was a widely-held opinion that women were incapable of the abstract thought required – *pace* Joan Clarke, while we know that several Wrens had university degrees, often in mathematics.

Deep-seated sexism in Oxford

The universities of Oxford and Cambridge were and are, of course, quite unrepresentative of the kind of education available to most students. Nevertheless, the shenanigans that were going on in the 1920s at Oxford reflect and are indicative of the state of play in the higher echelons of government, the civil service, law, medicine and the church with its ingrained nepotism, favouritism, exclusivity and sexism. As such they give us a good paradigm of the challenges a number of elite women still faced while trying to get on in this male dominated world, despite their ongoing achievements during the war. For educated women to progress in life and to realise their full potential at the highest levels they, of course, needed to be given the same opportunities to excel as their male colleagues.

Gilbert Murray, Regius Professor of Greek at Oxford, with all the power and prestige that eminent position brought, did his best to promote and champion the education of women in the days when female students were still denied the right to receive degrees. Among other things he chaired a meeting of the Oxford Society for Women's Suffrage when Vera Brittain was a member[2].

1919 Sex Disqualification (Removal Act)

The only consolation, for female students at least, was the passing in 1919 of the Sex Disqualification (Removal Act) which facilitated the admission of women to universities: hitherto women had only been allowed to attend lectures at Oxford under chaperone. It also permitted women to join the professions and professional bodies, to sit on juries and, whatever next?, to be awarded degrees. Marriage was no longer legally considered a bar to a woman's ability to work in these areas. The Act, nevertheless, was a compromise for a more radical private members' bill, the Women's Emancipation Bill. However, 1,159 women received their degrees at Oxford retrospectively in 1920-1921. The unfortunate women at Cambridge, however, had to wait until 1949 before they got their degrees. From 1922, women at Cambridge were awared "titles of degrees", but not the actual degrees.

In 1922, a Royal Commission sanctioned Cambridge's wish to remain predominantly male, and recommended that the number of female students should not be allowed to rise over 500, a tenth of the student body.

Seven years after the Act, male resentment was still very much in the air amidst the dreaming spires of Oxford: there was a debate about the introduction of a cap on the number of women accepted as undergraduates. The cap won and was set at 840 women in any intake, a mere sixth of total undergraduates. Frightening, given that a number of these lads went on to run the country in a time of war, and that, as Gilbert Murray pointed out, that these were women 'who certainly were more remarkable and interesting than the average of the men'.

The sexism and prejudice, of course, extended far beyond Oxford: Vera Brittain records how the generally industrious and courageous volunteers were avidly demonised, and how her return to Oxford terrified the authorities there:

> During the War tales of immorality among VADs, as among WAACS, had been consumed with voracious horror by readers at home; who knew in what cesspools of iniquity I had not wallowed? Who could calculate the awful extent to which I might corrupt the morals of my innocent juniors?[3]

Chapter 6

Women in Industry in World War I

Here is a summary of the other industries in which substantial numbers of women were employed, and in which they made a huge contribution to the war effort.

Shipbuilding

Shipbuilding is an interesting exception to Britain's typical intransigence in galvanising the war industries. German submarines were playing havoc with British merchant fleets who were bringing in cargoes of food and materiel to avoid starvation and mitigate ordnance shortages at the front. Between 4,000 and 5,000 merchantmen were sunk during the war. When it finally dawned on the Admiralty that it might be a good idea to replace some of these losses, the industry responded by permitting men to do work usually done by other trades and by allowing women to perform skilled work. Women could be found with the riveters, heating up the rivets and getting them to the riveters who drove them home; they were in the blacksmith's forge with the red hot iron, in the painting room, planing for the joiners, working screwing and boring machines, driving electric cranes and winches; shifting timber and iron, unpacking machine parts and unloading iron girders from trains.

Aircraft Manufacturing

The fledgling aircraft engineering industry could boast some household names at its inception: they include Geoffrey de Havilland at the Aircraft Manufacturing Company, later the Gloucestershire Aircraft Company in Cheltenham, and Frank Barnwell at the Bristol Aeroplane Company. Both firms employed women to meet demand; Bristol received an order for 50 fighter aircraft in the summer of 1916, followed by a top up order for 600. Typically, women were welcomed with some doubt and suspicion regarding their ability to do 'men's work' alongside men but, as usual, they acquitted themselves very well. Nevertheless, they were kept segregated and a separate canteen was built for them.

Women, however, developed a unique expertise in fuselages which required linen or flax to be stretched over the steel or wooden frames. To make them airtight and watertight they were treated, or 'doped', with a lacquer consisting of cellulose acetate imported from Basle in Switzerland and eventually Henri and Camille Dreyfus who ran the factory set up the British Cellulose and Chemical Manufacturing Co. in Derbyshire at the invitation of the War Office. Cellulose acetate, of course, is highly toxic and caused headaches, nausea and fatigue amongst the women workers in much the same way as the nitrocellulose used in the munitions afflicted the workers in that industry. Milk was prescribed but it proved quite useless.

Engineering

A good example of how women were determined to defeat the male, and official bias against them in industry, is their success in making inroads into the acute shortage of oxy-acetylene welders. Helen Fraser (pp. 42-43) tells how the London Society for Women's Suffrage, which was running the "Women's Service", had women volunteers for munitions in enormous numbers and tried to secure openings for them. It investigated and found that acetylene welders were badly needed. There were very few in Britain, although welding is essential for aircraft and other work, so they investigated if there were classes for training women, only to find that none of those in Technical Schools were open to women. One manager assured them that if women were trained satisfactorily in oxy-acetylene welding, he would give them a trial so the "Women's Service" decided to open a small workshop and secured Miss E.C. Woodward, a metal worker of long standing, as instructor. The school started with six pupils.

Fraser continues, adding that 'the first welders triumphantly passed their tests and gave every satisfaction in the factory, and the training went on and the School was enlarged. The oxy-acetylene welders turned out by this School went all over the country - 220 were trained and placed in the first year.

Other highly specialised engineering mastered by women included optical munitions and medical and surgical glass and X-ray tubes. Aeroplane propeller manufacturing also benefitted.

The Faculty of Technology at Leeds ran classes at the Central Technical School, Cockburn High School and at other schools to train women up to take in semi-skilled work at munitions factories. A former Leeds university student, May Sybil Burr (née Leslie), who graduated in 1906 became the chemist in charge of a munitions factory in Liverpool in 1916 and was awarded a doctorate by the University of Leeds for her research on explosives, which had included confidential wartime information.

Katharine (1859 – 1933) and Rachel Mary Parsons (1885–1956)

Katharine Parsons (née Bethell) was a founder member and second president of the Women's Engineering Society, and the first woman member of the North-east coast Institution of Engineers and Shipbuilders. In 1914, she married Charles Parsons, inventor of the steam turbine, who ran Parson's Engineering Works in Newcastle-upon-Tyne. Early in their marriage, Katharine would regularly accompany Charles on 7 am lake trials of his prototype torpedoes in Roundhay Park in Leeds. During World War I, Lady Parsons was heavily involved in managing the female workforces in Tyneside's converted armaments factories. She was critical of the removal of many women from such work under the terms of the Restoration of Pre-War Practices Act 1919; in a famous speech on 9 July 1919: 'Women's Work and Shipbuilding during the War', she deplored the way that women had been required to produce the 'implements of war and destruction' but then be denied 'the privilege of fashioning the munitions of peace.' Lady Parsons was also a co-founder of Atalanta Ltd, a company set up specifically to supply employment for women in engineering work.

Her pride in the factory girls' skills in precision engineering is palpable when she was able to report:

> Quite a large number of girls were able to set and grind their own tools, and a small proportion could set up their jobs from drawings. They could mill all the parts of the breech mechanism of howitzers, screwing the internal thread for the breech block, milling the interrupted screw and screwing the cone that fits into the breech block; milling firing pins and all the parts of gun sights...

Rachel Parsons, suffragette daughter of Katharine was one of the first three women to study Mechanical Sciences when she went up to Newnham College at Cambridge in 1910. Nevertheless, she was able to add theoretical knowledge to the practical skills she had already obtained at her father's factory. She went down in 1912 having taken the preliminary examination for Part I of the Tripos and a qualifying examination in Mechanical Sciences in 1911.

On the outbreak of war, she replaced her brother as a director at the Heaton Works of C. A. Parsons and Company in Newcastle-upon-Tyne where she oversaw the recruitment and training of women to replace the men who had left to join the armed forces. She became a leading member of the National Council of Women, and campaigned for equal access for all to technical schools and colleges, regardless of gender.

Rachel Mary went on to take a seat on the Parson's board and assumed a role in the training department at the Ministry of Munitions. She became a member of The Royal Institution of Great Britain in 1918.

The Northern Area Clothing Depot, Leeds and the Yorkshire shoddy works

Large parts of the textile factories were populated by women, girls and child workers; at the onset of war, women and girls were encouraged to knit and sew for victory – turning out socks and other items of warm clothing to make life a little more tolerable for the men in their cold, muddy and wet trenches. This extra demand for warming clothing caused by the war was increased further by the urgent need for uniforms, often met by the opening of special uniform distribution centres, again largely staffed by women and girls. The Northern Area Clothing Depot, for one, opened in Swinegate, Leeds in King's Mills, which the War Office had requisitioned and adapted for the "handling of pieces of khaki cloth and uniforms". By May 1915 more storage space was needed so the cattle market buildings in Gelderd Road were taken over to store cloth – up to nine million yards of it. Three million uniforms were also kept in another depot, belonging to the Aire and Calder Navigation. A Park Row premises saw 80,000 shirts inspected every week. All told, The Northern Area Clothing Depot patriotically produced 53 million shirts, 21 million pairs of army trousers, 8 million pairs of cavalry trousers, 10 million greatcoats, 24 million puttees, 89 million pairs of socks and 30 million pairs of boots. Apart from production and inspection, the depots also recycled uniforms and other clothing salvaged from battlefield casualties.

Before the Leeds depot opened the system for uniform manufacture and provision was cumbersome and inefficient, to say the least. Hitherto, cloth produced in northern mills was sent, by rail, all the way to the Central Army Clothing Depot in Pimlico, south London where it was checked and tested, and sent back to Yorkshire for making up. The new Leeds depot with its 150 staff revolutionised the process and answered the endless need for more and more khakis; it enabled cloth to be processed locally in a timely fashion. By the end of the war some 750,000 uniforms per week were passing through Leeds, some of which were produced by Edwin Woodhouse & Co. Ltd in Farsley.

Wool had to be available at the right time, in the right quantities and at the right price so the government took control of wool purchases. In 1918, according to the *Illustrated London News* the authorities ordered 95 million yards of cloth, 5 million yards of flannel, over 82 million items of hosiery, and 16 million blankets for processing through factories in Leeds, Shipley, Saltaire, and Keighley, Dewsbury, Batley, Heckmondwike, and Huddersfield[1]. In total the War Office bought 600 million lb. of British and colonial wool, costing £104 million.

Shoddy and mungo mixed with wool were the main constituents of uniforms and greatcoats. Workers, mainly women, were exposed with no protection to fibres and to fumes – a lethal slow burning cocktail of latent industrial disease which was just as deadly as a spell in the trenches or on the open battlefield[2].

Contemporary songs such as *Sister Susie's Sewing Shirts for Soldiers* would suggest that sewing for victory was work done in a cosy home by jolly girls and women on a trusty Singer sewing machine, just as if the rigours and privations of the Industrial Revolution had been nothing but a bad dream. In reality, sister Susie was confined in an airless, fluff fogged and cacophonous factory or workshop, lip reading in order to communicate with her colleagues hunched over their temperamental industrial Singers. There were many such sister Susies in and around Leeds. Arthur & Co, for example, employed 1,500 workers of whom 900 were women.

Montague Burton

Women were also very much in evidence in the factories operated by Burton's, which had been founded by Montague Burton in Chesterfield in 1904 under the name of The Cross-Tailoring Company.

By 1914 the number of Burton's shops increased to fourteen and their made-to-measure service was well on the way to becoming the largest in the world. World War I saw Burton's elevation to an official war contractor and a production change from suits to uniforms, clothing nearly 25% of the armed forces. Retail sales grew from £52,000 in 1915 to £150,000 in 1917 with a further £60,000 outstanding. In 1918 demob suits and bespoke suits were obviously very much in demand. In World War II Burton's were producing 25 percent of all British uniforms.

Uniforms and the demand for them are a natural by-product of war. Just as essential but perhaps less immediately obvious is the requirement for canvas bags, as explained in the Women's Factory Inspectorate Report 1915. The canvas bag factory was another instance of industrial development where 'women, girls and men have been employed in the making of nosebags for horses, engaged in sewing the bottoms to the bags'. Other products coming out of the factories included: khaki blankets, hosiery, fur coats, fur hats, shirts, boots and shoes, surgical dressings and bandages, stretchers, medical equipment, veterinary equipment, tin canisters and boxes for ammunition.

The china and earthenware trades

In 1914, 40 percent of workers in china and earthenware were women, 60 percent of whom were employed in and around Stoke. The war saw the number of women increase by 10 percent adding another 5,000 women to the workforce. Lead poisoning was an occupational hazard here, causing excessive cases of stillborn babies and gastric ulcers. It was not uncommon for women to hump loads of clay weighing up to 48 lbs. Girls under 18 were found by the Factory Inspectorate shifting barrows filled with up to 50 bricks at a time. Temperatures in the brickwork ranged from 108 to 120°.

The leather trades

In July 1914 there were 23,100 women employed in the leather trades producing, for example, saddles and reins, holsters and Sam Browns, rising to 43,000, one third of the workforce, by 1918 – most replaced men.

The chemical industries

The chemical industry in all its forms was undoubtedly the domain of men before the war with four times as many men as women employed. The women were confined to filling, labelling and finishing jars of or packets of chemicals.

The Royal Gunpowder Factory

The Royal Gunpowder Factory could boast over 3,000 women working at 'The Powder Mills' at Waltham Abbey during World War I[3]. During the war the percentage of women employees rose from 20 percent to 39 percent, making an increased total of 64,000 women, 34,000 of whom replaced men. Explosives were the main product although soaps and candles were also manufactured. Given the buoyant market, the factory grew quickly, turning out each new high explosive as it was formulated. Adjoining it to the west, an associated venture, the Explosives Loading Company, built a plant to fill bombs and shells in 1913. Both plants were high-tech state-of-the-art, with a power station, hydraulic mains and an internal telephone and tramway systems. Together they occupied an area of 500 acres (two km^2) – almost as large as the City of London.

At the start of World War I the two factories were requisitioned by the Admiralty and armed guards were duly posted. Production facilities were further expanded and many new staff recruited from Faversham town and elsewhere in east Kent. Road access for the workers was poor, so the Admiralty built a metre-gauge railway, the Davington Light Railway, to transport them from a terminus at Davington, near the Home Works, to Uplees.

The printing and paper industries

In Scotland women were allowed to work as compositors, a prestigious and skilled role, usually the preserve of men. Otherwise, for women in the rest of the kingdom it was just printing, paper making and paper bag manufacture. In bookbinding women were able to page, collate, fold and sew. The percentage of the total workforce rose from 36 per cent pre-war to 48 percent with 21,000 women replacing men.

Food and drink

Before 1914 women in the grain milling trade were confined to sack repair and light warehouse work. Bakeries employed them to clean up while biscuit manufacturers had women doing monotonous work like chocolate dipping, icing, lining of tins and packing. Brewing and malting was a female no-go area although they were permitted into bottling departments to bottle wash, stack and pack - women were considered to be more careful with all that glass. Overall the war saw a rise from 35 percent to 49 percent of women in the sector, largely replacing men. Flour mill owners were implacably opposed to the use of women but had to relent and let them sweep, repair sacks and trucks. In brewing, women later replaced men in filling casks, weighing and breaking hops, cask and pulp washing and testing.

Tetley's, Leeds

The introduction of conscription boosted the surge of women recruited by Tetley's, one of Leeds's biggest employers. Most were employed in the maltings and the offices, while some were given jobs in the mash room or worked as painters. The predictable gender pay gap was in evidence: women received 25 or 27 shillings a week, compared with 33 shillings for most men. By the end of the war the disparity was even greater.

Childcare and child welfare and children's work in WWI

Over 500,000 children lost their fathers in World War One - the biggest loss of fathers in modern British history. This had huge social and psychological consequences not just for the bereaved children but for their mothers, the 160,000 war widows. Their husbands and fathers would never return so the cessation of hostilities inevitably brought its own challenges in those anxious days before the welfare state. In the meantime, while the fighting continued, the widowed mother more often than not needed to take on paid work. Childcare, as ever, presented a problem and a hurdle.

The urgent need for women to work in munitions did prompt the government to provide some funds towards the cost of day nurseries for munitions workers, and by 1917 more than 100 day nurseries opened across the country. However, there was no provision for women working in most other areas of employment and the majority had to rely on friends and family to help care for their children while they were out doing war work.

Child war work

The Boy Scout's Association was among the first youth organisations to make a practical contribution to the British war effort. Generally, the Scouts rallied round: some guarded railway bridges and tracks, telephone and telegraph lines, railway stations, water reservoirs or any location of strategic military importance. From late 1917, many Scouts helped with air raid duties, including sounding the longed-for all-clear signal after an attack. Some were even trained in fire fighting. *The Scout Movement's Handbook* somewhat dramatically, instructed all Scouts to 'be prepared...to die for your country if need be'.

Girl Guides also assumed many duties. They packaged up clothing to send to front-line soldiers, made ready the hostels and first-aid dressing stations for use by those injured in air raids, tended allotments to help cope with food shortages, and provided assistance at hospitals, government offices and munitions factories. With Germany's submarines sinking and threatening the vital shipments that carried supplies of food, raw materials and materiel to Britain, Girl Guides joined many young Britons in responding to official public appeals to grow their own fruit and vegetables. By tending to allotments, Girl Guides aimed to help Britain cope with food shortages and provided a valuable complement to the Women's Land Army.

Sea Scouts were part of a network of observers that stood watch on the coast waiting patiently for German air attacks or a possible invasion.

Generally, children responded to the public appeals for people to grow their own fruit and vegetables to help stem shortages. Children also enthusiastically rooted around for and collected scrap metal and other essential materials that could be recycled or used for the war effort. They were also taken on by factories which had been requisitioned for war work, including converted aircraft factories and other manufacturers of materiel. These factories employed women, refugees, volunteers from the Empire, men too old to be conscripted and children. In 1917, Education Minister H. A. L. Fisher claimed that as many as 600,000 children had been 'prematurely' put to work.

Children generally worked on the land weeding, clearing and harvesting. Chemicals from conkers were used for filling shells and bullets so posters were put up in schools encouraging pupils to harvest conkers. Around 3,000 tonnes were collected by Britain's children in 1917.

Children also had a role to play in the nation's propaganda campaigns. One poster, depicting two children quizzing their father about what he did in the war, was conceived by Arthur Gunn, director of the London-based firm, Johnson Riddle & Co, who also printed it. He recognised the potential of a child's insistent question to a 'shirker' father; Gunn would know the power of such a message from his own personal feelings of guilt at having not volunteered himself. He is reported to have imagined himself as the father in question. In fact, after having a sketch of the scene made up by Lumley in 1915, Gunn joined the Westminster Volunteers. The poster depicts a young boy playing with toy soldiers on the floor at his father's feet. The young girl points to a page in a book and looks searchingly at her father asking "Daddy, what did You do in the Great War?" However, the use of children, emotional blackmail and shame to encourage enlistment proved unpopular with the public at large.

Baby Week 1917

One of the consequences of more women working and men away fighting was the alarming falling birth rate; this encouraged the government to establish an infant and child welfare scheme which took the form of a number of campaigns, one of which was National Baby Week, in July 1917. Queen Mary cut the ribbon, regaled by a guard of honour made up of 120 mothers and babies. Indeed pageantry and celebration were an important part of the event, and a welcome distraction from the war, enjoyed and embraced by women of all social classes.

Some women who led the event seized the opportunity to use it for constructive social and political purposes, in what was an unthreatening environment that celebrated motherhood. Their goal was to promote the material well being of, and state support for, women and children, and in this they succeeded. Baby Week was also an opportunity to showcase other welfare systems as a model for Britain to adopt, focusing in particular on New Zealand, with its free and comprehensive health service for infants[4].

Who's wearing the trousers now?

Women serving in the auxiliary services or working in manufacturing, transport and on the land wore a range of uniforms and work clothes; sometimes this involved trousers – attire which hitherto, despite its obvious practicality, was largely a stranger to the female wardrobe. Significantly, trousers also had no place in the ladies' clothes departments in shops. Although women's fashions were already evolving by 1914, the move to more practical clothing during wartime undoubtedly accelerated the pace of change in the wider community. By 1919 many modish young women were wearing shorter skirts and looser-waisted clothing, as well as the inescapable trousers. Needless to say, some men, and women, were appalled by such decadence. The war also opened the door for the 'new fangled bra' and closed the door on the restrictive corset. From now on corsetieres were a long elasticated tube which no longer pinched the waist but flattened the breasts. Skirts were pencil-shaped and getting shorter. The hair-do of choice in the 1920s and '30s was the masculine looking 'bob'. Women smoked in public now and wore make-up with impunity or without being dubbed a whore. The more 'outrageous' plucked their eyebrows and applied kohl, eye shadow and dark lipstick. The cosmetics industry targeted the canary munitions girls in particular with Oatine and Yen-Yusa: the Oxygen Face Cream. The more paranoid deplored 'the Jazzing Flapper, the social butterfly type… scantily clad…to whom a dance or a new hat [is] more important than the fate of the nations'. *The Hartlepool Northern Daily Mail* had still not got over it on 20 February 1920 when it thundered 'Fast young women even powdered their noses in public' while married women were 'hussies with three inches of powder on their faces'[5].

Women no longer had to be bothered with a chaperone when visiting a pub or going to the cinema. *La garçonne* had arrived.

To cap it all women were now playing organised football for real teams. As we shall see, the munitionettes were at the forefront of this popularisation of the women's game, largely because the middle class Welfare Inspectors hired by the factories regarded playing football a good and healthy way of keeping the women workers out of trouble during their time off. The fact that the men's game had been put on hold 'for the duration' can only have helped, as it left male fans with the option of watching the women or nothing. But the 'suits' and dullards at the FA were having none of it; they contrived a way to stop it dead in its tracks by banning women teams in 1921 from FA accredited grounds. That was it until 1968 when the ban was lifted. Since then the popularity has steadily grown with the women's national team winning the European Championships in 2022 in a 2-1 victory over Germany before 87,000 fans at Wembley.

In 2023 they reached the final of the World Cup – magnificent achievement and one which the men had got nowehere near since 1966. Who'd have thought?

The prejudices were still in evidence though: the kit sponsors refused to manufacture the goalkeeper's shirt (economies of scale, no doubt), and the pathetic non-welcome of the Lionesses back home was nothing short of disgraceful.

When the shooting stopped

With characteristic prescience *The Times* proclaimed the shape of things to come in its 12 December 1916 editions when it declared that the women who had clamoured to work in war work 'are not going to accept domestic service at any price' when the shooting stops. Indeed the days of the big house with downtrodden staff scuttling after a handful of aristocrats were numbered, as indeed were the days when women lived and worked without the vote: their record in war work was eloquent and persuasive with former opponents now converted to voting for the vote for women in 1918, Asquith, Prime Minister from 1908-1916, included. Women war workers had acquitted themselves admirably and it remains doubtful if Britain could have won the war without their blood, sweat and tears. Nowhere was this absence of gratitude more evident than amongst the war workers in the munitions industry. But:

> *On the 11th hour of the 11th day of the 11th month, the armistice was announced. We were all stopped, just like that, no redundancy, nothing.*
> *- Female factory worker, Southampton 1918*
> *(Southampton Oral History Archives)*

The Women's War Work Committee Archive

The archive, as mentioned, features mainly working class women in a wide range of industrial occupations. It gives a vivid picture of how extensive and varied women's war work was in World War I and includes the following[6]:

Munitions (grenade milling, shell production, chemical shell production, smoke shell production, gun cotton production), flour mill, shipbuilding, glass works, paper mill, textiles, foundry work, female doctor running a surgery for munitions workers, brewing, tin plate works, steel works, woman crane driver in steelworks producing railway tracks, range finding equipment for the army and navy, gas mask making, naval fire control systems, aircraft manufacturing, ammunition box production, brickmakers, stonemasons, cement workers, chemist in cement works, monumental masons, potteries, terra cotta workers, tannery workers, linoleum work, removing asbestos, sewing asbestos mattresses for the Royal Navy, tyre manufacture, women sludge pit workers in glassworks, plasterers, coopers, paper mill workers, rope makers, printing.

Chapter 7

Small arms manufacturing

The end of the eighteenth century saw the revolutionary introduction and use of interchangeable parts, as exemplified first (quite coincidentally) in the manufacture of muskets and, subsequently, other goods. Hitherto, each part of a musket (or anything else assembled from multiple components) had been individually shaped by a workman to fit with the other parts. In the new system pioneered by Eli Whitney (inventor of the cotton gin), the musket parts were machined to such precise specifications that a part of any musket could be replaced by the same part from any other musket of the same design. This ushered in mass production on assembly lines, and economies of scale, in which standardised parts could be assembled by relatively unskilled workmen into complete finished products.[1] In 1812 Whitney took his new idea to the United States government who, after a brilliant demonstration where the inventor spread the parts of ten muskets on a table and proceeded to assemble one musket out of all the parts, were sold on the idea. Samuel Colt famously developed the idea further in the production of his famous Colt revolver. How could the British now refuse to get on board with this 'American System'?

James Nasmyth, Scottish engineer and inventor, speaks of his experience in his Bridgewater Foundry in Manchester, showing how the wayward factory worker became his own worst enemy:[2]

> There was a great demand for skilled, and even for unskilled labour. The demand was greater than the supply. Employers were subjected to exorbitant demands for increased rates of wages. The workmen struck, and their wages were raised. But the results were not always satisfactory. Except in the cases of the old skilled hands, the work was executed more carelessly than before. The workmen attended less regularly; and sometimes, when they ought to have been at work on Monday mornings, they did not appear until Wednesday. Their higher wages had been of no use to them, but the reverse. Their time had been spent for the most part in two days' extra drinking.

Machines never got drunk, they always turned up for work, they never answered back, they may have broken down occasionally but they never went on strike, their hands never trembled and they were invariably accurate and on message ... the average worker simply could not compete.

In 1853 Naysmith was appointed to the Small Arms Committee which had been tasked with overhauling the Royal Small Arms Factory (RSAF) at Enfield. Subsequently the necessary machinery was shipped over from the Springfield factory into the north London works along with some of their best and most experienced workers and superintendents to take service under the British government[3]. The production expectation was 2,000 rifles per week, the making of which required 7,000 individual operations.

In 1895 the first Lee-Enfield rifle came off the production line with later modifications in 1902 allowing it to be used by infantry and cavalry as the Short Lee-Enfield, which was used in World War I and II. Some 17 million of these rifles were manufactured. On the ammunition side, George Kynoch set up on his own in 1868 and patented his version of the brass cartridge.

The repurposing of the Enfield factory had severe economic and social effects locally[4]. Part-time working was imposed while the new machinery was being installed; the Boer War had recently ended so re-armament was not on the agenda. The 2,000 or so workers were paid the miserly sum of £1 per week or less and the War Office was looking for 400 or more redundancies. Families were reduced to poverty, local shops closed down; large scale unemployment and starvation wages were the order of the day in Enfield and the surrounding area.

In 1905 an unsympathetic conservative prime minister Arthur Balfour turned the screw yet tighter when he ordained that the Enfield workforce should be reduced to around 1,900 and the wage bill was to be reduced to less to than £4,000; furthermore government ordnance factories, like Enfield, should henceforth not have more than one third of government orders and the rest should go to private companies. Enfield was left with a large amount of new equipment and tried to lessen the impact by suggesting they go into car production but this was rejected. The nearby Waltham Abbey gunpowder factory also had its labour force slashed by 400 workers. The Ordnance Factory at Smallbrook in Birmingham was closed down and sold off to Birmingham Small Arms Company (BSA) who inherited a share in Lee-Enfield production. While all this was going on, it was common knowledge that production at the giant arms company Krupp of Essen was continuing apace with 50 percent of its output headed for the German army. As an indicator of a likely impending conflict this had no peer. The only department at RSAF that had anything like a full order sheet was the department producing swords for the cavalry !

The declaration of war changed everything with twelve hour shifts, thirteen day fortnights and overtime galore. The people of Enfield and their town were prospering once again. Betting revived, the four pubs remained open until midnight except on Sundays when they closed at midday – not for any religious observance but to slake the thirst of the men on the Saturday night shift.

Recruitment took off with many more applicants than jobs, but those of fighting age (19-35) were excluded. In 1915 the minimum labourers' rate was 6d per hour for a 48 hour week with time and a half for overtime; Sundays were double time and an 82 hour week became the norm. Letters to *The Times* moaned that skilled workers were 'grossly overpaid'.

Small arms manufacturing

The influx of workers caused a housing shortage partly allayed by the construction of huts; dining facilities were inadequate until partly compensated for by local middle class ladies establishing refreshment services. Tram and train transport to north London was a shambles due to 'inefficient organisation'.

As with munitions, it was women who eventually provided the answer to the staffing issues. When conscription was introduced, 395 men left from Enfield and 516 from Waltham Abbey so by the end of 1916 nearly 1,000 women were taken on at RSAF Enfield along with younger boys under eighteen. By 1917 the labour force was almost 10,000 of which 15 percent were women and ten percent boys[5].

The Lee-Enfield was standard issue to every soldier and by 1917 10,000 were being made every week, as well as their accessories - the bayonet - and rifle repairs. But for rapid fire and mass destruction it was the machine gun that delivered the goods. Again, Britain turned to the US, in the shape of Hiram Maxim, who allegedly took the advice of a colleague who told him that the best way to make money from Europeans was to invent something that would make it easier for them to kill each other. Enter the Maxim machine gun, the first fully automatic centre fire machine gun manufactured in Britain by Mr Maxim with the help of Albert Vickers, introduced into the British Army in 1912 and remaining in service until 1968. Production took place at Erith in Kent, and some models that were fitted to early biplanes were also made there. The German Army's Maschinengewehr 08 and the Russian Pulemyot Maxim were both more or less direct copies of the Maxim[6].

The steel makers were followed by another American, Colonel Isaac Newton Lewis, who gave us the Lewis machine gun which BSA and Savage Arms made under licence. It was not just ground warfare that 'benefitted' from the gun; they soon found themselves fitted in aircraft. The United Kingdom officially adopted the Lewis gun in .303 British calibre for land and aircraft use in October 1915. The weapon was first issued to the British Army's infantry battalions on the Western Front in early 1916 as a replacement for the heavier and less mobile Vickers machine gun, which had been withdrawn from the infantry for use by the specialist Machine Gun Corps[7].

About the same time, the incendiary bullet was perfected with a phosphorus charge which ignited on contact with the air. They proved particularly effective against Zeppelins which had barely been troubled by regular bullets until now. When in August 1918 the L70 was hit and spectacularly burst into flames, the Zeppelin never flew again as a bomber over Britain.

Women, of course, were heavily involved in the manufacture of all small arms.

Chapter 8

Munitionettes – the canary girls

The Shell Crisis and other failures

August 1914 saw Britain rooted in the past militarily, and frighteningly unprepared as a consequence. New technologies in armaments and ordinance seem to have been disregarded because it was assumed that the ensuing war was surely going to be just like previous wars. Artillery bombardment would be followed by a headlong rush by the infantry, then the cavalry would show up to finish the enemy off. Britain would continue to rule the waves by blasting away at the German fleet until all their warships were sunk. Anthony Burton puts it well when he says 'guns would be hauled on the battlefield by horses just as they had been at Waterloo by teams of horses, and the most efficient way to send a message from one commander to another was to give it to a man on a horse.'[1]

The dependence on horses is evidenced by the existence of the Women's Forage Corps (WFC), and by some astonishing equine statistics: in the early days every infantry division of 18,000 men was accompanied by 5,600 horses; in 1917 there were still around 600,000 horses and 200,000 mules – even though motorised vehicles were increasingly available for a lot of the work[2].

The parlous state of Britain's preparedness before the outbreak of war in 1914 can, in part, be explained by the unbelievable ignorance of things military, as exhibited by Douglas Haig, Commander in Chief in France from 1915 and Lord Kitchener who was Secretary of War from 1914. Their squabbling did not help their country: the former believed that two machine guns per battalion (battalions can include up to about 1,000 soldiers) would be 'more than sufficient'; the latter begged to differ: he thought that perhaps four would be needed but certainly no more than that. Scenes from 'Blackadder Goes Forth' flash disconcertingly before the eyes; it was certainly not 'All Quiet on the Western Front'. So when the war started, the nation could boast 1,530 machine guns but by the end of the war close on 250,000 more had been manufactured. Lloyd George sardonically concluded: 'Take Kitchener's figure. Square it. Multiply by two. Then double again for good luck'.

Unfortunately, the ignorance did not end with the deadly effective machine gun. The chiefs of staff persisted in the belief, despite the bodies piling up before their eyes time and time again, that artillery barrages preceding casual advances into no man's land were the key to victory. But where were the shells going to come from - a good question given that shells played a crucial role in such bombardments?

Munitionettes – the canary girls

The shortage, indeed near absence, culminated in the 1915 Shell Crisis; Lord Northcliffe headlined it as the 'Tragedy of the Shells; Lord Kitchener's Grave Error'. All that did though was lead to a fall in circulation of the *Daily Mail* while the bodies continued to pile up.

But all this confirms how, when it came to munitions, arms and armour and other essential materiel, Britain was lamentably and alarmingly ill prepared in August 1914. She could call on a paltry three national factories producing munitions with 3,000 women workers. In response to the Shell Crisis, the British government passed the Munitions of War Act 1915 in a bid to increase government involvement and control of the industry. The Royal Arsenal at Woolwich was responsible for filling shells but could not keep up with demand so, in July 1915, the first National Filling Factories were opened at Aintree and Coventry to be run on business lines with real world procurement costings and profit margins. New factories and businesses sprang up while existing factories were converted into munitions manufactories, including such unlikely facilities as the HMV gramophone factory. By 1918 there were 150 national factories and over 5,000 controlled establishments which had exchanged the production of peacetime products for the weapons of war. The government spent £2,000 million keeping the guns firing and managed a workforce of three million. The factory gates soon clattered open to a steady stream of 'khaki girls', or 'canary girls', some of whom gave their lives and many of whom surrendered their long-term health and decimated their life expectancy. Initially, attempts were made to improve production by improving production techniques and using the existing male workforces but that was not enough; women were introduced into non-skilled capacities. The deployment of girls and women in the highly dangerous munitions industry was by far the most extensive, significant and visible war time deployment in respect of women's employment.

The newly created Ministry of Munitions regulated wages, hours and employment conditions in munitions factories. It also obliged the factories to take on more women to make good the deficiency in male labour. Between July 1914 and July 1918 the number of women employed in the munitions industry rose from 170,000 to 594,000 and to these 424,000 new employees we need to add the 232,000 women employed by the national factories. Some scholars, for example Angela Woollacott (1994), have estimated that approximately one million women were working in munitions industries by mid 1918 and that more women worked in munitions than in the Voluntary Aid Detachment, the Women's Land Army or other such organisations[3]. The vital area of work was in shell making which was carried out largely (60 percent of the total) by women who were engaged in all aspects, from roughing and turning the bodies to the final gauging of the finished shell.

The much-vaunted good wages were not always in evidence if this testimony by Olive Taylor, one of five women crammed in a room in a boarding house near the privately owned Morecombe Bay factory is anything to go by: 'the wages [were] terribly low…we had to pay the landlady 25 shillings out of the 27 we received, and there were no facilities for laundry'.

When rationing was imposed towards the end of the war the Food Controller reacted to the shortage of meat by allowing extra for manual workers, dividing manual workers into three categories: very heavy industrial workers, very heavy agricultural workers, and heavy industrial workers. Perhaps it comes as no surprise that women munitions workers who spent their day heaving heavy shells around, found themselves in the third category which offered the smallest meat ration. Worse still, it would appear that those under eighteen were considered to have no need to eat meat.

Women and engineering

At the end of the war a report compiled by the National Employers' Federation compared the performance of women with men and found that in sheet metal work women's quality exceeded that of men; in nine areas – from cartridge production to aircraft woodwork – women's quality equalled men's; the same was found in output, although for cartridge production it was 20 per cent higher. Only in shell production did women fall short of men.

But women faced the usual problems, not least the opposition from skilled male workers to the use of unskilled labour. Women gradually penetrated the engineering workshops, where they worked alongside the men. No doubt these men were alarmed by the fact that, for example, the national munitions factory in Gretna recorded that 36 percent of its workers had previously been in domestic service. From the women's point of view, how could making beds and washing up be more useful and patriotic than filling shells? The men saw it differently: how could a woman move from cooking and polishing the silver one week to filling shells the next?

The employment of women in munitions was greatly facilitated by the so-called "Treasury agreement" of 19 March 1915, relating to the trade-union rules that restricted the use of unskilled labour. In February 1916, the Ministry of Munitions issued *Notes on the Employment of Women on Munitions of War with an Appendix on the Training of Munition Workers*. Mr. Lloyd George's "picture book,'" as some of the women called it, is interesting because it discusses how far and well women were able to do the same work previously been done by men, and the methods that had been adopted to make certain tasks more suitable for women.

We have already noted the reality that in the early years of the war women – despite these invaluable contributions to the war effort - were still not considered as complete citizens – socially or politically: they did not have the vote and there were no female representatives in the House of Commons to speak up for them and to champion their rights. By far the majority of munitionettes, as these workers came to be called, and others in essential war work, were single, in their late teens and early twenties – the very demographic that was excluded from the franchise. So the sterling work these women carried out from day to day - risking their lives and long-term health – went disregarded and unrewarded when it came to representation at the ballot box.

Munitionettes and armaments were, as we have seen, the most visible manifestation of the huge job creation scheme which accompanied the declaration of war in 1914. Bullets, bombs, torpedoes, grenades and shells, bayonets and daggers, and the ordnance to unleash them is obviously pivotal to any country's war effort, as is the work, research and development which is conducted at specialist firms and factories. Hadfields Limited of Hecla and East Hecla, Sheffield, was a British manufacturer of special steels; it became heavily involved in the armaments industry, turning out shells and armour plate steel. Women made up a large part of the workforce: so important were Hadfields and its women to the war effort that Sheffield saw a breakthrough in child care when the government was forced into pioneering nursery provision between 7.00am and 6.00pm. They were lucky.

Sheffield's Women of Steel

If any city typifies the inestimable contribution women made to the world wars through industry then it is probably the city of Sheffield. The dangerous and physically demanding work they applied themselves to for six years is celebrated in a dignified and evocative sculpture in Sheffield city centre showing two indomitable women of steel. Sadly, the sculpture also epitomises the long, arduous wait for recognition which, to our shame, has been the fate of many other contributions by women in the world wars.

By June 1917, roughly 80 percent of the weaponry and ammunition used by the British army during World War I involved a munitionette. But munitionettes were paid less than half the rates of male workers; striking was made illegal and so there was no recourse to address this. Rates of pay varied significantly at different factories and, until 1917, women were also saddled with a job mobility restriction which prevented them from leaving one firm to move to another that would pay them better because they had to obtain a certificate from their previous employer stating that they had left with their employer's blessing. In the Munitions of War Act of July 1915, the certificate regulations were repealed. Munitions workers gave us an unusual case in the history of equal employment.

H.M. Factory, Gretna[4]

We can never beat Hindenberg [German field marshal] until we beat Krupp [huge German steel, artillery and ammunition manufacturer], and that is what these khaki-clad girls of Moorside [codename for Gretna] are going to do. Hats off to the women of Britain.

– Sir Arthur Conan Doyle

Gretna on the Solway Firth was the United Kingdom's largest cordite factory during World War I. The Devil's Porridge Museum at Eastriggs commemorates the superhuman efforts of workers there. Its scale and extent were truly breathtaking.

H.M. Factory Gretna stretched 9 miles from Mossband near Longtown in the east, to Dornock / Eastriggs near to the Scottish-English border in the west. The facility consisted of four large production sites and two purpose-built townships designed by Raymond Unwin, more famous as the architect for the garden cities movement. There were houses for families and hostels for unmarried girls which accommodated 120 or 90 girls each within a cubicle that could be curtained off, with personal storage space. Cook-housekeepers and maids did all the cooking and cleaning. No wonder 100,000 women and girls had deserted domestic service by 1916.

The 125 miles (201 km) of track laid there kept 34 engines busy. Electricity for the munitions manufacture and the townships was provided by a purpose-built coal-fired power station. The telephone exchange handled up to 2.5 million calls in 1918 alone. The townships had their own bakeries, laundry and a police force. The laundry could clean 6,000 items daily and the kitchens and bakeries cooked and baked 14,000 meals a day. Water was taken from the River Esk through a 42 inches diameter pipe to a pump house; from there it was pumped through a 33 inches (84 cm) main to a reservoir. A filtration/treatment works could handle up to ten million gallons every day.

Construction at Gretna started in November 1915; up to 10,000 Irish navvies worked on the site as well as building the two wooden townships to house the workers at Gretna and Eastriggs. To prevent any problems with this prodigious influx of construction and munition workers, the State Management Scheme was implemented which attempted to depress alcohol sales through the nationalisation of pubs and breweries in the vicinity. By 1917 the larger proportion of the workforce were women: 11,576 women to 5,066 men.

Munitions production started in April 1916. Engineers and chemists from nations from all corners of the British Empire were employed in the mass production of cordite. At its peak, *Grace's Guide* tells us that the factories produced 800 tons of cordite per week, more than all the other munitions plants in Britain combined. Cordite was colloquially known as the "Devil's Porridge"; the name comes from Sir Arthur Conan Doyle, who visited Gretna as a war correspondent in 1916. He later wrote, sparing no punches with regard to the inherent dangers:

> "The nitroglycerin on the one side and the gun-cotton on the other are kneaded into a sort of a devil's porridge; which is the next stage of manufacture...those smiling khaki-clad girls who are swirling the stuff round in their hands would be blown to atoms in an instant if certain small changes occurred".

The closure of Gretna in November 1918 left Waltham Abbey Royal Gunpowder Mills in Essex as the only government-owned cordite factory until an expansion programme started at the outbreak of World War II.

Munitionettes – the canary girls

The Woman Worker for February 1916 reported the situation in which girls were employed in core making for grenade bombs at Gretna. The girls were working five days from six in the morning to eight in the evening without any overtime allowance, and on Saturdays from six in the morning to five in the evening, Sundays from six in the morning to six in the evening. This was a working week, after deducting meal times, of 82 hours, with total earnings of 16 shillings and 8 pence, or something under 22 pence per hour. The night shift was extended from 6.00 am. to 6.00 pm. without any extra allowance for night work.

With absolutely no evidence, sexist employers and the Ministry still argued that "it was not considered that one woman was the equivalent of one man", and that women were a burden because they needed more supervision and required 'new amenities' whatever they were. Astonishingly, at the end of the war, "out of work" payments were only given to women who could prove that they had worked before the war. Everyone else was expected to return dutifully to their homes or to domestic service. The War Cabinet Committee on Women in Industry claimed to agree with equal pay in principle, but contrived to believe that due to their "lesser strength and special health problems" (whatever they were: periods?) the output of women was inferior to that of the male workers !

If munitionettes had 'special health problems' before they embarked on munitions work then the special health problems which over time afflicted many of them were even more special by and beyond the end of the war. The daily routine involved working with hazardous chemicals without adequate protection; personal protective equipment (PPE) was a thing of the future. Many worked with trinitrotoluene (TNT), and endured prolonged exposure to nitric acid that induced anaemia and toxic jaundice and which gave the women's skin a yellow hue, turning their hair a gingery blonde; this led them to be dubbed Canary Girls – not exactly the romantic and jolly nickname it has now become. But the effects were more than just cosmetic: research shows that ROF workers risked losing fingers and hands, burns and blindness: "In these factories, they would take the casing, fill it with powder, then put a detonator in the top that had to be tapped down. If they tapped too hard, it would detonate," said Amy Dale. "It happened to one lady, who was pregnant at the time, and it blinded her and she lost both her hands. She saw the pregnancy through, but the only way she could identify the baby was with her lips, which still had feeling." Ethel Dean, a worker at Woolwich Arsenal, recalls how 'Everything that that powder touches goes yellow. All the girls' faces were yellow, all around their mouths. They had their own canteen in which everything was yellow that they touched…chairs, tables everything'.

Exposure over a long period of time to chemicals such as TNT can damage the immune system, and cause liver failure, anaemia, and spleen enlargement; TNT can even affect a woman's fertility. Side effects commonly included breast and lower torso enlargement. Some 400 cases of toxic jaundice were recorded among ammunition workers in the war, of which 100 proved fatal. Some workers reported bone disintegration in later life, while others developed throat problems and dermatitis from TNT staining. Some women even gave birth to 'bright yellow babies' – they were called Canary Babies – according to Dr Helen McCartney,

King's College London. Gladys Sangster, whose mother worked at NFF Banbury, knows: she was one of them: "I was born [during the war] and my skin was yellow," she told the BBC. ..."Nearly every [worker's] baby was born yellow. It gradually faded away. My mum told me you took it for granted, it happened and that was it."

An urgent medical investigation was carried out by the government in 1916 to study, among other issues, the effects of TNT on munitions workers. The investigators were able to gather their data by masquerading 'as female medical officers posted inside the factories. They found that the effects of the TNT could be roughly split into two areas: irritative symptoms, mainly affecting the skin, respiratory tract, and digestive system; and toxic symptoms, including nausea, jaundice, constipation and dizziness'. The paper was published in *The Lancet* of August 12 1916 as 'Observations on the effects of tri-nitro-toluene on women workers', by Agnes Livingstone-Learmouth M.B., CH.B. EDIN., and Barbara Martin Cunningham M.D. EDIN.

Equally dangerous was picric acid which also was widely used in the manufacture of explosives. Picrid acid was commonly known as lyddite because it was first made in the UK at Lydd in Kent in 1888, later to be produced at Woolwich Arsenal. A bright yellow powder, it too produced that ominous yellow hue. Ironically picric acid was also used in the treatment of trench foot.

Mercury fulminate is another explosive material and is mainly used as a trigger for other explosives in percussion caps and detonators. During the late 19th century and for most of the 20th century, mercury fulminate became widely used in primers for self-contained rifle and pistol ammunition. It is far more insidious than the highly visible effects of TNT and lyddite; the effects of mercury fulminate are invisible and, when it gets to the eyes, causes mercurial poisoning.

The Health of Munitions Workers Committee

At Gretna, we have already noted that the mostly female workforce put in 12-hour shifts and lived in Spartan huts sharing beds with someone on the opposite shift to keep accommodation costs down. In general the Health of Munitions Workers Committee reported that "women have accepted conditions of work which if continued must ultimately be disastrous to health". It concluded that "to attain a maximum output women engaged in moderately heavy manual labour should not work for more than sixty hours per week," adding, perhaps as an after-thought, that it was "probable that the sixty hours per week were still too many to give the best total output."

Social life and women kicking balls: munitionettes, football and sexism

Social clubs, theatrical societies, bands and debating groups were formed in munitions factories; piano music and singing were especially popular. Such activities were often organised by workers and encouraged by welfare supervisors in a bid to increase morale, mindfulness and productivity. The similar situation which prevailed with British POWs in German prisoner of war camps is surely no coincidence.

We have already seen how, even by today's standards with its long-delayed and welcome resurgence, women's football was extraordinarily popular in the late 19th and early 20th century, especially at the factories, with many teams formed from munitions workers around the country during World War I. Their games were not just casual kickabouts, but were organised into prestigious competitions and took place at top class venues such as St James's Park in Newcastle, Preston's Deepdale and Middlesbrough's Ayresome Park.

In 1918, Bolckow, Vaughan in Middlesbrough, like other north-eastern manufacturing firms, had its own women's football team. Other women's clubs included Dorman, Long & Co; Teesside Ladies; Ridley's, Skinningrove; Skinningrove Ironworks; Smith's Docks; Richardson, Westgarth (both Hartlepool) and Christopher Brown (West Hartlepool). Matches attracted up to 53,000 spectators.

Some factories' management appear to have tolerated their staff participating in football as a "necessary evil" that increased productivity and discipline amongst women 'displaced from their traditional gender roles'.

The derailing of the women's game was doubly disappointing because not only did it deprive increasing thousands of spectators of enjoyable war-time entertainment when entertainment was exactly what the nation needed, it also denied numerous charities a vital source of funds. Women's football and charity had always gone hand in hand. For example, a match between the Scottish Filling Factory and Georgetown Girls in May 1918, raised £57 (about £3,756 today) for the Crewe Cottage Hospital Funds and the Red Cross. Dick, Kerr Ladies of Preston donated £600 (£49,500) after a match against Arundel Coulthard Foundry with Moor Park VAD Hospital for Wounded Soldiers.

Of course, not everyone wanted to follow a gruelling twelve hour day with yet more physical activity; many of the girls just wanted to relax and have fun. Dances were organised and the Gretna Tavern opened. Unsurprisingly, this was frowned upon by many a self-righteous observer: crime, domestic violence, alcoholism and syphilis were sure to follow. In the event, receipts from the Tavern showed that 70 percent of the takings came from food while more was spent on soft drinks than on alcohol. The pubs around Woolwich Arsenal were officially described as having 'a complete absence of brawling and excitement' and men and women alike were 'very good tempered'. A report in 1918 showed that there were but 17 cases of sexually transmitted infections amongst the tens of thousands of workers, and only 171 births registered to unmarried Gretna mothers.

UK World War I national filling factories

Raw materials used by the filling factories, such as TNT or propellants like cordite, were manufactured in National Explosives Factories and transported by train to the filling factories for filling into munitions. High-explosives like TNT had to be heated to melt them and the liquid was poured hot into heated shell cases. Extreme care was taken to ensure that there were no voids in the poured explosive charge as this could lead to the shell detonating in the gun barrel during firing[5].

Due to the risk of explosion at the factories, stringent regulations were obviously put in place to minimise those risks. Workers wore wooden clogs so as to obviate sparking from shoes with metal tips or heels. Other metal items were prohibited, including jewellery, hairpins, hair grips and bras with metal clips.

Nylon and silk clothing was also banned to eliminate static electricity. Women were strip searched every day. Workers were prohibited from carrying matches–something which cost Lilian Miles's friend her job at the Coventry Ordnance Works when their fore-mistress saw a match drop out of her pocket. The girl was imprisoned: 'She never got over it. Within a few months, she died. She was 20 years of age.'

As Amy Dale says with some irony: "Women weren't allowed anywhere near a gun, yet they were filling shells in factories. They were actively engaged in an act of war which I think made people uncomfortable.[6]"

The Ministry of Munitions owned up to 18 Filling Factories.

There were also some additional munitions plants built by the Ministry of Munitions but privately operated: for example, Chittening in Avonmouth was operated by Nobel Explosives. By November 1918, Chittening had turned out 85,424 mustard gas shells; but at a human cost of 1,213 cases of associated illness, including two deaths which were later mis- attributed to influenza[7].

National factories

The first few months of the Ministry's life saw the establishment of an impressive group of national factories so that by the end of December 1915, there were 73 new sites.

Over 8,700 companies and factories in the UK swung into action producing all sorts of munitions and related materiel. However, only 218 were directly administered by the Ministry of Munitions as National Factories. Of these, 170 National Factories were in England, with the rest in Scotland, Wales and Ireland. Many of the National Factories were adapted from existing works, while others were located in new, purpose built factories.

The National Projectile Factory, Lancaster[8]

In October 1918 there were 8,656 employees here of whom 47% were women. Lancaster was the largest UK NPF in terms of employment; the average was 4,500. Empty shell cases were manufactured, which were then sent, by rail, to the Filling Factories to be filled with explosives and have their fuses fitted. The website Documenting Dissent reveals that 'Altogether the factory produced over two million shells, including: 993,900 6-inch high explosive and chemical shells, 448,000 9.2-inch shells, 9,600 8-inch shells and 589,500 60-pounder shrapnel shells. During 1919, the factory was turned over to the manufacture of 250lb. and 500lb. aircraft bombs'.

A special court was regularly convened to deal with issues concerning the two munitions factories in Lancaster and Morcambe; it met weekly from October 1916 until the end of the war and focused mainly on safety. Of the 156 cases brought, fewer than 10% implicated women. The works police were ever vigilant, making regular searches of the workers. Four women were charged with having matches or cigarettes on their person in the NPF in Lancaster.

The National Filling Factory, Morecambe

More women were employed at Morecambe than at the NPF in Lancaster: 64.4% of the 4,621 employees in September 1917. Construction at Morecambe began in November 1915 on a 400 acre site. Here the NFF filled a range of shells with Amatol, a mixture of TNT and ammonium nitrate, but they also produced gas shells. Vickers produced filled shells for only 15 months before the site was almost entirely destroyed by fire in an explosion on 1 October 1917 killing ten people, mainly firemen.

There were three fatalities caused by cranes at the Caton Road works. An inquest, in January, 1917, reported on the third fatality: an electrical fitter, William Goodchild, from London, lodging in Morecambe, was accidentally crushed by a crane, driven by a female worker, Sarah McPhail. Source: *Documenting Dissent*.

Documenting Dissent goes on to tell how

> Gertrude Hardman, a 31-year-old widow and munitions worker (probably at the NPF)…had been in the local employment exchange when new female recruits arrived for the NFF at White Lund. Hardman talked loudly to one of them, so that all could hear her, saying "You don't know what you are going to. It's terrible; girls are fainting every minute; girls are dying every day. They take them out, and nobody knows anything about it." Hardman was arrested under the Defence of the Realm Act (DORA) and charged with making false statements. Witnesses in court repeated what Hardman had said: "There is a cemetery close by the factory where they bury them," and "If you are going to White Lund, then God help you. They are dropping dead every day at the works, and are being carried out." One witness who subsequently worked at White Lund said the stories of girls dying was false. She had never seen one. Another worker denied that girls were dying every day.

With so many workers congregated in one place it was inevitable that crime would rear its head; here are some examples:

Emily Pogson, 19, and living away from her home in Darlington for the first time, could not resist acquiring her colleague's possessions, including a raincoat and shoes, on three occasions. She was sentenced to one month's hard labour. Emily Hodges, from Bolton, stole plates and cutlery from the canteen to entertain her weekend visitors. In her defence she said that she could not afford to buy them and intended to return them after the weekend. More excitingly Kathleen Mulligan, a young Irish woman, stole a box of explosives from her workplace, intending to take them home to show her grandparents the tools that she used. Mulligan was remanded, outcome unknown.

Rosie Carling was sacked when it was discovered that she was only fifteen years old. She stole clothing from her co-workers, with whom she shared lodgings on the seafront at Morecambe, and fled home to Belfast. She was arrested and brought back to Lancaster to stand trial, admitting her guilt. A schoolmistress from Belfast undertook to escort Carling home if the Bench would set her free. This was agreed and she was bound over for £5 for good behaviour for twelve months.

There were other ways, of course, for women to make some extra money. Margaret Wilkinson, alias Taylor, was convicted of keeping a brothel at 3 Barratt's Yard, Brewery Lane, Lancaster. Her sister, Fanny Spandley, and Minnie Martin, a lodger, aided and abetted her. Three men, found on the premises when the house was raided by the police, were also charged with aiding and abetting. Each woman was sentenced to two months' hard labour. The men were fined £10 or 51 days' hard labour, if they could not pay.

Much more research is needed on the lives of munitionettes and the impact that their war work had on them during the war and afterwards.

The National Projectile Factory at Birtley, Gateshead

The National Projectile Factory at Birtley was built next to an existing works of Sir W.G. Armstrong Whitworth & Company and was taken over by the Belgian Government for munitions work. To house the workforce, a model village, Elizabethville (named after the Belgian Queen) was constructed from September 1915 using Belgian labour. Single-storey accommodation was provided for 1,600 workers and included 325 three bedroom houses, 342 two bedroom cottages, 22 timber huts, 24 hostels for single workers and two large dining halls. The village was run on military lines with its own local government, cemetery, church and hospital but opposition against the administration culminated in a serious riot in December 1916. The result was that Belgian Gendarmes were withdrawn and substituted with British police and the prevalent army discipline was relaxed. The workforce were repatriated to Belgium from 7 December 1918 and the houses were then transferred to the Ministry of Labour.

His Majesty's Cotton Waste Factories were the source of the cotton used in a nitration process to produce guncotton. In turn, guncotton was gelatinised with nitroglycerine to produce cordite - the most important propellant for shell firing guns and small arms used by Britain and her allies.

By 1918 mutionettes numbered more than 900,000, producing 80% of the weapons and shells used by the British Army. By June 1917 the factories were producing over fifty million shells a year. At the end of the war it is estimated that the British Army had fired around 170 million shells during the conflict.

Here is a roll call of disasters, which were often avoidable and which involved numerous women:

NFF Pembury[9]

Because of the necessary secrecy cloaking the NFFs, information is hard to come by, but at Pembury we have the diary of a Gloucestershire vicar's daughter named Gabriella West who had joined the newly formed *Women's Police Service* where she started working as a sergeant in 1917. According to Gabriella her job was to "control the women workers":

"The girls here are very rough and so are the conditions. Their language is sometimes too terrible! But they are also very impressionable. Particles of acid land on your face making you nearly mad - like pins and needles but much more so. They get on your clothes and leave brown specks all over them. They also get up your nose and down your throat and in your eyes so you are blind and speechless."

All of those symptoms were witnessed in the sulphuric acid section of the factory. When the war ended, the munitions factory at Pembury in Carmarthenshire went into reverse mode when it was used to deactivate and dismantle shells rather than to make them. On 18 November 1918, Mary Fitzmaurice (36), Jane Jenkins (21) and Edith Ellen Copham (19) were killed in an explosion. Two other women were injured. The women were dealing with a different type of shell than they had been used to. The explosion killed Jane immediately. Mary and Edith died in hospital that night.

A huge funeral procession was led from High Street by a brass band and followed by 500 munitions girls from the factory, wearing their uniforms. *The South Wales Weekly Post* said that the women 'had died as surely in the service of their country as any on the battlefield' and noted that the crowds of onlookers saluted as the funeral passed. Over a million shells were dismantled at Pembury without any further accidents.

Silvertown, West Ham

Friday, 19 January 1917 at 6.52 pm was a bad time in Silvertown, West Ham. This was precisely when an explosion occurred at the munitions factory: approximately 50 tonnes of trinitrotoluene (TNT) exploded, killing 73 people and injuring 400 more, 94 of them seriously, as well as causing widespread and substantial damage in the local area. Eighteen girls and women died in the blast although details remain sketchy. At least one was a factory worker: 16 year old Catherine Elizabeth Hodge (also known as Lizzie Lawrence of 53 Jersey Street). The eldest female to die was 76 years old, the youngest was four months, who died along with her grandmother[10].

The original factory was built in 1893 by Brunner Mond, a forerunner of Imperial Chemical Industries (ICI), to produce soda crystals and caustic soda. This ended in 1912 leaving part of the factory idle. In 1915 The War Office made a decision to use the factory's surplus capacity to purify TNT, a process more hazardous than manufacturing itself, ignoring the not insignificant fact that the factory was in a highly populated area. Despite opposition from Brunner Mond, production of TNT began in September 1915 using the method invented by Brunner Mond's chief scientist F. A. Freeth, who believed the process to be "manifestly very dangerous...the plant would go up sooner or later...we were told (by the Ministry of Munitions) it was worth the risk to get the TNT." The plant was only 200 yards from rows of workers' cottages and near riverside wharves containing other highly combustible materials such as oil, varnish and chemicals. The plant went on to purify TNT at a rate of 10 tonnes per day until it was destroyed by the predictable and predicted explosion.

Another plant, at Gadbrook, was built in 1916 producing TNT at a higher rate than the Silvertown factory, but away from populated areas and with more stringent safety standards.

Of the seventy-three people killed sixty-nine died instantly, four later from their injuries, and more than 400 were injured. Up to 70,000 properties were damaged, 900 nearby destroyed completely; the cost was put at £2.5 million. The comparatively low death toll for such a large blast was quite simply due to the time of day: fewer than 40 of the victims were in the TNT factory itself. Two firemen were killed or seriously injured in the explosion.

Reportedly, the explosion also blew the glass out of windows some miles away in the Savoy Hotel in the Strand and almost overturned a taxi in Pall Mall, London; the fires could be seen in Maidstone and Guildford, and the blast was heard up to 100 miles away, including at Sandringham in Norfolk and along the Sussex coast. The explosion was so powerful that the motor pump from Silvertown Fire Station was found over a quarter of a mile away.

The Ministry of Munitions had no option but to order an investigation; unsurprisingly it found that the factory's site was inappropriate for the manufacture of TNT. But it, and everyone else with any involvement, not least the residents, knew that. Management and safety practices at the plant were also criticised: TNT was stored in unsafe containers, close to the plant and the production process was risky. The report was conveniently not disclosed to the public until the 1950s.

Explosives Loading Company, Faversham

The worst ever explosion in the history of the 450 year UK explosives industry occurred in Faversham when at 14.20 on 2 April 1916 200 tons of TNT exploded (compared with the 50 tons involved in Silvertown). 115 people died including all of the men and boys of the works Fire Brigade. A memorial stands over the mass grave of 73 of the victims. The Love Lane Cemetery Register records that only 34 could be recorded by name as all the others were unidentifiablee, in which case the Register simply stated 'a male person unknown.' All the victims were men or boys from the factory – no women worked at the plant over the weekend - the oldest was 61, the youngest was 17. Thirty-five victims were buried elsewhere at the request of their families.

Faversham was home to England's first gunpowder plant, established in the 16th century.

The explosion killed at least 108 people - leaving many bodies unidentifiable - and injured 64. Windows were shattered in Southend-on-Sea 15 miles away; buildings in Norwich, over 100 miles away, shook and the explosion was heard in France. The usual official censorship and press blackout followed –the disaster remained one of the best kept secrets of World War I.

The National Shell Filling Factory, Chilwell, Nottinghamshire

Chilwell filled some 19 million shells with high explosives during World War I. From the start, women were employed here and may have influenced the choice of location because there was a tradition of women working in local textile factories in the nearby towns. Most of the factory was destroyed when eight tons of TNT exploded on 1 July 1918. In all 134 people were killed, of whom only 32 could be positively identified, and a further 250 were injured.

Barnbow Munitions Factory - National Filling Factory No. 1

Barnbow was a Leeds World War I munitions factory located between Cross Gates and Garforth. Tragically, Barnbow is best known for the massive explosion which killed thirty-five of the women workers in 1916.

The following gives some idea of the massive logistics, construction and facilities work which went into its operation. Much of it appears on the highly informative Barwick in Elmet Historical Society website. Platforms over 800 feet long were added to the nearby railway station to help the transport workers get to and from work at the site; the Yorkshire Power Company erected a 10KV overhead line to a sub-station. This, in conjunction with a boiler house and heating plant, provided power for the heating and lighting of the entire complex. The electric power cables extended for over twenty-eight miles. A water main was laid to deliver 200,000 gallons of water per day and a 90,000 gallon collecting and screening tank was built to collect waste, which was pumped to the Leeds Sewerage Works at Killingbeck. The service mains - water, sewage, and fire – extended for thirty-three miles, and the steam and hot water piping for sixty miles. Coal was supplied by rail from Garforth Collieries Ltd and Wheldale Coal Co. In April 1916, the first batch of thirty 4.5 shells were filled, the output then quickly increasing to 6, 000 shells a day, when the number of shifts was increased from two to three.

Around 130,000 female applicants were interviewed. One third of the staff was from Leeds while others commuted from York, Castleford, Selby, Tadcaster, Wetherby, Knaresborough, Wakefield, and Harrogate; by October 1916 the workforce exceeded 16,000 people, 93 percent of whom was women and girls - 'The Barnbow Lasses'. Thirty-eight trains per day, 'Barnbow Specials', transported the workers to and from work.

Ancillary services included canteens, nurse stations, administration and changing rooms. There were qualified nurses and an in-house doctor, two dentists with a fully equipped surgery to care for the workers. Fire was obviously a constant hazard, monitored by a fire brigade which had access to a 300,000 gallon reservoir to supplement the link to the city's water supply. Men of the Royal Defence Corps guarded the factory.

The local textile industry was heavily involved in supplying huge quantities of material for nearly 87,000,000 cartridge bags and 26,000,000 exploder bags and smoke bags – all these and smaller components were manufactured in Leeds. Leeds textile stores not only supplied Barnbow but all the filling factories in the country. There were six acres of floor space used in the four warehouses near Wellington Street. Here, staff dealt with over 27 million yards of textile materials in the piece, nearly 142 million yards of braids and tapes, 150 tons of sewing threads, and 9,354 tons of millboard and strawboard. This industry also fed into the local printing trade, leading to the invention of a new system of printing on the bags.

Some aspects of health and safety were encouragingly advanced. Sandbags and protective shields were distributed all around the place; sprinklers and drenchers were attached to the magazines; there were fireproof doors and protective earthworks. There was good ventilation in the work areas, especially in the AMATOL factories; initially staff were limited to a fortnight stretch anywhere TNT was handled. All workers had to pass a medical examination before starting their employment; those working in dangerous zones had a periodic medical examination. A female superintendent, supported by a staff of welfare workers, was appointed to make regular meetings with employees, either during work or at meal times. They also visited anyone who was off sick or absent from work for any length of time. Tennis courts were provided. The fire brigade was an early introduction: initially it was all men but later, girls were trained up. Eventually thirty girls and six firemen, under the command of an experienced firemaster from London, made up the brigade.

Units of the Royal Defence Corps provided security, maintaining a 24-7 hour patrol of the security fence and gates. The superintendent of police with three inspectors controlled the male police, while a female superintendent was in charge of policewomen of the *Women's Police Service* for female search purposes.

Munitionettes – the canary girls

All personnel were required to wear identity discs and to carry permits; there were frequent body and bag searches. Dangerous areas were under constant surveillance, with 'safe' areas reserved for smokers. There was a complete press blackout of the area.

Despite all of this Barnbow was still a very dangerous place to work. Workers who handled the explosives stripped to their underwear, and wore smocks, puttees, caps, rubber gloves and rubber soled boots to avoid sparks; cigarettes and matches were obviously banned except in safe areas as were combs and hairpins to prevent static electricity. Workers were allowed to drink as much barley water and milk as they liked and, to help with the milk, Barnbow had its own farm, with a herd of 120 cows producing 300 gallons of milk per day.

The explosion

On Tuesday 5 December 1916, 170 women and girls had just started their night shift in one of the fusing rooms: 4 ½ " shells were being filled, fused, and packed in Room 42. At 10:27pm there was a massive explosion which killed thirty-five women outright, maimed and injured many more. Many of the dead were only identifiable by their identity disks. The injured were taken to the Leeds General Infirmary with the help of the factory medical staff, the ambulance corps and the voluntary motor transport section. Despite the magnitude and horror of the catastrophe, production was interrupted only for a short time, and once the bodies were recovered, other girls immediately stepped up and volunteered to replace them in Room 42.

For reasons of 'national security', none of this was revealed to the public until 1924; at the time death notices appeared in the *Yorkshire Evening Post,* simply stating cause of death as 'killed by accident' and other such euphemisms. There were two further explosions at the factory; the first in March 1917 killing two girl workers, the other in May 1918 killing three men.

Apart from setting up the dignified memorial, in 2012 the people of Leeds named a number of parks, buildings and streets in memory of the 'Barnbow Lasses'. The names of those who died are listed in the roll of honour in Colton Methodist church, and in York Minster near to the Five Sisters Window[11].

Louise Birch, from Local and Family History, Leeds Central Library has researched some very tragic and moving details about the casualties, as given in her *Remembering the Barnbow Tragedy: 100 Years Ago Today.* Here are just a few of the thirty-seven selected at random, highlighting the desperate and tragic circumstances of the women and of their surviving families:

> K. Bainbridge of Leeds, 40 years old at the time of her death, Kate was married with four children. Her husband William served with the West Yorkshire Regiment, but had become ill with pulmonary tuberculosis and spent most of 1916 in hospital. On December 6th, 1916 his doctor recommended permanent discharge with the following report: "Not a result but aggravated by active service

exposure. Permanent is getting worse. Total incapacity. Very hard case. Wife killed last night in Barnbow explosion, and he has 4 children, eldest 9. He is extremely ill and urgently needs money. Earnings – nil." William Bainbridge died Febrary 27th, 1918.

Edith Sykes of Leeds, died aged 15: Edith's older sister Agnes also worked in Barnbow's Room 42 but the night of the explosion Agnes was home sick with flu. Edith was injured in the explosion and taken to Leeds Infirmary where died several weeks later. Her older brother Herbert was in the Army, based in York and borrowed a gun carriage from his Barracks to carry Edith's coffin.

Eliza Grant of Castleford, died aged 39: Leaving 7 children aged 6 ~ 17, all now considered as in "Partial dependency of her income of 19s 6d". They were granted £65 compensation from the Ministry of Munitions. A story passed down from Eliza's descendants says that December 5th was Eliza's day off however as she had completed all her housework before the last bus left for the factory she decided to go in on the advice of a friend. Eliza was killed as she arrived, walking through the door of Room 42 as it exploded.

Hooley Hill Rubber and Chemical Works, Ashton-under-Lyme

The Ashton-under-Lyne munitions works exploded on 13 June 1917 when the Hooley Hill Rubber and Chemical Works caught fire. The factory was engaged in the production of TNT and was completely destroyed. Forty-three people died and most of the surrounding area was left devastated[12].

The casualties also included more than 120 hospitalised and several hundred with minor injuries. Amongst the dead were 23 employees of the Chemical Works, and eleven adults and nine children from the surrounding area: railway workers on the nearby line and children making their way home from St Peter's Primary School. Another child died as he swam at Ashton Baths when the windows were blown in by the explosion. The youngest victim was aged just four.

A relief fund was set up to help those affected, with more than £10,000 raised within a couple of months - a huge sum. An enormous crowd of around 250,000 followed the funeral corteges. A public inquiry and the inquests gave a verdict of accidental death.

Women and girls were, of course, engaged in other vital war work:

Chapter 9

Balloons & policewomen

Observation balloons

In 1878 the Royal Aircraft Establishment was set up as part of the Royal Engineers. Captain James Templar was in charge – himself a keen amateur balloonist who turned up with his own balloon at Woolwich. Challenges in these early days of aviation included how best to use hydrogen efficiently; this was resolved by having the gas compressed in cylinders and by finding the best material for the balloons. Templar discovered that goldbeaters' skin made from the large intestine of a calf – a parchment used in the manufacture of gold leaf - was perfect for the job. Women took on the role of preparing the skins and stitching the 2 ft square pieces together in the balloon factories - their first foray into the aviation industry. A large proportion of the workforce was women: out of a total of 297 employees, 270 were female.

> During World War I, all major combatants used observation balloons to observe their enemies' trench lines, [artillery] and troop movements. Observers provided real-time information through telephone and telegraph wiring. They were so effective that early air forces made enemy balloons a target priority. In turn, they were heavily defended by rings of anti-aircraft guns.

By the end of 1917 there was, under the Home Defence Scheme (DORA), a requirement for kite balloons for the anti-submarine programme. A National Balloon Factory was established in a converted cinema in Finchley. Production of Caquot & Nurse type observation balloons began in April 1918: the total number of balloons up to 8 February 1919 (when the factory closed), was 118[1].

The Women's Police Volunteer (WPV)/Women's Police Service (WPS)[2]

From 1914 about 4,000 women adopted a policing role carrying out voluntary patrols to ensure basic security and orderly behaviour in parks, YMCA huts, railways stations and other public spaces. The Women's Police Service was originally established by Nina Boyle and the musician and philanthropist Margaret

Damer Dawson, who had met when Damer Dawson was working for the Criminal Law Amendment Committee in 1914.

From its foundation onwards the WPS's role was delimited to enforcing the Defence of the Realm Act (DORA), public decency, and supervising and searching female workers, particularly munitionettes[3]. Indeed, ninety percent of the approximately 1,000 Women's Police Volunteers (WPVs) trained from 1914 were employed in munitions factories as supervisors and searchers of women workers to ensure that they did not take anything into the factories which might spark explosions. They were paid a weekly wage and also developed a special interest in the law affecting women and children. Another of the main responsibilities of the Women's Patrols - as they were first known - was to maintain public order and monitor women's activities around factories or hostels.

Both Boyle and Damer Dawson observed the troubles faced in London by Belgian and French refugees, particularly the danger of their being groomed for prostitution on arrival at railway stations, sex trafficking in modern parlance. They were also concerned about existing career prostitutes loitering near railway stations used by the increasing number of servicemen passing through the capital. The two women obviously felt that a uniformed woman police service could do much to help. The breakthrough came when the pair gained the approval of Sir Edward Henry, Commissioner of Police of the Metropolis, to train women, who would then patrol the streets of London on a voluntary basis offering advice and support to women and children, primarily to help prevent sexual harassment and abuse. To them this was a response to a need for more understanding and sympathetic treatment of women and children than the male police force was deemed able to give.

Sadly, it is a matter of some shame in the early 21st century that we cannot point to much progress in this regard: while women police officers are now commonplace and rightly so, women in the community (51 percent of our population) remain prey to the same constant harassment and many are fearful of walking alone, not just at night.

Qualifications for entry were as follows: a minimum height was established at 5 feet 4 inches, considerably lower, of course, than that for men; women with dependent young children were barred from service; women officers were not to be sworn in as constables; they had no right to a pension.

Boyle's background was in the *Women's Freedom League (WFL)* and so for her the WPV was an opportunity for women to assist in catching predatory criminals and to disrupt the male monopoly in the legal profession, particularly in relation to sexual issues - in other words to be an instrument to help and support women rather than to control their activities. Boyle, however, was increasingly alarmed that her organisation and other similar initiatives were being used to support anti-female propaganda and to curtail women's civil liberties. She also deplored the adoption of Regulation 40D, an anti-prostitution amendment to the 1914 Defense of the Realm Act, that in many people's view revived some of the objectionable features of the nineteenth-century Contagious Diseases Act[4]. She described Regulation

40D, which punished women for their sexual relations with members of the armed services, as 'besmirching' the good name of women.

In February 1915 Boyle and Damer Dawson fell out over the use of the WPV to enforce a curfew on women of so-called 'loose character' near a service base in Grantham; this proved unacceptable to Boyle and her values. Boyle also denounced the use of the Defence of the Realm Act by the authorities in Cardiff to impose a curfew on what were described as 'women of a certain class' between the hours of 7 pm and 8 am. In contrast, Damer Dawson took a more pragmatic line, with the support of most of the WPV's members. Dawson changed the name of WPV to the *Women Police Service* and severed all links with Boyle and the WFL.

Dawson's new service enjoyed great success, not least where its members' role was searching women working in Ministry of Munitions factories. In August 1915 in Grantham, Edith Smith of the WPS was appointed the first woman police constable in England with full power of arrest. In 1916 the Admiralty embedded a member of the WPS as an undercover worker in an attempt to expose espionage and drug taking at the Scapa Flow Naval Base. By the end of the war the *Women's Police Service* could boast over 357 members: Damar Dawson asked the Chief Commissioner, Sir Nevil Macready, to make them a permanent part of his force. He refused, saying (interestingly) that the women were "too educated" and would "irritate" male members of the force. Macready instead elected to go his own way and recruit and train his own women.

In February, 1920, five members of the WPS were charged with wearing uniforms too similar to those worn by the Metropolitan Women Police Patrols. After a four-day hearing Macready won his case and the WPS was forced to change its uniform and its name; they thus continued as a voluntary service, becoming the *Women's Auxiliary Service* in 1920. Significant changes in society triggered by World War I contributed to the desire to develop and maintain women as career police officers. For example, one of the more astonishing observations was that the 'public' was no longer viewed as exclusively masculine – the work done by women in munitions factories was instrumental in burying that particular notion. As the first uniformed women's police services, both the WPS and the WPV made valuable progress in gaining acceptance of women's role in police work.

Chapter 10

Between the wars

November 11, 1918 – what happened next?

With the end of the conflict most people, no doubt, assumed a return to some form of normality; but the exact nature of that normality would be impossible to define in this new, confused 'land fit for heroes'.

The December general election returned the coalition, the complexion of which was unmistakably a landslide for the Conservatives with their 338 seats compared to Labour's miserly 42. Even Conservative Stanley Baldwin was less than impressed with the new intake, and on his own benches he could only perceive 'hard faced men who looked as if they had done well out of the war'. Nevertheless, the electorate was now theoretically more representative of the British people as it embraced men over 21 (and postal votes for men still overseas, but no lunatics, criminals or members of the Lords !). In addition middle-aged women (over 30) who occupied or owned land to the value of £5 per annum were now being enfranchised for the first time. For women, that requirement whittled it down quite a bit and kept the working classes, the very women who did much of all that war work, out in the cold for now and denied citizenship. As things stood, many fewer had jobs and most still lived in the hovels they had always lived in but without that 'pin money' coming in for those 'nice little extras'.

For women, any expectation that they would be kept on in their wartime occupations was naïve, but unfortunate all the same. They had in general acquitted themselves superbly and deserved better than a directive to go back home, do the sewing and look after the house...and the kids... and the husband[1]. But the (necessary) legislation - the 1919 Restoration of Pre War Trade Practices Act efficiently saw to it that the men returning from the various fronts had jobs to go back to – to support the very families their women had supported singly for the last four years. It had to be thus: the labour market could not absorb or accomodate huge numbers of men and women workers at the same time.

Before the war most working women were, as we have mentioned, employed in domestic service or in the textile industry. In 1917 the *London Gazette* surveyed women who had done or were doing war work and found that 70,000 had been in service. Two years later, in 1919, 65 percent vowed never to go back into domestic service while a further five percent said they would, but not on the pre-war terms. Their demands were a minimum of £40 per year, two and a half days off every week and to be able to choose their own uniforms. This demonstrates that women now

Above left: 1. Sheffield's Women of Steel, Women of Steel, Sheffield.

Above right: 2. Sister Edith (Edie) Appleton, Queen Alexandra's Imperial Military Nursing Service.

3. This photograph is of three sisters, May Winifred, Maud Elizabeth and Dorothy Evelyn née Lewis who served as Voluntary Aid Detachments for the British Red Cross during World War I. Their three brothers saw active service where two sadly died in France and Belgium and the survivor was injured. Thanks to Richard West, their great nephew for permission to use it. See https://www.qaranc.co.uk/VAD-WW1-Uniform-Photo-Three-Sisters.php and www.qaranc.co.uk for more details. May was born in Hartlepool in 1883.

Above and below: 4. Women workers at Gretna, 'stirring the porridge' and bale breaking. (Courtesy of The Devil's Porridge Museum)

5. A VAD poster appealing to the patriotism of the people.

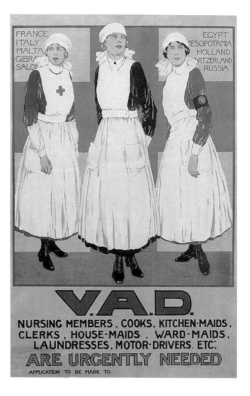

6. Queen Mary's Army Auxiliary Corps Tending graves in the cemetery at Etaples, 1919. (NAM. 1994-07-239-5 National Army Museum, Out of Copyright)

7. The grave being tended by the Women's Army Auxiliary Corps (WAAC) gardener was that of Betty Stevenson. (NAM. 1995-01-24-1 National Army Museum, Out of Copyright)

Above left and above right: 8. Vital war work at the London Rubber Company to help reduce the rampant spread of STIs which had afflicted military personnel in London and other ports and cities where troops, sailors and pilots mustered in WWII. On the left we have inflation testing and on the right electronic testing of condoms on the Automated Protective Line. (Both copyright Waltham Forest Archives and Local Studies Library, Vestry House Museum and published in *Protective Practices: A History of the London Rubber Company and the Condom Business* by Jessica Borge, McGill-Queen's University Press, 2020)

9. A member of the Women's Land Army (WLA) operating a single-furrow plough on a British farm. (Public Domain)

10. Preston Army Pay Office Ladies' Football Team, 1918. (NAM. 1994-07-249-1 National Army Museum, Out of Copyright)

Above: 11. Women's Army Auxiliary Corps typing pool, 1918. (NAM. 1995-01-23-3 National Army Museum, Out of Copyright)

Left: 12. A number of ATS women were selected for training as radio operators and undertook Special Operator Training at Trowbridge and, in 1942, the Isle of Man. This image shows three such special operators, courtesy of Christine Chalstrey. Alma Careswell, Christine's mother, is on the right; she served in the ATS Signals Corps in Harrogate and on the Isle of Man.

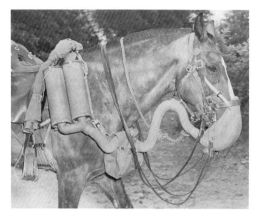

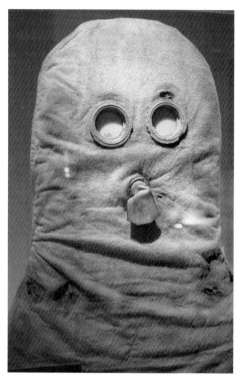

Above and right: 13 and 14. Much work in and around the World War I years was focussed on chemical warfare and mainly involved toxic, asphyxiating and blistering gases. The associated images, artworks, memoirs, novels, films and poetry all remain etched on our minds. And it wasn't just soldiers who had to be protected, as these stunning images show us. Dogs, horses, donkeys and mules all benefited from specially adapted gas masks throughout the war.

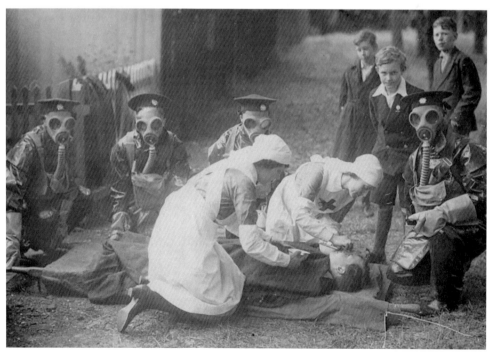

15. Two VADs performing first aid on a patient on a stretcher, surrounded by four men wearing gas masks and three curious young boys.

Above: 16. 'The lady window cleaners of Newcastle-upon-Tyne'.

Left: 17. A WW1 fitter of the Women's Royal Air Force working on the Liberty engine of a De Havilland 9A. The de Havilland DH9A, known as the 'Ninak', was developed as a medium bomber.

18. The Hospital Supply Depot at Newport, Essex with nurses.

19. Women carriage cleaning.

20. Women of the Women's Mounted Emergency Corps, 2nd Field Artillery.

21. Auction sale aboard a Red Cross barge – selling a German helmet, Peronne, June 1917. (NAM. 1999-11-70-48 National Army Museum, Out of Copyright)

22. Munitionettes boring and milling in the Hartlepools National Shell Factory.

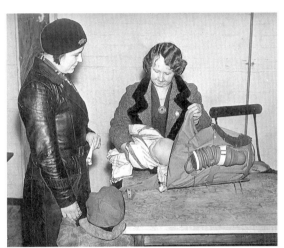

23. Gas masked baby.

24. One of the Stockport Air raid tunnels.

Above: 25. Women's Land Army Women on their knees thinning turnips on a farm near Kendal.

Below left and below right: 26. Two graphic posters aimed at US military personnel warning of the epidemic of STIs which afflicted them (and us) after their arrival in Britain in preparation for D Day 1944.

Above: 27. Auxiliary Territorial Service personnel manning an anti-aircraft searchlight, 1940. (NAM. 1994-07-279-58 National Army Museum, Out of Copyright)

Below left: 28. Auxiliary Territorial Service personnel at an anti-aircraft gun station, 1942. (NAM. 1994-07-279-45 National Army Museum, Out of Copyright)

Below right: 29. A West Indian member of the Auxiliary Territorial Service, 1943. (NAM. 1994-07-283-1 National Army Museum, Out of Copyright)

30. Women welding, probably in a shipyard. (NAM. 2006-12-102-52 National Army Museum, Out of Copyright)

31. October 1942: ATS women working on a Centurion tank at a Royal Ordnance Corps depot.

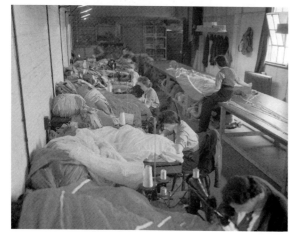

32. WAAF women in May 1944 packing parachutes for the impending Normandy landings.

33. Naafi break: tea, biscuits and buns.

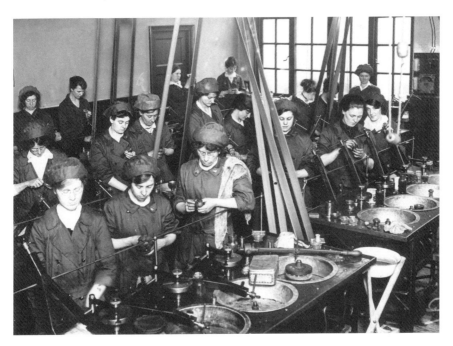

34. Women war workers grinding lenses October 1916. Note the complete absence of eye protection.

Above left and above right: 35. WWII National Fire Service firefighters in action; twenty-three NFS firewomen lost their lives.

36. See you again soon! Members of QAINS arrive at the Normandy bridgehead, June 1944. (NAM. 2006-12-103-18 National Army Museum, Out of Copyright)

Between the wars

recognised their worth due to having worked efficiently in a diverse range of industries and services where most often the gender of a worker was irrelevant and that they could now claim heightened self respect, were empowered and independent and were no longer going to tolerate being virtually enslaved. Women saw quite clearly that they had a proven, positive and productive contribution to make to their country's economy, society and politics. Even *The Times* declared acidly that 'mistresses seeking maids have to adopt a more democratic attitude...and pay a wage they would have thought ample for their own dress allowance'. The upshot of it all was that in 1919 there were four vacancies for every woman looking for work in service.

The Ministry of Labour was unsympathetic and unbending, spitefully relieving 22,000 girls of their unemployment pay 'because they did not like it [the work]'. The officials failed to see that new-found self esteem and dignity were valid levers in their claim for a fair wage and conditions, and that by fostering that self esteem rather than crushing it, morale and production would have been enhanced to the betterment of the country.

Over 750,000 British men died during the First World War - 9% of all British men under the age of 45. At the time much of the feeling was that the slaughter amounted to nothing less than a 'lost generation' of young men. During the 1920s, newpaper editors wrung their hands, intolerant newspaper headlines moaned gloomily of 'surplus' women who would never find husbands. While many middle class women did remain unmarried due to the lack of available men in the relatively narrow social sphere in which they moved, some women in this period remained single by choice or by financial necessity. Professions such as teaching and medicine were opening up to women, but only if they remained unmarried.

At the end of WWI the WAAC, WRNS and WAAF were disbanded. Time for these experienced, mature and highly trained women to go back home. The FANY however, being independent and self-funding, could not be abolished. They did have many supporters in the military establishment who were appreciative of their war-time service; from 1921 the War Office provided Army accommodation and training assistance for Annual Camps and the FANY continued to train so that they would be ready to provide support in any time of national emergency.

In the 1926 General Strike, FANY was the only women's Corps officially employed by the War Office – on 1 May, Commandant Franklin was summoned to the War Office and asked to provide twenty private cars and drivers to take War Office staff to and from their homes. This work led to the inclusion of the Corps in the monthly Army List, although government funding was still withheld.

The Vera Brittain view of post war prospects for the war working woman

Vera Brittain's thoughts on the quickly revised role of women and their prospects in the immediate post-war period are instructive, after all that gushing about how well they had done, keeping the country going, helping us to beat the Germans. She makes it very clear what a great and unique opportunity it was.

'It was impossible to remain very long preoccupied with the effect of the War upon one's own position when the opportunity for changing the position of all women…was there to be seized for the first time in history'.

She goes on to acknowledge that 'straight after the Armistice 'numerous women's organisations…began to emerge from the all-pervading military fog which …had enveloped all movements for social reform'. Although they were lacking resources and 'had to rely on such ignominious expedients as jumble sales for raising funds, they all had definite and intelligent political plans for the pursuit of such objects as the retention of the wartime women police, the introduction of women establishment officers into Civil Service departments, pensions for widows, and the extension of the franchise to all women'. Nevertheless, Brittain points out that Cambridge University was still denying Degrees to women and limiting their intake of women to five hundred while the London Hospital closed their doors to women students altogether 'using the now time-worn argument about the difficulties of teaching 'certain unpleasant subjects of medicine' to mixed audiences'. At the same time, due to the shortage of nurses 'the age of admission was being lowered by the same hospital, and girls under twenty-one were accepted for training without questions of 'delicacy' being raised. Things had undoubtedly changed but there was a huge amount that remained immutable and confined to male strongholds.

Fifteen years after the Armistice in 1933, the Women's Health Enquiry carried out some valuable research on the general health of working class women: the report concluded that working class housewives, particularly those with children, worked a 12-14 hour day, usually confined to one room, mostly on her feet. That was the situation which prevailed before, and during, World War I, after the war and before and during World War II.

In the 1920s we know that women at Viners in Sheffield, for example, had no facilities to wash properly and had to use buckets as toilets. In the same city the 1918 Spring-knife Worker's Report did not mince its words when it reported that some workshops were ' not fit to keep animals in'.

As war clouds gathered in the 1930s, plans evolved to form an all-embracing women's service. This would provide drivers, cooks and clerks for the Army and RAF. Reluctant to lose their independence but conscious of their patriotic duty, in 1938 the FANY undertook to supply trained driver/mechanics, to be part of the new *Auxiliary Territorial Service (ATS)*. They also set up an officer and NCO Training Centre at Camberley. As a concession, the FANYs were allowed to wear their own flash on their ATS uniform sleeves. In 1939 the *FANY London Motor Companies* were ordered to also make their HQ in Camberley, thus separating them from London HQ. Those FANYs not in the Motor Companies became known as the 'Free FANYs' and during the next war were to undertake a variety of valuable roles.

PART TWO
WORLD WAR II

Introduction

Britain had significant levels of unemployment to thank for the pool of labour available in 1939. However, as World War II loomed ever closer many of the men were either conscripted into or volunteered for the various armed services. Many who did not were detained in reserved occupations in order to keep the country going and the forces equipped, and to generally amplify the war effort at home. Such occupations included railway and dockworkers, steelworkers, miners, farmers and other agricultural workers, bakers, gardeners, lighthouse keepers, teachers, police officers, the National Fire Service (NFS), nurses and doctors. The industries with most exemptions were the various areas of engineering; engineering included munitions work.

As in World War I women were ready, willing and waiting to fill the jobs vacated by the men as they left for the various fronts. From March 1941 it was compulsory for women to register at employment exchanges while in December that year the National Service (No 2) Act introduced conscription for women for the first time in British history, largely because insufficient women were volunteering for the auxiliary units of the armed forces[1]. Britain was the only country to conscript women as well as men. Initially the Act applied to unmarried women aged between twenty and thirty and all childless widows, but it was soon extended to married women, except women who were pregnant or had young children[2]. Later the age limit was expanded from nineteen to forty-three (fifty for WWI veterans). The early encouragement was for more women to enlist in the various women's branches of the military services but their national service could just as well be spent in industry, Civil Defence or in the Women's Land Army, for example. By 1943 about 90 percent of single women and eighty percent of married women were doing war work of one sort or another.

Conscription, along with government re-direction of women's existing labour from work in shops, offices and restaurants led to the proportion of women working in essential industries – steel, engineering, chemicals and shipbuilding – increase from 14 percent of the workforce in 1939 to 33 per cent in 1943. For example, in South Yorkshire that year, 37 percent of the female workforce was making munitions. Many worked at the ROF in Maltby while others worked as crane drivers in the Sheffield and Rotherham steelworks, or built planes at Cravens in Sheffield; some worked on the coal wagons in Darnell Goods Depot and produced bottles at Beatson Clark in Barnsley.

Even married women with children were involved: they could do part-time work while older women neighbours looked after their children, encouraged by

Introduction

the advertising slogan which asserted that 'Caring for war workers' children is a National Service'. As production demands increased, the government responded by setting up day nurseries for workers' children in industrial towns and cities. They had arranged for the rapid expansion through local authorities of day nurseries as well as asking them to prepare a register of "minders". Pre-war fees would apply - about sixpence a day - and the Government would match this for the child care.

1945 brought much the same official reaction to women and work as there had been in 1914, much to the chagrin of many women. However, the loss of men in 1945 made it a buyer's market for women with plenty of jobs available for which women were in a strong negotiating position. In a remarkable reversal of fortunes, Dixons steel workers in Sheffield had problems recruiting women buffers and had to resort to hiring men[3].

Chapter 11

Women workers in the military services – here we go again

The WRNS

- "Join the Wrens and free a man for the Fleet".

The WRNS, having been disbanded at the end of WWI, was hastily reformed in April 1939. The imperative need to have women's naval service in preparation for World War II was foreseen back in 1937 by Dame Katherine Furse, a year before an indecisive Admiralty conceded that she was right. Recruits were allocated posts which attempted to reflect their recent experience in civilian life. Most would pass through the Central Training and Drafting Depot in London with its six main divisions plus Raleigh Divisions for training cooks. These recruits would be gradually assimilated into the Royal Navy; then the novice Wren would be posted to her first placement in a naval base or establishment. Further training followed for a wide number of trades, which included: air mechanic technician; automatic Morse transcriber; anti-aircraft target operator; boat driver, meteorological, parachute packer, photographic assistant, radio mechanic, torpedo. From 1941 there was Special Duties Linguist training for Wrens with language skills; these were drafted to stations around the coast to intercept and translate enemy signals. Around the same time the first WRNS arrived at the Government Code and Cypher School, Station X, Bletchley Park.

At its peak in 1944 the WRNS had 75,000 active servicewomen. During the war 245 WRNS members were killed in action and 22 wounded. WRNS were operating radar and communications equipment and providing weather forecasts. The Naval Censorship Branch was staffed by WRNS clerks and censor officers either working in mobile units or in London. Many Wrens were involved in the planning of naval operations, including the D-Day landings in June 1944.

'The BBC People's War' tells how Wrens operated small harbour launches and tugs close to shore. Some Wrens were trained to serve as pilots on D-Day, taking the smaller ships across the Channel and towing disabled vessels back into port for repairs, which were often carried out by WRNS mechanics.

WRNS were posted to every home and overseas naval unit: thousands of Wrens served overseas and saw work in the different branches of the Royal Navy, including the Fleet Air Arm and the Royal Marines. The Women's Royal Indian Naval Service (WRINS) contributed significantly to the running of Royal Indian Navy shore establishments.

Women workers in the military services – here we go again

The Women's Auxiliary Air Force (WAAF)

The WAAF had its second incarnation in 1939 when it assumed the role, again, of the female auxiliary of the Royal Air Force during World War II, absorbing the forty-eight RAF companies of the ATS which had existed since 1938 making just over 1,700 members stationed throughout the country in 47 Companies. When war was declared another 10,000 women volunteered. The Defence (Women's Forces) Regulations were passed in April 1941 which made WAAF members subject to RAF rules. Numbers exceeded 180,000 at its peak in 1943, with over 2,000 women enlisting per week. The WAAFs soon proved themselves, with up to 95 percent directly replacing airmen and 70 percent in skilled trades.

Recruits were given basic training at one of five sites, West Drayton, Harrogate, Bridgnorth, Innsworth and Wilmslow. From 1943 all WAAF basic recruit training was at Wilmslow.

Cathy Pugh, in *The Work of Women in the Women's Auxiliary Air Force* tells how new recruits were usually accommodated in Nissen huts with up to 23 girls sharing; they were kitted out, endured the repellent 'FFI' (Free From Infection) checks, inoculated twice, and given dental inspections. One window was always left open overnight whatever the weather while rats and mice roamed freely over the serried ranks of camp beds. Bathroom facilities might be some distance away requiring a draughty dressing-gowned trek while bath water was rationed to below a 4" line painted in the bath. The one sign of humanity came from a man: Lord Nuffield, William Morris, the well known philanthropist, who generously provided WAAFs (and Wrens) with one packet of sanitary towels per month, known by the grateful recipients as 'Nuffield's Nifties'. Eighty years later we are, to our shame, still living with period poverty. On his 62nd birthday, on 10 October 1939, Nuffield slotted a cheque into a nurse's collecting box at the Mansion House. The logo on the poster the nurse was holding read 'Give freely' to the Lord Mayor's Red Cross Fund'. When the cheque was unfolded it was found to be in the sum of £100,000 (about £4 million in 2016).

WAAF recruits attended lectures on service history, current affairs, discipline, welfare, First Aid, gas, fire and hygiene and were tested for and designated to trades. Primary training introduced them to pay parades, inspections, drill and tough discipline.

Margaret Sturges recalls:

> We had instructions for folding and placing our clothes in a certain order in a cylindrical canvas duffel bag that could be carried on the shoulder. A small bag held mending kits and other non-uniform items such as cosmetics, shoe polish and stationery. Hair had to be worn one inch above the collar.

Ethel Vine, training to be a teleprinter operator in Signals, preferred to wear her own underwear: I didn't like the underwear, we had 'twilights' and 'blackouts' in the knickers, and the 'twilights' were grey woolly things that came down to your knee - like old ladies wore, and the 'blackouts' were like silky bloomers!'

Only women in the civilian *Air Transport Auxiliary (ATA)* flew as aircrew. Nevertheless, the range of essential duties for the flightless was extensive, to say the least, and included: parachute packing, crewing barrage balloons, catering, meteorology, radar, aircraft maintenance, transport, communications duties including wireless telephonic and telegraphic operation. WAAFs worked with codes and ciphers, analysed reconnaissance photographs, and performed intelligence operations. WAAFs were vital in the control of aircraft, both in radar stations and as plotters in operation rooms, most famously during the Battle of Britain. By 1943 WAAFs made up 47 percent of all Balloon Command personnel with 1,029 sites staffed by all female crews (Young Amazons). For reconnaissance photography the WAAFs were trained to develop, print and make up photograph mosaics and trace maps for aircrew. A number of WAAFs were recruited into the SOE.

Electricians completed what was in peacetime a rigorous three year course in nine months. Assistant armourers learned weaponry. By 1944 most plotters and radio controllers were women, 32,000 of them. Early in the development of radio control it was discovered that women's voices carried more clearly over the cockpit cacophony than the voices of their male colleagues. Fast communications were either by words ('Clear') or Morse for home to overseas. German speaking WAAFs were later used to create mayhem amongst Luftwaffe night pilots by issuing contradictory instructions and information. The development of Radio Detection Finding (RDF), later radar, was rapid from 1939 and resulted in an unbroken chain of stations along the south, west and east coasts; here WAAFs with their innate 'anti-hamfistedness' became the perfect operators and were code-known as Special Duties Clerks.

WAAF Nursing Orderlies, known as the Flying Nightingales, flew on RAF transport planes to evacuate the wounded from the Normandy battlefields in 1944. *The RAF Air Ambulance Unit* flew under 46 Group Transport Command from RAF Down Ampney, RAF Broadwell, and RAF Blakehill Farm. Training for air ambulance nursing duties included instruction in the use of oxygen, injections, learning how to deal with broken bones, missing limbs, head injuries, burns and colostomies; and to learn the physiological effects of air travel and altitude.

WAAFs were posted abroad: wherever the war moved, the services obviously moved too. They were to be seen in the British High Commission in New York in 1940; in Egypt and Palestine, Syria and Iraq in 1941 (where they were spat at and stoned), and as far away as Bermuda, the Bahamas, Newfoundland, Labrador, Algeria and the Far East.

At its height in 1943 there were just under 182,000 WAAFs making up sixteen percent of the total RAF strength. They worked in 22 officer branches and in over 80 trades. Overall, during the war 250,000 women passed through the WAAF while 600 or so died in service. Without the WAAF, the RAF would have needed 150,000 extra men – a number which they could not possibly have recruited.

WAAFs were paid two-thirds of the pay of male counterparts in RAF ranks. WAAF was renamed the Women's Royal Air Force in 1949.

Special Operations Executive (SOE)

Times had moved on and along with their still vital, clerical and domestic duties, women were driving and maintaining vehicles, manning anti-aircraft guns and RADAR stations, ferrying aircraft from factories to airfields, deciphering coded German messages in secret naval communications units and, most courageously and dangerously of all, working as agents in the Special Operations Executive (SOE).

Here, women were priceless assets in their varied roles: as couriers, spies, saboteurs and radio operators in the field. Female agents received the same training as the men, and even the most stubbornly opposed men had to grudgingly admit that female spies had distinct advantages over the men on the ground. For example, women could travel freely because they were not expected to be at work during the day. In her *The Female Spies of the SOE*, Kate Murphy Schaefer neatly sums it all up with 'the female spies of the SOE were successful because they learned to be inconspicuous'

During the war thirty-nine of the 470 SOE agents in France were women, with sixteen more deployed to other theatres of war. In 1981, the official historian of the SOE, Michael R. D. Foot, said that the staff of SOE consisted of about 10,000 men and 3,000 women. Of that number, "A few highly accomplished and gallant [women] were agents operating in France or Yugoslavia." Foot cautioned that "On these few there is a large popular literature, almost all of it worthless and much of it about the wrong people".

The Government Code and Cypher School, Bletchley Park

"I was given one sentence, 'We are breaking German codes, end of story'", Ruth Bourne, cipher-breaker

The https://www.techrepublic.com/article/the-women-who-helped-crack-nazi-codes-at-bletchley-park/ website, Hacking the Nazis, reminds us that because of Alan Turing's individual achievements, we often forget that more than 10,000 other people worked at the Government Code and Cypher School, of whom more than two-thirds were female. These servicewomen played a pivotal role in an operation that, classified until 1971, decrypted millions of German messages and which is credited with significantly shortening the war and saving countless lives.

As Annie Burman, in her 2013 MA thesis, *Gendering decryption - decrypting gender: the gender discourse of labour at Bletchley Park 1939-1945,* says:

> The impact of Ultra, the intelligence gained from Enigma, on the Second World War was immense. It allowed the Allies to evade German U-boat wolf-packs during the Battle of the Atlantic, which saved Britain from starvation. It made it possible to cut off Italian

supply-lines to the German Army in North Africa. It assured the Allies that the misinformation fed to the Germans in preparation for D-Day had been accepted as true, allowing the invasion of Normandy to go ahead. The work done at Bletchley Park also led to great advancements in computer science and cryptology. The world's first programmable computer, Colossus, was constructed and used at Bletchley Park for breaking German telegraph ciphers, and several war-time employees became leading [experts] within the new discipline of computer science.

Women, in one role or another, must take credit for a significant part of all this.

"Station X", "London Signals Intelligence Centre", and "Government Communications Headquarters" were all cover names for Bletchley during the war. The formal, official name for their posting for the many "Wrens" working there, was to *HMS Pembroke V.* Royal Air Force. Other names for Bletchley Park and its outstations included RAF Eastcote, RAF Lime Grove and RAF Church Green. The postal address that staff had to use was "Room 47, Foreign Office".

According to Marion Hill in *Bletchley Park People*, 'personal networking drove early recruitments, particularly of men from the universities of Cambridge and Oxford'. And, rather patronisingly 'Trustworthy women were similarly recruited for administrative and clerical jobs...this eclectic staff of "Boffins and Debs" - scientists and debutantes, young women of GC&CS to be whimsically dubbed the "Golf, Cheese and Chess Society"'.

Many of the Bletchley women came from middle-class backgrounds and held degrees in mathematics, physics and engineering. Among them were Eleanor Ireland who worked on the Colossus computers and Ruth Briggs, a German scholar, in the Naval Section. The female staff in Dilwyn Knox's section were sometimes termed "Dilly's Fillies". Marion Hill adds that Knox's methods enabled Mavis Lever (who married mathematician and fellow code-breaker Keith Batey) and Margaret Rock to crack another vital German code, the Abwehr cipher.

However important the cryptanalysis may have been at Bletchley Park, it was only a means to an end. The most central part of the organisation's work was the translation, interpretation and dissemination of intelligence it spawned (Burman, p. 32).

Joan Clarke, a Cambridge undergraduate, was one of the few women employed at Bletchley as a full-fledged cryptanalyst. Lynsey Ann Lord describes how

> Her first placement was humble enough, joining a large group of women, generally referred to as "the girls" who were engaged in routine clerical work in Hut 8. Even though the ratio of women to men working at Bletchley Park was 8:1, women were mostly employed in clerical and administration work and not the more intricate cryptology, which was a male dominated area. During her time at Bletchley Park, Clarke only ever knew of one other female

mathematical cryptanalyst. Clarke was originally paid £2 a week - but as this was an era of female discrimination in the workplace, similarly qualified men received significantly more money[1].

Clarke became deputy head of Hut 8 in 1944, although she was prevented from progressing because of her sex.

The Germans changed the settings on the Enigma machines on a daily basis and each branch of their military intelligence and civil services used different enigma settings. Not knowing the settings meant that the chances of being able to decipher a message was an astonishing 150 million million million to one.

Before cipher equipment and codes were fortuitously captured, German wolf packs had sunk 282,000 tons of shipping complete with invaluable cargoes a month between March and June 1941. The situation was getting ever more desperate and Britain was fast running out of food. We learn from https://mathshistory.st-andrews. ac.uk/Biographies/Clarke_Joan/ that 'in early May 1940, matched plaintext and Enigma cyphertext became available from a German patrol boat, Schiff 26, captured off the Norwegian Coast. Joan Clarke's first task on arriving at Bletchley Park was to use a new key-finding aid called the Bombe, against the recovered data. This successfully resulted in Clarke and her colleagues breaking approximately six days of April traffic over a period of three months'. By November, Clarke and her team successfully reduced the number of tonnage sunk to 62,000 tons. Hugh Alexander, head of Hut 8 from 1943 to 1944, described Clarke as "one of the best Banburists in the section". Banburismus was a new code breaking technique invented by Turing; it got its name because it involved the use of long sheets of paper printed in Banbury[2].

Burman, in her thesis, interestingly explores 'the gender discourse of labour at Bletchley Park and how it relates to the wider context of wartime Britain'. Not only does this throw valuable light on the Bletchley Park workplace but it also adumbrates the situation in many other areas of women's wartime work covered in this book. 'This is done through the theoretical concepts of gendering (the assignation of a gender to a job, task or object), horizontal gender segregation (the custom of assigning men and women different jobs) and vertical gender segregation (the state where men hold more prestigious positions in the hierarchy than women)'.

Burman achieves this through 'interviews, letters and memoirs by female veterans of Bletchley Park, kept in the Bletchley Park Trust Archive and the Imperial War Museum's collections, and printed accounts. Unusually for the literature, 'Using accounts created by female veterans themselves as the main source material allows for women's perspectives to be acknowledged and examined. This becomes especially important in a field of research where the focus lies almost exclusively on male actors and their achievements'. As such, by giving these women a voice, it allows us to experience their experience and provides a relatively uncommon viewpoint of, and is relevant to, many other areas of women's war work, 'relating it to patterns of women's work in Britain during the Second World War'. In effect we get a more balanced idea of the Bletchley Park wartime experience for women in an environment where 'The Bletchley canon: male intellect and female invisibility' conceals the real story: 'gender remains one of the most prominent of the forms of bias. Of all forty- six monographs published on the subject of Bletchley Park in the UK, only eight are written by women. Of these, five...are memoirs, and two were written by the same person'. It is reasonable to assume that similar bias prevailed in the other services, the factories and on the farms. Here's how it happens:

The focus on individuals forms a canon of great names, such as Turing, Welchman, Dillwyn Knox, Tommy Flowers and Hugh Alexander. All these men (because in such a canon, there are never any women) made important and oft-described contributions to the work at Bletchley Park, and there are often interesting, captivating or even amusing stories about them. By contrast, the Typex girl, the Wren machine operator or the typist is a nameless female, most often uniformed into anonymity, and, if she is a civilian, still not distinct enough to catch the interest of the authors.

If it happened at Bletchley (admittedly the most celebrated example) it probably happened too at Gretna, RAF Scampton and at BSA in Birmingham – in fact anywhere where women were not running the show (as at the Women's Institute, for example). 'This has implications for any study of women's work in the World Wars and must be taken into account'. The 'temporary men' were often invisible women at one and the same time.

Political Warfare Executive (PWE), Woburn Abbey

The Political Warfare Executive (PWE) was a clandestine service set up with the aim of spreading both white and black propaganda to enemy and enemy-occupied countries. White propaganda is propaganda that does not conceal its origin or nature. It is the most common type of propaganda and is distinguished from black propaganda which is intended to create the impression that it was created by those it is supposed to discredit. The aim was to damage enemy morale while sustaining the morale of countries occupied by Nazi Germany. The Executive was formed in August 1941, reporting to the Foreign Office. The staff came mostly from SO1, which had been until then the propaganda arm of the Special Operations Executive.

> Unlike the better-known Ministry of Information and its domestic propaganda, the PWE's existence remained hidden due to its function as a psychological warfare arm involved in subversion and disinformation. These activities included rumour campaigns, broadcasts, leaflet drops, underground publications, and forgeries. They were designed to undermine the enemy's will to fight, embolden resistance forces abroad, and create a sympathetic view of the Allies as the liberation of Europe occurred.
> - *https://www.leverhulme.ac.uk/research-project-grants/political-warfare-executive- covert-propaganda-and-british-culture*

The Leverhulme website goes on to explain how material was garnered for these operations: the PWE secretly employed a range of notable authors including the novelists Muriel Spark, David Garnett, and Graham Greene, the poet Stephen Spender, the Bloomsbury writer Quentin Bell and the historian A. J. P. Taylor. 'Although such PWE service remained sensitive after the war, the PWE's legacy still manifested in far-ranging ways, including in fictional and autobiographical writing, and in the continued evolution of its rumours and techniques in cultural discourse'.

Beatriz Lopez, in https://writersandpropaganda.webspace.durham.ac.uk/2019/02/01/muriel-spark-and-plausibility/ finds traces of Spark's wartime service in the PWE in two novels deeply concerned with the appearance of truth: *The Comforters* (1957) and *Loitering with Intent* (1981).

> In her autobiography Curriculum Vitae (1992), she describes her role in the Political Warfare Executive which involved writing down intelligence provided by recently returned aircrews – 'the details of the bombing, the number of planes that had gone out and those (not always all) that had returned' – for black propaganda boss Sefton Delmer. Propaganda is usually understood as biased or misleading information, but Spark's intelligence gathering here shows that it was often based on truth (or...the appearance of truth).

Lopez explains how PWE agents studied German newspapers to find the names and addresses of real people, building up a 'file of personalities' to provide the 'characters' to populate deceptive stories. The propagandists then took pains to highlight only those details needed to infuse a deceitful story with plausible detail.

In her *Muriel Spark and the Art of Deception* Lopez explains how Spark's propaganda work informed her later writing but, at the same time, gives us an idea of her methodology (and presumably that of her colleagues) when working for the PWE.

> This was a formative experience which allowed her to develop an understanding of literal truth as elusive and historically contingent – even a constructed effect – as well as an interest in fictional fabrication and deception. Drawing on an account of the methods of WWII British black propaganda, Spark's biographical accounts, and heretofore untapped archival documents from the Political Warfare Executive Papers (National Archives).

The Allied Central Interpretation Unit (CIU), Medmenham

Women were also very much in evidence in Photographic Intelligence (PI) based at Medmenham, in Buckinghamshire, the Headquarters of the Allied Central

Interpretation Unit and part of the RAF Intelligence Branch. Later in 1941, the Bomber Command Damage Assessment Section was subsumed, and amalgamation was completed when the Night Photographic Interpretation Section of No 3 Photographic Reconnaissance Unit, RAF Oakington, was integrated with CIU in February 1942.

It was here that the air photography, snapped by reconnaissance aircraft flying over enemy territory and occupied Europe and the Mediterranean, was analyzed by photographic interpreters: the intelligence produced from their reports impacted virtually every Allied operation planned and carried out during the war. For example, when new photographs were compared with earlier ones of the same areas it swiftly became apparent when the Germans were developing weapons or other facilities. These could become targets for Bomber Command.

In 1945 the figures were astonishing with the daily intake of material averaging 25,000 negatives and 60,000 prints. By VE-day, the print library, which documented and stored worldwide cover, held 5,000,000 prints from which 40,000 reports had been produced.

An analytical mind, curiosity, the ability to sniff out clues, and spot the unusual were prerequisites for the interpreters and were found in men and women from scientific and artistic backgrounds. By mid 1944 there were over 1,700 personnel on the unit: women made up half the workforce, observing, scrutinising and analysing all aspects of enemy activity.

As Celia Lee says in her *Women in War*, Churchill's daughter Sarah Oliver served as an aircraftswoman plotter for six months before training as a PI. She was posted to RAF Medmenham where it was her role to maintain a daily monitor on Kiel Harbour in order to identify the German vessels in port and track their movements. In the summer of 1942, with the build up to the North African landings underway, Oliver transferred to an inter-Allied, inter-Service team, and worked intensively for several months on preparations for the top-secret invasion of North-west Africa, 'Operation Torch'.

We learn from *RAF Medmenham – The Clearest View* (28 October 2020) by Paul Stewart that some of the most secret, important and successful work done at Medmenham was L Section's identification of the destructive German V Weapons programme. This section focussed on the German aircraft industry and new types of aircraft; it was commanded by Flight Officer Constance Babington Smith; formerly a journalist on *The Aeroplane* magazine, Babington Smith's knowledge of aircraft led her to volunteer for the WAAF. While studying photographs in 1943 she spotted scorch marks on the runway grass at Peenemünde in Germany, showing that the Germans had developed a twin-engine jet, the Me 163 Komet as well as providing evidence of the test flights of the Messerschmitt Me 262 jet fighter. Later that year she also noticed a rocket-like object at the same site – making her the first person to identify a V1 'Doodlebug'. This discovery resulted in a special team being created to study the V Weapons programme in detail. Between late 1943 and early 1944 this team, known as Crossbow, successfully identified all V1 heavy launch sites.

Another woman of prodigious talent was Dorothy Garrod who read history at Newnham College Cambridge before training as an archaeologist. She became the first female professor at Oxbridge, volunteered for the WAAF and was posted to RAF Medmenham as a PI because of her archaeological expertise.

Working with Winston Churchill

According to Lawrence James in his review of Cita Stelzer's *Working with Winston: The Unsung Women Behind Britain's Greatest Statesman*[3] 'daily life in Churchill's service was full of quirky incidents. It was also enormous fun, extremely demanding and occasionally alarming'. Stelzer's book is an anthology of the memories of eleven women who were Churchill's secretaries between the mid-30s and his death in 1965. The female secretaries 'were hired on an ad hoc basis through newspaper advertisements, an employment agency and social connections'. None of that 'modern rigmarole of interviews, vetting and psychological profiling' for Winston Churchill. After all, there was a war on for six of those years. Job requirements were equally unfussy and straightforward: 'good humour, tolerance, and above all, uncomplaining adaptability'.

Kathleen Hill, divorced wife of an Indian Army officer and Girl Guide organiser came on board in 1936 to look after the repair of Churchill's shotguns. She found life at Chartwell 'alive', 'restless' and 'vibrating'. Churchill was concerned about the wellbeing of his girls 'warning them not to risk heart attacks by running upstairs and carrying heavy articles'. His notorious 'mercurial temperament was a constant hazard' but the explosions were short-lived and followed, like the sunshine after the storm, by profuse apologies. Once reduced to tears after a typical Churchillian rebuke, Miss Hill was 'quickly restored to equanimity by Churchill's praise of her typewriting'.

Initially, sanitation in the Central War Rooms left much to be desired: as late as June 1939 the only convenience was a row of buckets lined up in the sub-basement or 'dock'.

Leading aircraftwoman Myra Murden who worked in the Map Room recerived some encouragement when apprised by an RAF officer, 'Of couse you know young lady if the Thames is bombed...we will be drowned'. Myra goes on to reveal how they did 12 hour nights and 12 hour days so daylight was never seen. Sun lamp treatment was obligatory once a week.

The Mechanised Transport Corps (MTC)

The Mechanised Transport Training Corps (MTTC) was set up in 1939 under the Ministry of Transport mainly for women who preferred to do part-time work, in this case driving for civil defence purposes. By 1940 the corps was sending units to France, having changed its name to the Mechanised Transport Corps (MTC), and was contracted to work for a number of foreign governments, British government ministries and the *American Ambulance of Great Britain*. Its members were conscripted and paid. Some volunteered to drive ambulances in France; in 1944 they landed with the Royal Marine Commandos as part of the *Hadfield-Spears Ambulance Unit,* who became known as the "Spearettes".

Members drove staff cars, including those for foreign dignitaries whose drivers were not accustomed to driving on British roads, and also ambulances in the Blitz. Postings followed to Syria, Kenya, Palestine, and Egypt; in 1943 a Security Unit was sent to Algiers, moving on to Italy in 1944. They also drove SOE agents to airfields where they would board the planes that parachuted them into occupied France.

Training included map reading, stretcher practice, vehicle maintenance, breakdown procedure, convoy driving, gas, respiratory practice and first aid. By 1943 there were 3,000 MTC members; the MTC also set up the *Girls' Training Corps.*

The following women's units were affiliated to the military services:

The Girls' Training Corps

"To serve and Train for Service"

The first Girls Training Corps units were formed in 1941; their purpose, as with other cadet organisations at the time, was to prepare young people for wartime service to their community and then to support in the war effort on reaching adulthood. For the Girls' Training Corps this meant training in military drill in order to prepare the girls for serving in the Auxiliary Territorial Service (ATS).

The following cutting describes what the GTC were, and what they weren't. *The Knaresborough Post* on 13 February 1943 reported on the Knaresborough Recruiting Campaign:

> 20 No. 357 Company, Knaresborough, of the Girls' Training Corps, which was begun on June 8 1942, when about 15 cadets were enrolled, has now just passed a membership of 50. Knaresborough Company of the Girls' Training Corps ends its recruiting week tomorrow (Sunday) with a church parade at 10.30am to the Parish Church. After the service, the salute will be taken in the Castle Grounds by Mrs C. H. Tetley. This evening, the girls of the company are giving a concert at King James's Grammar School. The G.T.C. had helped Knaresborough during the "Holidays-at-Home" Week and the "Tanks for Attack" campaign, and would no doubt be called upon to help in the "Wings for Victory " effort.

Mrs Smith took pains to emphasise that membership of the GTC did not involve any of the 20 women's services, though it gave girls excellent training for them, and said there was 'nothing of the Hitler Youth about the movement'.

What did they get up to? An impressive range of activities – and varied skills required to master them - included learning to be bicycle couriers, learning Morse code, aircraft recognition, gymnastics, homemaking, craft-work, public affairs, land navigation, learning first aid, marksmanship, firefighting, and assisting with air warden duties. During the war and after, GTC companies and members were active in volunteering in the community, such as "sitter-ins" in hospitals.

Within a year, over 120,000 girls had joined a GTC company. Unlike their male counterparts, members of the GTC had to provide their own uniforms using valuable clothing coupons. The plan was that after the war the GTC would be disbanded, but there was still sufficient support in 1945 and, following advice from the Youth Advisory Council, the GTC was saved, but, as Claire Duchen writes in her 2001 *When the War Was Over* there was a disappointing greater emphasis in the GTC training programme to recognise the girls as "a potential wife and mother". In 1964 the GTC and WJAC amalgamated to become the *Girls Venture Corps*.

Girls' Nautical Training Corps

The Girls' Nautical Training Corps was formed in 1942, for girls aged 14 to 20, with the majority of units being located in the south of England. It provided training in Royal Navy drill and seamanship, preparing girls for service in the Women's Royal Naval Service, similar to the training and aims of the Sea Cadet Corps.

Women's Junior Air Corps (WJAC)

At first, the WJAC did not receive official support from the Air Ministry. The uniform was modelled on that of the RAF and WAAF; WJAC was formed in 1939 and provided training and activities including drill, Morse code, marksmanship, physical training, first aid, motor maintenance, and aircraft recognition. Optional training courses included anti-aircraft operational duties, radio location, signals, engineering and electrical work, and clerical and office duties. The core and optional training available were used to prepare girls for service in the Women's Auxiliary Air Force and the Air Transport Auxiliary (ATA). Both WJAC and the GTC were also active in supporting local governments in areas such as health initiatives, for example providing vitamins to school children. They were also given training with a limited number of aircraft, such as the Fairchild Argus II, to provide pleasure flights and basic flight instruction.

High achieving female pilots were officers in the WJAC, and included:

Diana Barnato Walker, ATA pilot and the first British woman to break the sound barrier

Freydis Sharland, ATA pilot and founding chairwoman of the British Women Pilots' Association

Jean Bird, first woman to be awarded RAF wings, was a flying instructor in the WJAC.

The Girls Venture Corps Air Cadets (GVCAC)

A voluntary uniformed youth organisation for girls aged between 11 and 20; it received no funding from the Ministry of Defence. GVCAC originated in 1940 as part of the National Association of Training Corps for Girls, the umbrella organisation responsible for the Girls' Training Corps (GTC), Girls' Nautical Training Corps (GNTC) and Women's Junior Air Corps (WJAC).

The Auxiliary Territorial Service (ATS)

September 1938 saw the formation of the Auxiliary Territorial Service (ATS). Many former members of the *Queen Mary's Army Auxiliary Corps (QMAAC)* were among the first recruits.

Davina Blake in her *Wool, Women and World War II* says

> English women recruited to the Auxiliary Territorial Service (the ATS) in World War II found themselves the proud possessors of a mountain of kit mostly made from wool: two itchy khaki uniforms, four pairs of lisle stockings, three pairs of khaki lock-knit knickers (ouch!), two pairs of striped men's pyjamas, eight starched collars, including the studs to attach them, and a greatcoat meant for a man.

The ATS was the women's branch of the British Army, formed on 9 September 1938, initially as a women's voluntary service; it was operational until 1 February 1949, when it was merged into the *Women's Royal Army Corps*. The decision was made that the ATS would be attached to the Territorial Army, and that the women serving would receive two thirds the pay of male soldiers. Companies were raised on a county by county basis under County Commandants. By September 1939 over 1,000 officers had been trained. The FANY formed Motor Driver Companies for the ATS.

The first recruits to the ATS got to work as cooks, clerks and storekeepers. At the outbreak of war, 300 ATS members were posted to France; some ATS telephonists were among the last British personnel to be evacuated with the remnants of the BEF. As more and more men left for the various fronts, ATS numbers reached 65,000 by September 1941. Women between the ages of 17 and 43 were allowed to join; duties also expanded with ATS orderlies, draughtswomen, drivers, postal workers and ammunition inspectors. In 1942 the first ATS military police (Provosts) reported for duty.

Over the six years of the war, about 500 ATS personnel were trained to operate the Cinetheodolite, a specialist camera used in, for example, gunnery practice, with the highest number being in 1943–44, when 305 ATS were in active service using this equipment.

ATS members, in common with members of the other women's voluntary services, gradually took over an increasing number of support tasks, such as radar operating,

Women workers in the military services – here we go again

forming part of the crews of anti-aircraft guns, and military police. According to the Imperial War Museum, there were 717 casualties during World War II.

The ATS and the Royal Signals

The ATS enjoyed a special relationship with Royal Signals and their communications role. Many members of the ATS had worked for the GPO before the war and were drafted into the Royal Signals to mitigate severe manpower shortages. The trades included Teleprinter, Switchboard and Cipher Operator with some stationed overseas, including Africa, Burma and India.

As the war wore on ATS communications responsibilities and numbers increased: by 1944 they had assumed responsibility within the UK for signal and cipher offices, switchboard operating, line circuits and many of the static anti-aircraft communication systems. Indeed, by the war's end over 15,000 ATS members were deployed on indispensable signals duties.

A number were selected for training as radio operators and undertook Special Operator Training at Trowbridge and, in 1942, on the Isle of Man to join the men of the Corps.

One such member of the ATS selected for this vitally important intelligence work because of obvious special skills was Alma Marion Careswell who trained as a radio operator and/or interceptor (see plates section). Once the required standard of Morse Code was reached and the women were conversant with German procedure signals, they joined the men of the Royal Signals at secret listening and intercept stations across Britain, including Harrogate at Forest Moor Y station, and at Kedleston Hall near Derby.

Alma was one of those women. Her three daughters, Lynne, Gill and Christine recall that that she was stationed on the Isle of Man after induction training in Harrogate. Alma, along with the other listeners, would have copied thousands of coded messages and passed them along to the Bletchley Park team for deciphering.

The entire operation was obviously guarded and the Nazi High Command never realised that the Allies knew their secret plans within hours. The secret work undertaken by these ATS women played a pivotal role in an operation that decrypted crucial German messages and in doing so significantly shortened the war and brought peace to Europe. Their contribution was not publicly acknowledged until decades later.

The Royal Signals Museum (https://www.royalsignalsmuseum.co.uk/women-secrets-and-signals/ tells how in 1943, following training in Shenley for radio intercept overseas, elements of 4 ATS Y wing and 5 ATS Y wing were posted to Cairo and Saraband. This freed up male personnel to staff 2 Special Wireless Group which moved to the desert (its mobile section attached to HQ 8 Army with an advanced base at Mustafa Barracks, Alexandria).

At Trowbridge with the reserves for the Y sections preparing for D-Day landings, attention turned to building sections for the war against Japan in Burma, and so the ATS joined with the men in learning the intricacies of Japanese, Morse, Kana and Katana. Women were posted to India and Ceylon – Mountbatten's HQ, to replace Royal Corps of Signals operators who would join field sections in the jungles of Burma.

In the end, the ATS made up 10 percent of the Royal Corps of Signals.

Harrogate's association with the military lives on to this day. Harrogate was central to the Coats Mission, a secret plan for the evacuation of the Royal Family from London. Newby Hall was identified as a possible evacuation place for the Royal family and a wing of Grove House, Harrogate, as accommodation for Winston Churchill, should he need to overnight following any audience with the King. Grove House stood opposite a secret RAF bunker. On 8 September 1940, Buckingham Palace was bombed and the Coats Mission was put on standby but it went no further than that. The Coats Mission was a special British army unit established in England in 1940 for the purpose of evacuating King George VI, Queen Elizabeth and their immediate family in the event of a German invasion of Britain during the Second World War.

Harrogate was the home of a Women's Auxiliary Air Force (WAAF) training centre. Today it remains the location of the Army Foundation College - the only British Army establishment that delivers initial military training to Junior Soldiers. And then there is RAF Menwith Hill which continues the clandestine military intelligence work commenced with the ATS. It provides communications and intelligence support services to the United Kingdom and the United States. The site contains an extensive satellite ground station and is a communications intercept and missile warning site. It is probably the largest electronic monitoring station in the world.

In February 1945, at the age of 18, Princess Elizabeth joined the ATS 'in order to get an insight into what the women in the Services are actually doing in this war' with the blessing of the War Cabinet who saw this as a powerful propaganda coup. Tessa Dunlop, from her research in the princess's military archive at the National Army Museum for her *Army Girls* (p. xviii), describes her as 'a modest teenager' whose service 'saw her become the symbol for a generation of women who went to war in unprecedented numbers'. Elizabeth was a pawn in a greater game and even when she was allowed out of Windsor Castle (her 'castle closet') ...her experience was minutely controlled', her war was 'choreographed'.

Contemporaries 'treasure the friendships forged in their communal living quarters...but that rite of passage was not available to the Princess, she slept at Windsor Castle'. One contemporary (Irene) remembers that she always had lunch in the Officer's Mess.

Searchlight detachments

The primary role of searchlight units was to light up and expose enemy aircraft and facilitate their destruction by pinpointing them for British and allied night fighters. The ATS Remembered website reveals how other routine tasks included sweeping the seas to locate ditched aircraft and air crew; exposing enemy shipping, submarines and mines; providing 'moonlight' for infantry and artillery; shining directly at hostile pilots so they became disorientated; flashing Morse code so that 'friendly' planes could find their way home (a Homer beam) - areas were designated a letter, for example 'B', and a 90 cm searchlight with a shutter would signal this letter in Morse code so that pilots knew how to find that area. Searchlights were used horizontally to help find survivors in bombed out buildings – dangerous as there was a chance that someone could look directly at the arch which generated the light and end up being blinded. It was the Homer beams which the women operators found most gratifying.

The plan in 1935 was to have a male force of nearly 100 searchlight companies with 2,334 lights, 3,000 Lewis guns, 464 three-inch guns and 43,500 men. But by 1941 it was clear that these men were required elsewhere so an untypically pragmatic and enlightened General Officer Commanding-in-Chief Anti-Aircraft Command 1939–1945, General Sir Frederick Pile, urged the use of women of the Auxiliary Territorial Service (ATS) to man these operational roles. They were first deployed to heavy anti-aircraft (HAA) gun units to work the AA guns, radars and command posts. Pile later wrote "The girls lived like men, fought their lights like men and, alas, some of them died like men…They showed themselves more effective, more horror inspiring and more blood-thirsty with their pick-helves than many a male sentry with his gun, as several luckless gentlemen found to their cost". For the time, rare praise indeed. Pile added that the women should have a more practical uniform and should be given the same rates of pay as the men if they were doing the same job.

The replacement of men by women in searchlight units was, however, initially thought to be problematic. The women would be scattered in small detachments in isolated conditions suffering hardship and few amenities. S/L sites were subject to enemy attack and usually had light machine guns for self-defence, but Defence Regulations prohibited women from firing them.

On 23 April 1941 54 A.T.S. members were sent for training at Newark. They were aged between 19 and 35; "the Army Intelligence tests showed the general intelligence to be rather higher than that of the men: the members were fairly representative of A.T.S. personnel." This secret trial clearly demonstrated that women were after all capable of operating heavy searchlight equipment and coping with Spartan conditions on the often desolate searchlight sites. Subsequently, members of the ATS began training at Rhyl to replace male personnel in searchlight regiments.

In July 1942 the first searchlight troop was formed with ATS members. There were six detachments to each troop, four troops to each battery, three batteries to a regiment. Each detachment had fourteen women commanded by a sergeant with a corporal as assistant. Each troop was commanded by an ATS subaltern. On 25 October 1942 the 93rd (Mixed) Searchlight Regiment was formed at Gerrards Cross, with 301, 342 and 495 Searchlight Batteries. Apart from 301 Bty, which was already an all-female battery, the regiment was still 50 percent male when formed, but the wholesale transfer of ATS in, and male gunners out, started immediately.

By the time the regiment was fully converted in August 1943 there were approximately 1,500 women in the regiment, apart from the Commanding Officer and the Battery OCs. In October that year the all-women 301 Battery was transferred to the new 93rd (Mixed) Searchlight Regiment, the last searchlight regiment formed during World War II and the first and only all female Regiment in history. The regiment was deployed in 38th Light Anti-Aircraft Brigade, which was part of the defences of London. Later it moved to the 47th AA Brigade defending Southampton. Many other searchlight and anti-aircraft regiments on Home Defence followed, freeing men aged under 30 for transfer to the infantry.

Before the widespread use of radar, duties within the detachment included:

Spotters: situated about 75 yards from the searchlight projector equipped with binoculars; The Long Arm Operator – manoeuvred the searchlight on instructions from the Spotters via headphones; Bearing Sound Locator and Elevation Sound Locator; Generator operator; Cook/R.T. Operator.

http://www.atsremembered.org.uk/historysearch.htm tells us how

> in some instances [we] were allocated a 'token man' who would arrive with the searchlight troop when the alarm was sounded. He would start the generator and then disappear into the night. Some troops had a Number 9 (the person in charge of the generator) who would start it themselves and these girls became known as Lister Twisters. Lister being the manufacturer of the generator. Later on during the war electric starts were put on generators which saved a lot of the problems…The only immediate contact with the outside world was a small radio transmitter for detachment personnel to give and receive messages from the troop officer. A dispatch rider would arrive each day with details of how friendly aircraft could be identified and deliver personal mail. The ration lorry visited detachments once a week to deliver the rations.

Each site was armed with a Lewis machine gun for use against enemy aircraft, and later each man was issued with a rifle with five rounds of ammunition. Three coshes were also supplied which consisted of a Tate & Lyle syrup tin with nails protruding, embedded in concrete. And three pikes which were six foot gas pipes with a bayonet stuck on the end in concrete.

The First Aid Nursing Yeomanry - FANY (PRVC)

As we have seen, the First Aid Nursing Yeomanry (FANY) was originally formed in 1907. While at the end of World War I the WAAC, WRNS and WAAF were disbanded, the FANY, being independent and self-funding, could not be stood down. From 1921 the War Office provided Army accommodation and training

Women workers in the military services – here we go again

assistance for Annual Camps and the FANY continued to train for readiness to provide support in time of national emergency.

According to their website(https://www.fany.org.uk/history)

In the 1926 General Strike, they were the only women's Corps officially employed by the War Office when on 1 May, Commandant Franklin was summoned and asked to provide 20 private cars and drivers to take War Office staff to and from their homes. This work led to the inclusion of the Corps in the monthly Army List, although funding was still withheld. The Corps title was revised, and they were briefly known as the *Ambulance Car Corps (FANY)*. The name never stuck but it did signal to the wider world the Corps' move post WW1 from a first aid role to one of transport. In 1937 the name was officially changed to *Women's Transport Service (FANY)*.

This higher profile boosted recruitment and small sections were formed away from London in the 1930s - for example, in 1936 Lady Sidney Farrar formed a FANY unit in British East Africa (now Kenya), the first overseas women's unit ever to be formed. In 1933, HRH The Princess Alice, Countess of Athlone, became the first Commandant-in-Chief of the Corps.

Being on the Army List also began the formal recognition of the FANY as military drivers - both by themselves and by the authorities, and formal Army tests for driver mechanics were organised. The War Office also provided War Department vehicles – ambulances and six-wheeled lorries – for Annual Camp in 1936, thus allowing training for drivers/mechanics on convoy work and care and custody of tools.

In November 1939 when Russia invaded Finland, FANY responded by sending a convoy of ten ambulances with forty FANY drivers to Finland via Sweden the following February. They arrived just after the fighting had stopped but stayed on to help evacuate hospitals and refugees from Karelia which had been yielded to the Russians under the terms of the armistice.

After the German invasion of Poland in 1939, 24,000 Poles escaped to re-form into fighting units in Scotland. The FANY got involved with these Free Poles from 1940 until the end of the war, supplying drivers, clerks, cooks and administrative services. A FANY mobile canteen unit was in France with the Poles, returning via St. Malo during the BEF withdrawal.

The website continues:

> Free FANYs were attached to the British Red Cross, the American Ambulance Corps GB and the British Committee for the French Red Cross from 1940 to 1945. In September 1944, 23 FANYs of No 1 Motor Ambulance Convoy were amongst the first women to cross the Channel [to help liberate France].
>
> SEAC Welfare Unit: as the war in Europe drew to a close, FANYs from the Polish Units and the BRCS were recruited for service in the Far East. Thousands of starving Allied prisoners-of-war were freed over the next few months. The FANYs served in Burma, Vietnam, Thailand, Malaya, Japan and the East Indies.

Other FANYs worked during the war as radio officers, encryption specialists, wireless operators, radar operators, personal assistants (drivers, coders and decoders) in the UK, North Africa, Italy, India, Ceylon and the Far East.

However, the most famous role played by the FANY in WW2 was in Special Operations Executive (known as the SOE). The Corps' strength in WW2 was 6,000, of which 2,000 were in SOE.

FANY and the SOE – 1940 - 1945

One major contribution by the FANY to the work of the SOE was in communications, in both the Signals and Cipher departments, where they received intensive training on Morse code. Many FANYs were posted to Grendon Underwood listening station in Buckinghamshire, waiting to receive messages from the agents, because wireless was the most valuable link between the FANY operators based in the UK and the agents on the ground.

Others acted as FANY agents in the field, working mainly in France. Thirty-nine of the 50 women sent into France were FANYs. The FANY had to have perfect knowledge of France, excellent French, and few family ties.

They did their initial training at Arisaig in Scotland in silent killing, weapon handling, fieldcraft, and sabotage; and made parachute jumps at Ringway aerodrome, Manchester. They were proficient in operating wireless sets, which were carried in cases disguised as ordinary leather suitcases. Thirty-nine FANYS went into the field, of whom 13 were captured and murdered by the Gestapo.

Some of the most celebrated, and brave, include:

Noor Inayat Khan, who was part of the ill-fated Prosper network which operated around Paris. Noor was eventually the only SOE wireless operator in Paris. She was arrested but under torture revealed nothing, and twice tried to escape. She was sent to Dachau, where she was shot in September 1944.

Odette Sansom was arrested after seven months, and brutally tortured (with a red hot poker on her back, and having her toenails pulled out), but somehow she managed to convince the Gestapo she was married to Peter Churchill, another agent with whom she had been arrested, and that he was closely related to Winston Churchill. She was sent to Ravensbrück Concentration Camp, where she was kept in solitary confinement in a room next to the furnaces with the heating turned on full blast throughout the summer to try and break her. She survived pneumonia and the war and lived to become one of our most venerated veterans.

Violette Szabo was captured after a major shoot-out, only being taken when she ran out of ammunition. She was shot at Ravensbrück in January 1945. Others included **Lise de Baissac** and **Nancy Wake**. Violette Szabo, Odette (Churchill) Hallowes and Noor Inayat Khan were all awarded the George Cross, Violette and Noor posthumously.

Women workers in the military services – here we go again

In occupied France, and in other countries, women fought in the local Resistance. Catherine Dior was the 26 year old younger sister of Christian Dior who was destined to become France's greatest coutourier. What few people know is that she was also a member of the French Resistance and was arrested by the Gestapo on July 6 1944. Her later witness statement tells us:

'This investigation was accompanied by brutalities: punching, kicking, slapping etc... was taken to the bathroom. They undressed me, bound my hands and plunged me into the water [which was filled with ice], where I remained for about three quarters of an hour...from time to time they submerged me completely and immediately afterward they questioned me...I lied to them as much as I could'.

Catherine was imprisoned in Fresnes awaiting her deportation to Ravensbrück where she was starved and enslaved with the other inmates. From there she was cattle-trucked to Markkleeberg, a subcamp of Buchenwald for more of the same.

Catherine's life as a *Resistante* began in unoccupied Provence where she met Hervé des Charbonneries, a Resistance hero in a radio shop in Cannes. She started carrying messages for agents first in Cannes and then Paris where she was arrested in the Place du Trocadéro and taken to the Gestapo at 180 Rue de la Pompe. The place was notoriously *infernale* with a decadence which saw guards with their gun in one hand and a glass of champagne in the other. Surviving the camps and the death march from Markkleeberg she arrived back in Paris in May 1945 so emaciated her brother did not recognise her[4].

All those FANYs who lost their lives are commemorated on the FANYs' memorial at the FANY church, St Paul's, Knightsbridge.

Chapter 12

Women workers in the civilian services

Air Transport Auxiliary (ATA)

The RAF was adamant that women would, under no circumstances, be permitted to fly operationally, and the only women who did fly were those who flew for the ATA, delivering new, damaged and repaired planes from factories to bases or from base to base, to maintenance units and scrapyards. The female pilots (nicknamed "Attagirls") enjoyed a high profile in the press.

On 14 November 1939 Commander Pauline Gower was put in charge of organising the women's section of the ATA. Thirty WAAF were permitted to join – out of 1400 applicants. The first eight women pilots were accepted into service as No 5 Ferry Pilots Pool on 1 January 1940; at first they were only cleared to fly de Havilland Tiger Moth biplanes from their base in Hatfield. Overall, during World War II there were 166 ATA women pilots, one in eight of all ATA pilots, with volunteers from Britain, Canada, Australia, New Zealand, South Africa, the United States, the Netherlands and Poland.

A welcome, albeit a solitary instance of pay parity, was the fact that from 1943 ATA women received the same pay as men of equal rank. This was a landmark policy because, for the first time, the British government had agreed to equal pay for equal work within an organisation under its control. At the same time American women flying with the Women Airforce Service Pilots (WASP) were receiving as little as 65 percent of the pay of their male colleagues.

And it was not just with equal pay for women that the ATA broke new ground. Diversity was high on the agenda too when forward looking officials made it a policy to recruit pilots who were considered unsuitable for either the RAF or the Fleet Air Arm for reason of age, fitness or gender. Physical disabilities were ignored if the pilot could fly a plane safely – thus, there were one-armed, one-legged, short-sighted and one-eyed pilots, humorously referred to as "Ancient and Tattered Airmen" (ATA). As noted, the ATA also took pilots from other countries, both neutral and combatant. Representatives of 28 countries flew with the ATA.

The initial plan had been that the ATA would carry personnel, mail and medical supplies, but the need for women to replace RAF pilots to allow them to assume combat roles changed all that. At one point there were fourteen ATA ferry pools as far apart as Hamble, near Southampton, and Lossiemouth, near Inverness.

Women workers in the civilian services

ATA pilots also flew service personnel on urgent duties and performed some air ambulance work.

Ferrying was not without its risks and as many as 174 pilots, women as well as men, were killed flying for the ATA during the war. The most celebrated casualty was Hull born Amy Johnson who crashed while delivering an Airspeed Oxford from Prestwick to RAF Kidlington near Oxford in January 1941. Johnson went off course in bad weather: reportedly out of fuel, she bailed out as her aircraft crashed into the Thames Estuary near Herne Bay.

Here are some little known statistics relating to the ATA:

During the war the ATA flew 415,000 hours and delivered more than 309,000 aircraft of 147 types, including Spitfires, Hurricanes, Mosquitoes, Mustangs, Lancasters, Halifaxes, Fairey Swordfish, Fairey Barracudas and Boeing Fortresses.

The average aircraft strength of the ATA training schools was 78. A total of 133,247 hours were flown by school aircraft and 6,013 conversion courses were delivered. The total flying hours of the Air Movement Flight were 17,059, of which 8,570 were on domestic flights and 8,489 on overseas flights. About 883 tons of freight were carried and 3,430 passengers were transported without any casualties; total taxi hours amounted to 179,325, excluding air movements.

This gives an idea of the size of the ATA:

16 ferry pools (1944); Air Movement Flight Unit; 2 Training Units; 1,152 pilots (male) 168 pilots (female); 151 flight engineers; 19 radio officers; 27 ADCC, ATC, and sea cadets; 2,786 ground staff.

The British War Relief Society (BWRS)

The British War Relief Society (BWRS) was a US-based humanitarian umbrella organisation devoted to the supply of non-military aid such as food, clothes, medical supplies and financial aid to people in Great Britain during the early years of World War II. The organisation acted as the administrative hub and central receiving depot for items donated from other charities which were then despatched to its affiliate organizations in the US and to Britain.

As the war wore on, and the British need for aid grew, a large number of charities emerged across the US to aid Britain - amongst them were *American Ambulances in Great Britain, the American Committee for Air Raid Relief, American Hospital in Britain, British American Ambulance Corps, the British Hospital Association* and *Bundles for Britain.*

Merle Curti in *American Philanthropy Abroad (1963)* p. 421, tells how Bundles for Britain was started in 1940 by Natalie Wales Latham as a knitting circle in a shop front in New York City. Knitted goods – socks, gloves, hats, sweaters, and scarves – were made and shipped to Britain. Within sixteen months, Latham expanded Bundles into an organization with 975 branches and almost a million contributors, and by the spring of 1941, it had delivered 40,000 sleeveless sweaters, 10,000 sweaters with sleeves, 30,000 scarves, 18,000 pairs of sea-boot stockings,

50,000 pairs of socks, and 8,000 caps. By 1941, moreover, Bundles had also shipped ambulances, surgical instruments, medicines, cots, blankets, field-kitchen units, and operating tables, along with used clothing of all sorts. The total value of goods shipped reached $1,500,000; another $1,000,000 was raised in cash.

Mrs. Latham was rightly recognized for this wartime effort, being invested by George VI as an honorary Commander of the Order of the British Empire in 1946, the first non-British subject to receive this honour.

The Women's Voluntary Services for Air Raid Precaution (WVS)

'The WVS never say no'.

Another organisation that women could join was the Women's Voluntary Services for Air Raid Precaution (WVS), set up in June 1938; it was the forerunner of the WRVS[1]. Their mission statement was that every woman should be given the opportunity to contribute to the defence of the country against enemy air attack. Initially their main duties were evacuation and making medical supplies, bandages (made from old sheets), nursing gowns and pyjamas. February 1939 brought about a name change to the *Women's Voluntary Service for Civil Defence*, which was more apt because much of the work of a WVS member revolved around the aftermath of the air raids, but most people continued to refer to them as WVS.

One of its first jobs was to evacuate one and a half million children from the big cities to the country. In London children under five went to one of three WVS receiving nurseries. Every child had its head washed to destroy the ubiquitous louse, and was given any clothes he or she lacked before being then personally escorted in a train or car by a WVS member to a country nursery. In two years 30,000 small children were evacuated. One WVS member travelled 126, 490 miles in three years and escorted 2, 526 children under five[1].

Refugees were high on the agenda too. In May 1940 WVS St Pancras branch, for example, visited and classified about 1,350 billets in advance and dealt with 150 arrivals. Helpers met trains at St Pancras filled with confused and anxious refugees from Belgium, the Netherlands, Poland, Malta and Czechoslovakia; by August there were 517 refugees resident in the borough. The WVS ran English classes, clubs and craft classes for them. In Dulwich the WVS organised a tea party attended by 100 refugees.

At its height 960,000 women were involved in the WVS, working alongside local authority personnel and the Air Raid Precaution Service.

The work they undertook broadened to include salvage drives under a mobile Salvage Officer, involving actions such as the removal of iron railings from public buildings. Recycling schemes included highly successful and efficient WVS paper/rubber drives and the collection of aluminium pots and pans, kettles, jelly moulds and even artificial limbs. Old (animal) bones were processed for use as glue and garden fertilisers; rosehips were harvested and turned into a vitamin enriched syrup handed out to mothers and babies; the Housewives Service involved each volunteer being allocated an area of the town or city in which they lived, to assist with immediate aid when emergencies arose following air raids; they delivered water in tankers where the water supply had been disrupted; WVS volunteers would also run information centres, assisting those affected most by the bombings, including tracing missing or injured people and, under a Food Leader, they would work in rest and mobile canteen services serving hot drinks and snacks to Civil Defence workers and those people 'bombed out', as well as providing temporary accommodation for destitute people whose homes were destroyed. The WVS were responsible for the Re-homing Scheme to assist people who had lost all of their belongings during air raids. They organised talks on such issues as 'Make do and Mend (says Mrs Sew and Sew)' and avoiding the 'Squander Bug', a nasty cartoon character who unpatriotically encouraged housewives to waste resources. Clothing too deposited in WVS clothing stores for people who had been 'bombed out'. Mothers were able to exchange garments which their children had outgrown. The organisation of campaigns such as Warship Week, Wings for Victory and Salute the Soldier also fell into their remit.

Some of the more innovative ways in which frugality helped the nation included:

- Making wartime JEWELLERY from old beer bottle tops, cup hooks and corks
- Supplementing a shortage of CLEANING MATERIALS by crushing egg shells for use as a scouring compound and cutting squares out of old stockings for use as dishcloths
- Using the dregs of cold tea to clean WOODWORK
- Varnishing the soles of CHILDREN'S SHOES to prolong the footware's life
- Cutting up old Mackintoshes to make BIBS for babies

From Portsmouth in November 1943, we hear how the WVS Centre's "dog hair expert" attended a special demonstration day at Harrods which taught volunteers how to salvage fur from dog grooming and spin it into a warm and hardwearing alternative to wool.

Bales of wool were supplied in regulation colours and the WRVS would wind the wool into skeins and issue it to women. Knitting was what women did on buses and trams - to not knit was regarded as unpatriotic.

The Women's Institute (WI)

By 1939 the WI was already a well-established pillar of rural life in Britain with institutes in more than 5,500 villages (one in three English and Welsh villages), with 328,000 members[2]. It was the largest non-military voluntary women's organization in the country. Their problem was reconciling work on the home front with their official anti-war position, having in 1929 passed a resolution that the movement should consider 'how best to further the cause of world peace'. Pacifist Quaker members had to be considered too. Nevertheless, this conundrum was overcome and generally speaking the WI continued with their good peacetime work in the war-struck community, mostly helping the other civilian services, focusing on looking after evacuees and working on rural food production.

To that end they were active in Dig for Victory and organised the National Fruit Preservation Scheme, as well as helping with recruitment to the Women's Land Army. WI markets sold surplus produce – mainly fruit and vegetables – from WI members and from smallholders and allotment holders. The WI also helped the WVS to distribute and sell pies to agricultural workers as part of the Rural District Pie Scheme. In 1940 there was a serious shortage of onions; the WI organised the distribution of onion seeds and sets, the Oxfordshire WI harvested 13 tons in 1942. WIs also distributed tomato seeds and seed potatoes in large numbers and sold other seeds to their members at a preferential rate[3].

Oranges were also scarce and as an important source of vitamin C were given to children before adults. To make up the shortfall, the WI helped the WVS with 500 tons of rosehips which were used by pharmacists to make rosehip syrup which was very rich in Vitamin C. Oxfordshire WI members collected foxgloves and belladonna which were dried to make the drug digitalis, efficacious in patients with heart conditions.

The war saw the WI boost their production of jam: in 1939 the government asked them to set up 200 preservation centres so people could make jam with surplus fruit. The next year they asked them to set up 1,000 centres and by the end of 1940 they had established 5,000 in private houses, farm kitchens, outbuildings, village halls and school kitchens. Canning operations received a further boost when the American Federation of Business and Professional Women donated six mobile canning vans to the WI[4].

In 1939, to avoid much of the fruit from the summer's bumper harvest going to waste, WI's headquarters secured sugar supplies direct from the Ministry of Food for £1,400. In the subsequent first wave of jam making, it is estimated that the WI saved 450 tons of fruit from rotting and made 1,631 tons of jam. The American Associated Countrywomen of the World 'sent 500 Dixie Hand Sealers (home canners) along with a complete Food Preservation Unit and oil stoves, tea towels, jam jars, bottling jars, jam pot covers and special discs for pickles and chutneys' (Stamper, p. 7)[5]. Between 1940 and 1945 over 5,300 tons of fruit was preserved in this way. Sir Henry French, permanent secretary to the Ministry of Food told a WI conference that 'the output of the last four years had been the equivalent to a year's jam ration for more than half a million people in this country'.

Members were active in billeting and receiving evacuees and helping to settle them into rural communities. Early in 1939, they assisted the Government's evacuation scheme in which 1.25 million mothers and children were evacuated from urban areas over three days by carrying out a survey of rural homes to find out how many might be able to take evacuees. They promoted 'Make Do and Mend'

Women workers in the civilian services

and advised on how to eke out rations and arranged knitting drives for evacuees, hospital patients and those who had been bombed out.

In 1940 the President of the National Savings Committee asked the WI to help raise the profile of the National Savings Campaign. Each WI branch displayed posters and distributed leaflets and set up its own National Savings Scheme. Stotfold in Bedfordshire raised £8,190 (the equivalent of £283,000 today) in just two years.

The NFWI agreed to an unusual project in 1943 for the Board of Trade: *Propaganda and Instruction in connection with the Domestic Front and the use of rabbit skins to line coats for Russia* in support of Churchill's Aid to Russia Fur Scheme. This was seen more as a gesture to curry favour with the Russians as allies than anything to do with clothing Russians. Coats, waistcoats, hoods and caps lined with rabbit fur flew off the WI home production lines; members not only made the clothing but they reared the rabbits and cured the pelts. In all 2,071 fur lined garments were sent to Russia via the Red Cross (Stamper, p. 11).

Despite all their good, patriotic work Francis White reveals that for the WI 'their biggest difficulty was petrol rationing...because they were a pacifist organisation the government mean spiritedly refused to give them bulk supplies of petrol so they had to beg, steal and borrow transport in order to get their goods to market'.

Air Raid Precautions (ARP)[6]

Air Raid Precautions (ARP) consisted of a number of organisations and guidelines dedicated to the protection of civilians from the peril posed by air raids. In September 1935, prime minister Stanley Baldwin published a circular entitled *Air Raid Precautions*, inviting local authorities to make plans to protect their people in event of a war. Some towns responded by arranging the building of public air raid shelters, built of brick with roofs of reinforced concrete. However, predictably, some local authorities ignored the circular and in April 1937 the government set up *The Air Raid Wardens' Service* to report on bombing incidents – it was looking for 800,000 volunteers; some 200,000 people had joined by mid-1938, and following the Munich Crisis of September 1938 another 500,000 had enrolled.

The use of gas in World War I was obviously a factor in the decision that every single person in Britain would need a gas mask, which meant nearly 40 million respirators were required. Air raid shelters, the evacuation of people and blackout regulations - passive air defence – were other issues. Cellars and basements were requisitioned for air raid shelters and trenches were dug in the parks of large towns. The government also ordered the flying of barrage balloons over London.

On 1 January 1938, the Air Raid Precautions Act came into force, compelling all local authorities to establish their own ARP services: air raid shelters (for example the external Anderson and internal Morrison shelter) were distributed from 1938 and within a few months nearly one and a half million of these Anderson Shelters were distributed to people living in areas expected to be bombed by the Luftwaffe;

ARP wardens; messengers; ambulance drivers; rescue parties and liaison channels with police and fire brigades were all put in place.

Wardens

The job of ARP wardens was crucial: under their wide ranging remit from 1 September 1939, ARP wardens enforced the "blackout". They managed the air raid sirens and ensured people were directed to shelters. They issued and checked gas masks, evacuated areas around unexploded bombs, rescued people where possible from bomb damaged properties, found temporary accommodation for those who had been bombed out, and reported to their control centre about incidents and fires. Obviously they also called in other services as required.

Messengers

Often Boy Scouts or Boys' Brigade members aged between 14 and 18 were designated as messengers or runners, taking verbal or written messages from air raid wardens and delivering them to either the sector post or the control centre. Bombing would sometimes sever telephone lines so messengers performed an important role in giving the ARP services a broader picture of events and generally keeping lines of communication open.

First aid parties

These were trained to give first response first aid to those injured in bombing incidents.

Ambulance drivers

Casualties from bombing were taken to first aid posts or hospital by volunteer drivers. There were also stretcher parties that carried the injured to posts.

Rescue services

The rescue services were involved in removing the dead and injured from bombed premises.

Gas decontamination

Specialists were trained to deal with and clean up incidents involving chemical weapons.

Fire guards

Following the wholesale destruction caused by the bombing of the City of London in late December 1940, the Fire Watcher scheme was introduced in January 1941. All buildings in certain areas were mandated to keep a 24-hour watch. In the event of fire these fire watchers could call up the rescue services and provide access to buildings so that incidents could be properly dealt with.

The Auxiliary Fire Service was set up in 1938 to support existing local fire services, which were amalgamated into a National Fire Service in 1941.

From 1941 the ARP changed its name to the Civil Defence Service to reflect the wider range of activities it had assumed. During the war almost 7,000 Civil Defence workers were killed. In all some 1.5 million men and women served within the organisation during World War II. Over 127,000 full-time personnel were engaged at the height of the Blitz but by the end of 1943 this had fallen to 70,000.

ARP personnel were issued with Mk. II British helmets, which were not made to the same levels of protection as those issued to soldiers, to reduce costs. These helmets had less resistance to ballistic impact – something of a concern in an environment where bombs were falling all around and the air was thick with shrapnel and masonry.

Women ARPs

Women were integrated into ARP services through the *Women's Voluntary Service* in May 1938. It was prescribed that the ideal warden should be at least 30 years old, but men and women of all ages became wardens. In certain instances, even teenagers were wardens. ARP work was open to both men and women but only men could serve in gas contamination, high explosive and incendiary bombs, heavy and light rescue and demolition services. Decontamination squads were also limited to men. From 1 September 1939 a small number of ARP wardens were full-time and were paid a salary (£3 for men, £2 for women), but the majority were part-time volunteers who carried out their ARP duties as well as their full-time jobs. Part-time wardens were ideally on duty about three nights a week, but this increased greatly when the bombing was at its heaviest. One in six was a woman, and amongst the men there were a large number of World War I veterans.

When the war started there were more than 1.5 million people involved in the various ARP services. Full-time ARP staff peaked at just over 131,000 in December 1940, nearly 20,000 were women. By 1944, with the decreasing threat from enemy bombing, the total of full-time ARP staff had dropped to approximately 67,000, 10,000 of whom were women. Volunteers in 1944 numbered nearly 800,000, of which 180,000 were women.

Charity Bick

The youngest recipient of the George Medal during the war was fourteen year old Charity Bick (1924 – 2002), an ARP despatch rider, decorated for her bravery during a raid on West Bromwich in 1941. She had lied about her age, claiming to be sixteen.

During the raid on 19 November 1940 she and her father attempted to neutralise a German incendiary bomb which was lodged in the roof space of a local shop. When she discovered that the standard issue stirrup pump was broken, she successfully doused the fire with handfuls of water. Then while she was leaving, the damaged roof supports gave way and she plummeted into the shop below. Luckily Charity suffered only minor injuries and she and her father made their way to the local ARP Post, where he was the Post Warden. As they arrived high-explosive bombs were falling and houses nearby were hit[7].

After the incident she was presented with a new bicycle for her ARP duties. Charity later joined the RAF, serving until 1962, retiring as a Warrant Officer with 22 year's service.

Stockport Air Raid Shelters

Opened in October 1939, these fascinating shelters were the largest purpose-built civilian air raid shelters in the country. Originally designed to provide shelter for up to 3,850 people, an unsurprising extra demand led to them being extended to accommodate as many as 6,500 people providing shelter and a way of life for families in and around Stockport.

This unique labyrinth of tunnels offered basic amenities: electric lights, benches and bunk beds, 16-seater flushing chemical toilets, a first aid post, canteen and sick bay, and facilities for nursing mothers. Smoking was permitted so the atmosphere, as well as being claustrophobic, was decidedly unhealthy.

The Brinksway shelter in nearby Edgeley had 1,085 bunks and 1,735 seats. The Dodge Hill shelter in Heaton Norris could hold around 2,000 people.

With many men away serving in the forces, women were in the majority, often accompanied by their children. Women were largely responsible for the frequent patriotic sing-alongs which filled the tunnels.

The Royal Observer Corps

In the absence of a comprehensive radar system, the next best thing for spotting an impending air raid on your town, or for observing enemy aircraft movements, is the human eye. The Royal Observer Corps provided those eyes in an organisation which until April 1941, when it was honoured with the 'Royal' prefix, was a men-over 30 only unit. In June that year it was accepted that the physiology of the human eye is exactly the same irrespective of gender, and women were permitted to join. Initially, of the 32,000 observers, only 4,300 were women but that figure soon rose to nearer 16,000 – half, and roughly in line with the 50 percent of people who go to make up our general population.

Composed largely of civilian part -time volunteers, ROC personnel wore a Royal Air Force (RAF) style uniform and latterly came under the administrative control of RAF Strike Command and the operational control of the Home Office. In 1925 the formation of an RAF command concerning the Air Defence of Great Britain led to the provision of a Raid Reporting System, itself delegated to a sub-committee consisting of representatives from the Air Ministry, Home Office and the General Post Office; the GPO at that time operated Britain's national telecommunications system.

During World War II, the ROC complemented and sometimes replaced the Chain Home defensive radar system with an inland aircraft tracking and reporting function, while Chain Home provided a predominantly coastal, long-range tracking and reporting system[8].

Apart from the high power Royal Navy-issue binoculars provided to observers, it was initially all a bit rudimentary: observation posts often consisted of a wooden garden shed next to a telegraph pole, enabling a telecommunications link to be established with a control centre, often via a manual switchboard at the local telephone exchange.

The YMCA National Women's Auxiliary (WA)

The YMCA set up the National Women's Auxiliary which recruited large numbers of volunteers for its war work. During World War II, the mobile canteen, known as the "Tea Car", was introduced to supply food and drinks to troops, other war workers and those made homeless by bombing. WA members could access PoW camps and provided refreshments there to enemy prisoners. They delivered to anti-aircraft installations in remote locations, otherwise deprived of refreshments. At the end of the war 500,000 women had worked in the WA at home and overseas in 2,500 purpose built YMCA centres, or 'huts', canvas marquees, and 1,000 of those mobile canteens.

The Young Women's Christian Association (YWCA)

Over 180 bright and cheerful YWCA 'huts' provided rest and privacy for off duty military women and nurses in often remote camps and airfields in the UK and Middle East with an opportunity to play games, meet friends and enjoy dances. At home they ran hostels for women on leave, Land Girls and munitions workers.

Women's Home Defence /The Home Guard

When MP Dr. Edith Summerskill had the temerity to ask the War Office to allow women to join the Home Guard, the door was resolutely slammed in her face. Smarting from this slight, other groups sprang into existence such as the *Amazon Defence Corps* headed by Venetia Foster in London and the *Women's Defence Corps* set up by Miss Watson-Williams in Bristol.

The Amazon Defence Corps

The Bartitusu Society tells how

Legally prevented from carrying firearms, the Amazons nevertheless practiced with rifles in shooting galleries set up in public amusement arcades and members' homes. Weighted beanbags served as facsimile hand-grenades and Molotov cocktails. The Amazons also trained in unarmed combat.

The Corps contributed a series of five illustrated photo-features to the *Daily Mail*. Titled "At Him, Girls!", the articles instructed readers in some basic jiu jitsu techniques and also included advice on how to wield an umbrella, walking stick or fireplace poker if attacked by an invading enemy soldier. Its members included Marjorie Foster who a decade earlier had become the first woman to win the coveted Bisley King's prize for shooting.

Unlike the War Office, knowing that there is strength in numbers, these different groups and others were consolidated into the *Women's Home Defence* with appeals to allow the training of its members to include the handling and use of firearms; this was flatly rejected. The number of women on the books soon grew to 20,000 in 250 units, and in September 1944 reached 32,000.

The Oxfordshire Home Guard website reveals that despite it all, many women joined the Home Guard in an 'unofficial' capacity and got on with administrative tasks, first aid training, cooking, typing and the like. Finally in 1943 the War Office capitulated (again) and gave permission for women to become members of the Home Guard on the proviso that women were to be recruited solely in non-combatant roles. To avoid any misunderstandings the enrolment form invited candidates to select from being (a) a driver, (b) a typist, (c) a telephonist or (d) a cook. There was no uniform but you did get a plastic/bakelite badge.

Regardless, many women took part in full HG duties learning unarmed combat, marksmanship and other distinctly un- sanctioned activities previously jealously guarded as the exclusive domain of the men.

There was, however, some concern over the fate of the women if the Germans invaded and occupied Great Britain. *Francs-tireurs* ("free shooters") were irregular military formations deployed by France and had a poor reputation with the Germans going back to the Franco-Prussian War. *Francs-tireurs* were routinely shot and it seemed likely that the captured women of the Home Guard may suffer that fate. Accordingly, they were issued with an official 'protection certificate', which confirmed they were 'authorised to follow the Armed Forces of the Crown' and entitled to PoW status if captured.

The Navy, Army and Air Force Institutes (NAAFI)

The website of the NAAFI, always a significant employer of women, ((https://naafi.co.uk/) describes how 'The British Government established NAAFI on 9th December 1920 by combining the *Expeditionary Force Canteens (EFC)* and the *Navy and Army Canteen Board (NACB)* to run the recreational establishments needed by the Armed Forces, and to sell goods to servicemen and their families.

At the outbreak of WWII NAAFI grew exponentially to support the troops on active service, with the number of employees rising from 8,000 to a peak of 110,000, and the number of trading outlets growing from 1,350 to almost 10,000, expanded from less than 600 canteens and 4,000 personnel in 1939. Many staff were recruited from the ATS. NAAFI facilities included bakeries, warehouses, stores, 800 canteens on ships, 900 mobile canteens, and launderettes. During the Normandy landings the NAAFI fed 500,000 troops in the field. Over the course of the war it has been estimated that they served 3.5 million cups of tea and sold 24 million cigarettes every day.

Tragically, 550 NAAFI employees lost their lives supporting the war effort overseas.

NAAFI personnel serving aboard ships are part of the *Naval Canteen Service (NCS)*, wear naval uniform and have action stations, but remain ordinary civilians. NAAFI personnel can also join the *Expeditionary Force Institutes (EFI)*, which provides NAAFI facilities in war zones. EFI personnel are members of the Territorial Army serving on special engagements, bear ranks and wear uniform. NCS personnel can similarly volunteer to join the Royal Navy when it goes on active service.

Male EFI personnel were members of the Royal Army Service Corps until 1965, then the Royal Army Ordnance Corps. Female personnel were members of the ATS until 1949.

The Entertainments National Service Association (ENSA)

NAAFI also ran *ENSA*, the forces entertainment organisation established in 1939. In the 1940 Battle of France alone, the EFI had nearly 3,000 artists and 230 canteens and ran 2, 656, 565 shows between 1939 and 1946.

Women, of course, were the stars of many a show; celebrities included Vera Lynn, Joyce Grenfell, Vivien Leigh, Margaret Rutherford and Gracie Fields.

Tap dancer and acrobatic Vivienne Hole, stage name Vivienne Fayre, a 19 year old civilian was the only ENSA member killed in the war. On 23 January 1945 in Normandy, she was being driven between shows as a passenger aboard a truck carrying stage scenery which strayed into a minefield. She was buried with full military honours in Sittard War Cemetery.

War Correspondents

If you were to scan a list of war correspondents for 1942-43 you might be forgiven for believing that war reporting was (another) all male stronghold to which women had no access[9]. However, women were certainly included in the press corps for World War II and played a major part in bringing back the news of the war. Here are some of them:

Clare Hollingworth OBE (1911 – 2017) was an English journalist and author who was the first war correspondent to report the outbreak of World War II, described as "the scoop of the century. Hollingworth had been working as a *Daily Telegraph* journalist for less than a week when she was dispatched to Poland to

145

report on growing tensions in Europe. She persuaded the British Consul-General in Katowice, John Anthony Thwaites, to lend her his chauffeured car for a fact-finding mission into Germany. While driving along the German–Polish border on 28 August, Hollingworth observed a massive build-up of German troops, tanks and armoured cars facing Poland, after the camouflage screens concealing them were disturbed by wind. Her subsequent report was headlined: *"1,000 Tanks Massed on Polish Frontier; 10 Divisions Reported Ready For Swift Stroke; From Our Own Correspondent."* On 1 September, Hollingworth called the British Embassy in Warsaw to report the German invasion of Poland. To convince sceptical embassy officials, she held a telephone out of the window of her room to capture the sounds of German forces. Hollingworth's eyewitness account was the first report the British Foreign Office received about the invasion of Poland[10].

Her telephoned reports ignored censorship rules and she is reported to have once avoided arrest by stripping naked[11]. In 1941, she went to Egypt and subsequently reported from Turkey, Greece and Cairo. Her efforts were hampered and diminished because women war correspondents did not receive formal accreditation.

Hollingworth was also a prolific charity worker, helping and working with Czechoslovak refugees in Poland as part of her work with the British Committee for Refugees from Czechoslovak (BCRC). It is estimated she helped two- to three-thousand people escape from the Nazis as the takeover of their country scared many into seeking refuge[12].

Betty Knox (1906 – 1963) was an American dancer and journalist. When she hung up her dancing shoes she became a journalist for the *London Evening Standard* and was subsequently a war correspondent in Normandy and a reporter at the Nuremberg trials. In 1943 Michael Foot (*Evening Standard* editor, and future leader of the Labour Party) gave Knox her own thrice-weekly column which she called *Over Here,* celebrating the contrasting cultures of the British and the increasingly ubiquitous American GI ('overpaid, oversexed and over here'). Her first column featured an interview with John Steinbeck, who had recently returned from Capri where he was war correspondent with the United States Navy.

In July 1944 Knox filed her first story from Normandy. As was routine with most female war correspondents she was expected to cover the war from a woman's angle – with on-the-spot reports from military hospitals and articles on food shortages. However, she often bent the rules, and on one occasion hitched a ride with the French Resistance and went Nazi hunting[13]. During this period she worked closely with fellow war correspondent Erika Mann (the eldest child of novelist Thomas Mann).[14]

After the war Knox remained in Germany reporting from the Nuremberg trials. Freda Utley's book *The High Cost of Vengeance* (1948) was highly critical of the conduct of the Nuremberg trials, especially the subsequent trials of those further down the chain of command. Utley spoke to Knox, who had transcribed the last words of three prisoners and (together with fellow journalist Josie Thompson) witnessed their executions. According to Utley, neither Knox nor Thompson "were ever likely to forget their terrible experience".

Erika Mann (1905 –1969) was a German actress and writer and a vocal critic of National Socialism. After Hitler came to power in 1933, she moved to Switzerland, and married the poet W. H. Auden, purely to obtain a British passport and so avoid becoming stateless when the Germans cancelled her citizenship. She continued to attack Nazism, most notably with her 1938 book *School for Barbarians*, a critique of the Nazi education system. During World War II, Mann worked as a journalist in London, making radio broadcasts, in German, for the BBC throughout the Blitz and the Battle of Britain. After D-Day, she became a war correspondent attached to the Allied forces advancing across Europe. She reported from battlefields in France, Belgium and the Netherlands, entered Germany in June 1945 and was among the first Allied personnel to enter Aachen.

Mann attended the Nuremberg trial every day from the opening session, on 20 November 1945, until the court adjourned a month later for Christmas. She was present on 26 November when the first film evidence from an extermination camp was shown in the courtroom. She interviewed the defence lawyers and ridiculed their arguments in her reports and made clear that she thought the court was indulging the behaviour of the defendants, in particular Hermann Göring.

Evadne Price (1888 – 1985) was the war correspondent for *The People* from 1943, covering the Allied invasion of Europe and many major war stories, including the Nuremberg Trials. She was the first woman journalist to enter Belsen concentration camp. Her husband was a prisoner of war in Japan, and was presumed dead for two years.

Muriel Audrey Russell, MVO (1906 – 1989) was a BBC Radio journalist (then called a "commentator"), the BBC's first female news reporter, and, in 1944, the first accredited female war reporter[15]. She landed in mainland Europe just after D-Day and reported from Belgium, the Netherlands, Germany, and Norway. Her World War II military uniform (although non-combatants, war correspondents held military rank) is in the Imperial War Museum.

Elizabeth "Lee" Miller (1907 –1977), was an American photographer and photojournalist. She was a fashion model in New York City in the 1920s before going to Paris, where she became a fashion and fine art photographer. During World War II, Miller was a war correspondent for *Vogue*, covering events such as the London Blitz, the liberation of Paris, and the concentration camps at Buchenwald and Dachau.

In 1940 Miller was living in Hampstead when the Blitz began. As the official war photographer for *Vogue* she documented the Blitz and was accredited with the US Army as a war correspondent for Condé Nast Publications from December 1942. According to the Fitzrovia Chapel website Miller's accreditation allowed her 'to record the efforts of the women in the armed forces and other war efforts. The first article she wrote and photographed for British Vogue was nurses at a US army base in Oxford. She photographed these American nurses at work – in their uniforms and in the operating theatre...and there is the wonderful image of a nurse with rows of surgical gloves being dried and sterilised'.

Her first article in Europe just after D-Day reported on American nurses at the 44th Evacuation field hospital in France, and was published in both British and US

Vogue. Here she captured the daily life of nurses showing their resourcefulness and resilience as they went about their ablutions outside or took part in operations in makeshift hospital tents.

During this period, Miller photographed dying children in a Vienna hospital, peasant life in post-war Hungary, corpses of Nazi officers and their families, and finally, the execution of Prime Minister László Bárdossy.

Chapter 13

Nursing & other health care workers

By the end of the war 14,000 nurses were working in one military nursing service or another.

Queen Alexandra's Royal Naval Nursing Service (QARNNS)

In 1939 large numbers came forward from the civilian hospitals to sign up, some proceeding abroad without first serving in naval medical establishments at home. Some saw action during the fall of Hong Kong in December 1941.

Queen Alexandra's Imperial Military Nursing Service (QAIMNS)

Some QAIMNS nurses went with the BEF to France in 1939; all were evacuated safely in 1940. Before leaving their area, the nurses helped destroy medical equipment, while the Royal Engineers demolished the field hospital– all carried out under fire from German aircraft. QAIMNS nurses found themselves serving all over the world, including Norway, Iceland, Greece, Ceylon and South Africa. Others worked during and after the fall of Singapore in February 1942 where some were subjected to atrocities and others murdered by the Japanese. Others still were held in internment camps for the rest for the war where at least they could do some good for their fellow internees.

The Territorial Army Nursing Service (TANS)

The Territorial Force Nursing Service (TFNS), later Territorial Army Nursing Service, was originally formed to staff the territorial force hospitals at home, so most of its members spent their wartime service in the United Kingdom, not only in the 25 territorial hospitals, but also in hundreds of auxiliary units throughout the British Isles. Soon they were also employed in the eighteen territorial hospitals abroad, and alongside their QAIMNS colleagues in military hospitals and casualty clearing stations in France, Belgium, Malta, Salonica, Gibraltar, Egypt, Mesopotamia and East Africa. TANS was formed in 1920, when the Territorial Force was renamed the Territorial Army.

Queen Alexandra's Royal Army Nursing Corps (QARANC)

QARANC, known as the QAs, is the nursing branch of the British Army and part of the Army Medical Services[1].

Princess Mary's RAF Nursing Service (PMRAFNS)[2]

In 1943 1,126 PMRAFNS sisters and staff were deployed in 31 RAF Hospitals and 71 Station Sick Quarters. 12 June 1944 saw Mollie Giles and Fluffy Ogilvie the first women to land in Normandy with 50 MFH. Subsequently they were both awarded the MBE. From June 1944 onwards 300,000 case vacs were carried out, the largest ever carried out in the history of the service.

Voluntary Aid Detachments (VADs)

With World War II, all male VADs were absorbed into the RAMC. Women were mobilised as and when required for services in military hospitals. During the war VADs resumed their provision of nursing and general support to the medical organisations of all three services, both overseas and in the UK.

District (Queen's) Nurses

The QNI website tells how during World War II district nurses were again called upon to help the war effort, particularly on the Home Front[3]. One of their main roles in the early part of the war was to help organise the reception of evacuees from London and other cities to the countryside. The *Queen's Nurses'* magazine describes how district nurses met evacuated mothers and children at railway stations. Children were given medical examinations to determine which needed special care before they proceeded to host families. District Nurses were also responsible for training members of the *Civil Nursing Reserve* of whom there were almost 100, for example, in West Sussex in March 1940. Nurses also attended a two day meeting in London on Moral Re-Armament, and the health producing and psychological value of a positive, fear-free environment.

Queen's Nurses also served abroad.

Nursing & other health care workers

The Joint War Organisation (JWO) – the Order of St John (parent body of St John Ambulance) and British Red Cross working together

The JWO was formed from the *Order of St John of Jerusalem*, the *Home Ambulance Service* which from 1919 operated under the aegis of the Joint Ambulance Committee of the British Red Cross Society and St John Ambulance Brigade. The women who joined were mostly trained to replace men as ambulance drivers and attendants.

Food parcels

The JWO did invaluable work for PoWs, sending international relief parcels to them (British Red Cross & Order of St John War Organisation parcels) in their camps and providing a support network for their families back home. In addition to the Red Cross Parcels, the JWO also sent special food parcels for invalids, medical supplies, educational books and sports equipment worldwide. During World War II over 20 million standard food parcels were despatched in the International Red Cross distribution system. The food parcels cost on average 10 shillings which was covered mainly by the Penny-a-Week Fund.

Comforts Bags were also sent containing the basic essentials a wounded man admitted to hospital might need such as soap, face flannel, toothbrush, toothpaste, shaving brush, razor and razor blades.

From spring 1941 ICRC ships were able to transport parcels from Lisbon to the south of France, for onward transport to Geneva and subsequent distribution to POWs. The JWO helped the Channel Islands in the winter of 1944–45, averting starvation with over 100,000 food parcels sent to Guernsey and Jersey during their occupation by German troops from late June 1940 to 9 May 1945. Food parcels, flour, grain and coal were brought by the ICRC ship *SS Vega* to the local JWO's who had operated throughout the war in the occupied islands.

Others worked as volunteer hospital supply workers in Central Hospital Supply Stores preparing various supplies, dressings, swabs and bandages. The organisation also worked in hospitals, care homes, nurseries, ambulance units and rest stations with much of the funding coming from the Duke of Gloucester's Red Cross and St John appeal, which had raised over £54 million by 1946[4].

In World War II, Red Cross ambulances carried 1,013,076 casualties and patients and covered 9,142,621 miles.

The Wounded, Missing and Relatives Department

The Red Cross established the Wounded, Missing and Relatives Department to help people searching for information about servicemen who were reported missing or wounded. Red Cross volunteers ran a search service in hospitals to obtain information from patients about men who had been reported missing. They also responded to queries about the condition and progress of men in hospitals around the world.

The Red Cross gave out patterns for sweaters, balaclavas, socks, mufflers, fingerless mittens (which allowed soldiers to keep their hands warm while firing), and toe covers for injured soldiers with legs in casts.

On 15 April 1945, British and Canadian troops liberated the Bergen-Belsen concentration camp only to find, to their horror, over 13,000 unburied bodies and around 60,000 inmates, most of them extremely sick and starving. On 21 April, five British Red Cross teams were sent to Belsen. Red Cross doctors and nurses staffed the hospital, welfare officers took care of children suffering from malnutrition, and cooks established canteens to feed the inmates. Others set up first aid posts, handled stores of fuel and clothing supplies and drove patients from the camps to hospital.

The Hadfield-Spears Ambulance Unit

This unit was established early in the war with £100,000 donated by Sir Robert Hadfield, the British steel tycoon. It was an Anglo-French volunteer medical unit which served initially with the 4th French army in Lorraine, from February 1940 until it was forced to retreat on 9 June ahead of the German advance. Its official French name was *Ambulance Chirurgical Légère de Corps d'Armée 282*. *Ordinary Heroes* novelist Mary Borden (Mrs Spears) agreed to take charge of the largely British female personnel – the nurses and drivers of Lady Hadfield's new field hospital with its 100 beds. The French military '*Service de Santé*' agreed to provide the male staff for the medical unit, including doctors, orderlies and drivers for the unit's heavy trucks[5].

Drivers arrived from the American Field Service, and hospital orderlies from the *Friends' Ambulance Unit* in London – the latter all conscientious objectors or pacifist Quakers. Vehicles, tents, beds, cookers and ward equipment were purchased from the War Office. The vehicles included fifteen 3-ton Bedford trucks, and the same number of 15-hundredweight lorries, as well as five Ford V8s to transport the nurses and officers. *The Mechanised Transport Corps* provided twelve drivers.

Under the designation of *HCM (Hôpital chirurgical mobile) 3 Ambulance Hadfield-Spears*, it was attached to the Free French forces (1st Free French Division) in the Middle East, North Africa, Italy and France before being dissolved in Paris in June 1945.

American Ambulance, Great Britain (AAGB)

A humanitarian organisation founded in 1940 by a group of Americans living in London to provide emergency vehicles and ambulance crews to the United

Nursing & other health care workers

Kingdom. Funding came from private donations, both from Americans expatriates living in the United Kingdom and from the United States. Within six weeks of being set up £140,000 had been raised. By the end of 1940 the organisation had raised around £700,000.

They eventually operated a fleet of around 300 vehicles; the 400 staff were British women aged between 18 and 45, some of whom were seconded from the *Mechanised Transport Corps (for Women)* and the *Women's Transport Services (FANY)*.

Full details can be found at https://aagb.org.uk/the-organisation/

Chapter 14

The Emergency Services

The Auxiliary Fire Service (AFS)

As the threat of war intensified an Act of Parliament was passed to authorise the formation of a voluntary fire service. The Auxiliary Fire Service (AFS) formed in January 1938 as part of the Civil Defence Service and *ad hoc* fire stations were set up in schools, garages and factories. A recruitment campaign was launched, with over 28,000 firefighters needed to support the Brigade's 2,500 officers and firefighters. However, as most younger men had joined the armed services, the AFS welcomed those too old or too young to fight. Significantly, it also marked the first time women joined the Brigade.

Jane Stern, Museum Curator at the London Fire Brigade Museum, tells

> 'Though women did train, they didn't actually fight fires in the Second World War. They became fire watchers and drivers, and managed the communications networks. A rank system for women of the fire service was developed during the war to recognise their service and bravery – many were awarded for their remarkable achievements.
>
> *- https://www.london-fire.gov.uk/museum/history-and-stories/ firefighters-of-the-second-world-war/*

The National Fire Service (NFS)

To provide a unified service throughout the country, the National Fire Service (NFS) took control on 18 August 1941 when all the auxiliary fire services reorganised to form a new national service. The NFS had both male and female members with women usually taking on administrative duties such as staffing communication centres. By 1943 over 70,000 women had enrolled in the NFS.

The Fire Watcher Service

The Fire Watcher Service was formed in September 1940 due to lessons learned during the London blitz in which many offices and commercial buildings had been

The Emergency Services

left unattended, resulting in incendiaries causing fires that could have been dealt with if detected sooner. The Fire Precaution (Business Premises) Order made it compulsory for owners/occupiers of commercial and business premises to have fire watchers on duty at all times. They were to deal with incendiaries as best they could and call on the assistance of the fire and rescue parties as required. The Access to Property Order granted to Wardens and others the right of access to private dwellings and commercial buildings to tackle incendiary bombs.

January 1941 saw compulsory recruitment of civilian men and women to join part-time fire watching and fire party duties. Fire Guards (men aged 16-30 and women aged 20-45) were called up for duty and volunteers were also accepted (men up to age 70 and women to the age of 60). Long nights spent fire watching were tedious and highly unpopular.

Fire Guards were issued with a helmet, armband, torch, a stirrup pump for dealing with small fires, a scoop for picking up incendiaries and a bucket of sand in which to extinguish them.

By December 1943 some six million people were enrolled in the Fire Watcher Service.

Women's Auxiliary Police Corps (WAPC)

In early 1939 the Government published its *National Service Handbook;* conspicuous by their absence were women with no plans for enrolling women as Special Constables. However, the Women's Auxiliary Police Corps (WAPC) - known as 'waspies' by their male colleagues - was set up that August, for women between the ages of 18 -55 for the duration of the war. Duties were wide-ranging and included clerical work at the police station, operating the police control room, vehicle repairs, and driving duties.

One of the most important tasks was documenting bomb sites and casualty numbers in the police station 'war room'. In October the Home Office notified forces that up to 10% of the local police forces could be made up of women. If you worked full time you were paid; those working part-time did so on a voluntary basis. The women were unsworn, that is, they had no powers of arrest; drivers were part-time and so unpaid. If Gloucester is anything to go by, shifts could be long, sometimes lasting from 4.00am until midnight, and could involve driving up to 130 miles in a day[1].

In Manchester, Chief Constable John Maxwell reported to the City Council Watch Committee in late 1939 that six women were carrying out plain clothes police duties in the force – mainly taking statements from women and children, escorting female prisoners to court and dealing with "special enquiries of a delicate nature"[2]. Maxwell was living proof that vision and diversity were, albeit rarely, alive and well amongst men in the higher echelons of public service.

He also referred to the Home Office report about the WAPC when he informed the Watch Committee that he had already had a number of applications from women to join the WAPC, and it was now time to reorganize women in the Manchester Police. He recommended that the existing six policewomen be given full police powers, granted the status of Constable and issued with a uniform. He also believed that the newly formed military camps in the area were attracting undesirables and causing problems with prostitution, which could best be dealt with by women police. He therefore recommended that twenty women be enrolled in the WAPC for the city. The report was acted upon in early 1940.

But this was in a strictly limited way and in 1941, Herbert Morrison, the then Labour Home Secretary, while encouraging greater numbers of women to serve in the police, remarked: "It is true that police duty is, for the most part, a man's job, but such work as driving cars, typewriting and attending the telephone can be done by carefully selected women. There is no reason why canteen duties should not be taken over entirely by women". The old guard, including Labour MPs, persisted and prevailed with their sexist outlook while progress left the room[3].

Women prison officers

Not strictly an emergency service but absolutely essential and usually passed over in the literature on womens' war work. The working lives of female prison officers in general is, as Helen Johnston says, relatively under-researched, partly because the prison wartime records are still locked up in the custody of their respective Governors.[4] Her article aims to uncover the working lives of female officers, the role and daily duties of officers and the development of training schools for female staff.

In World War II female prisoner officers, like their male colleagues, had to deal with four main offences the incidence of which had increased greatly. They were: shoplifting – a reaction to clothes rationing; neglect of children; brothel keeping, and industrial absenteeism.

Heather Creaton records a long report (M-O file 2198) January 1945 which gives us a glimpse of life as experienced by a temporary officer who served in Holloway for four months, with no previous experience of the prison service. She speaks of 'conditions and pay, the formalities of joining and the uniform, day-to-day routines, bribery and tobacco smuggling'. She admits that 'staff conditions generally are slack' and 'the majority of the regular officers are extremely dull, mentally and physically'. It was obviously not a pleasant experience for her, complaining of 'unhappy, bitchy staff and dirty, smelly prisoners'. The worst duty was on the VD [STI] wing but the women in 'for neglecting their children are the most despised, and next to them the petty pilferers'. The drug addict was considered of 'a higher rank than the majority, but the most respected are the abortionists and the grand scale shoplifters (hoisters)'. The Sound Archive at the IWM has nearly 400 recordings relating to wartime imprisonment.

Chapter 15

Women on the farms, in the fields and in the forests

The Women's Land Army (WLA)

One choice open to women who preferred the fresh air to a stint in the services or a shift in a factory was to join The Women's Land Army, resurrected in June 1939 when 17,000 volunteers had already registered with the 52 county offices. At its peak in 1943, there were over 80,000 'Land Girls'.

Recruitment posters portrayed a healthy, wind in your hair outdoor lifestyle – although it never rained or sleeted in these posters. The reality was that living on a farm, as many of the girls and women did, could be very lonely with more than a little home-sickness. So hostels were set up and by 1944 to foster camaradery, friendship and company; eventually there were 22,000 land girls living in 700 hostels.

It wasn't just the Nazis the WLA was fighting: any notions of a bucolic idyll were quickly shattered when we learn that during the war there were over 50 million rats in Britain. The WLA rose to the task of winning their own personal war against these ubiquitous vermin: the Imperial War Museum tells how 'teams of land girls were trained to work in anti-vermin squads. Two land girls are reputed to have killed 12,000 rats in just one year. Land girls in anti-vermin squads were also trained to kill foxes, rabbits and moles' (https://www.iwm.org.uk/history/what-was-the-womens-land-army).

Land girls received their wages directly from the farmers who employed them. The minimum wage was 28s per week and from this, 14s was stopped for those living on the farm for board and lodging; in the meantime, the average wage for male agricultural workers was 38s per week. The working week for land girls was 48 hours in winter and 50 in summer. At the start there were no holidays – paid or unpaid, just a free travel pass for which they had to wait six months. However, conditions improved after 1943 with the introduction of the 'Land Girls Charter' which brought in one week's holiday per year, raised the minimum wage, introduced half day Saturdays and Sundays off, and sick pay.

Some farmers took advantage of their Land Girls by illegally insisting they also help the farmer's wife with the housework, lugging coal and cleaning out the grate.

Unsurprisingly, city girls did not always make natural land workers, and, to the annoyance of many a farmer, there was much damaging of machinery, even confusion between the sex of some animals and, with some justification, about the absence of toilet facilities out in the fields. As a consequence, there had to be some basic training which took the form of six week programmes on model farms and in agricultural colleges. Courses included milking by hand and machine, animal husbandry, tractor driving, hoeing – all followed by written and practical examinations.

The Women's Timber Corps

In 1942 the Women's Timber Corps (WTC) picked up where the Women's Forestry Corps (WFC) left off in 1919. Wood was in demand for replacement housing after the Blitz and the V1 and V2 raids; in addition there was an ongoing need for railway sleepers, telegraph poles and pit props. Barrack huts and PoW camps also required wood, as did ammunition boxes. Railway sleeper production increased from 800,000 to just under two million per year.

Although over 75 percent of our timber needs was homegrown, production rose from 450,000 tons to nearly four million tons per annum. In 1942 the German occupation of Norway began to have a serious effect on timber imports. One of the major difficulties the women faced was in finding accommodation and many householders were reluctant to take the Lumberjills in as they considered them 'dirty' or were prejudiced against women workers. One woman recalled that she stayed at over 80 different billets in two years[1].

What did the Lumberjills do? Their work included felling, snedding, loading, crosscutting, driving tractors and trucks, working with horses and operating sawmills[2]. A more specialist skill was measuring - assessing the amount of timber in a tree, measuring the amount of timber felled, surveying new woodlands and identifying trees for felling.[3]

Basic training consisted of a four to six week course at one of the Corps depots at Culford (four miles north of Bury St Edmunds), Hereford, Lydney (Gloucestershire) or Wetherby before being posted elsewhere[4]. The work was heavy and hard[5], but eventually farmers and foresters had to admit that the women of the WTC were as good as the men they had replaced. Pay ranged from 35 to 46 shillings per week for treefellers with measurers earning more at about 50 shillings per week.[6] The women were paid piece-work rather than a set wage as paid to the women of the WLA, this resulted in the average WTC wage being higher than the WLA[7]. The overall wages though were lower than the national average of just over 62 shillings per week being earned by women in industry during the later war years[8]. At the end of the war some of the women were considered skilled enough to be posted to Germany to help salvage the sawmills there.[9]

When the WTC was disbanded in 1946 each member was awarded a personal letter signed by Princess Elizabeth. Other than this no recognition of the WTC (or the WLA) was made and it was not until 2000 that former members of the WTC were allowed to take part in the annual Remembrance Sunday parade in London.

Women on the farms, in the fields and in the forests

In 2007, the Department for Environment, Food and Rural Affairs announced that all surviving members of the WTC would be entitled to wear a new badge to commemorate their service in the Corps.

Salvage

Women too were involved in the national drive to recycle iron, steel and aluminium, and the raw materials to produce them, all of which were, pre-war, imported from or via enemy territories to some degree. Regulation 50 of the Defence (General) Regulations 1939 (to allow the effective prosecution of the war) demanded that all iron objects be surrendered, including garden railings, gates, bedsteads and old white goods[10]. The response was such that a surplus accumulated and much of it was discreetly sold off. About 6,000 tons of iron was salvaged from blitz scrap. In the end some of the salvage was found to be 'the wrong sort of iron' and this, with the surplus, was quietly dumped in the North Sea. Salvage leaders led the salvage drives, often organised by the *Women's Voluntary Service*; children too played their part as Junior Salvage stewards known as 'cogs'. The compulsory recycling of paper formed a key part of a wider National Salvage Campaign. From 1942, those refusing to sort their waste could be fined £2,500 and face two years in prison.

The public were educated in how their donations were being used through magazine and newspaper advertisements: who would have known that 'twenty periodicals make one seat for a pilot'? Or that bones (not human bones) could be magicked into cordite, glue, soap or fertiliser? Rubber was reformed and old clothes were repurposed into camouflage netting or gun wadding.

Chapter 16

Women in the war factories

This war is a war of machines. It will be won on the assembly line.
– Time Magazine, September 1940

One of the final actions relating to World War I in 1919 was the adoption of the 'Ten Year Rule' which, championed by Winston Churchill who in 1919 was Secretary of State for War and Air, demanded that the three services were to set their budgets on the assumption that they would not be involved in a major conflict within the next ten years. Former Prime Minister Arthur Balfour failed to persuade the Committee of Imperial Defence, which adopted the rule, of the blindingly obvious fact that 'nobody could say that from any one moment war was an impossibility for the next ten years ... we could not rest in a state of unpreparedness on such an assumption by anybody. To suggest that we could be nine and a half years away from preparedness would be a most dangerous suggestion'[1]. We only have to observe the abject naivete and complacency of NATO powers in the years after the fall of Communism in 1989 and the invasion of Ukraine by Russia in 2014 and 2022 to appreciate the truth in that statement.

The Ten Year Rule

In 1928 Churchill, when he was Chancellor of the Exchequer, heaping folly on folly, convinced the Cabinet to make the rule self-perpetuating; in effect it was now in force unless specifically countermanded. In 1931 the Prime Minister Ramsay MacDonald wanted to abolish the Ten Year Rule because he thought it unjustified based on the international situation. This was bitterly opposed by Foreign Secretary Arthur Henderson who succeeded in keeping the rule.

Consequently there were savage cuts in defence spending which plummeted from £766 million in 1919–20, to £189 million in 1921–22, to £102 million in 1932[2]. The Ten Year Rule was eventually ditched by the Cabinet in March 1932, but with the caveat that "this must not be taken to justify an expanding expenditure by the Defence Services without regard to the very serious financial and economic situation" which the country was currently in due to the Great Depression. The U turn was due in large part to First Sea Lord, Sir Frederick Field, who reported to the Committee of Imperial Defence that the Royal Navy had declined not only in relative strength compared to other Great Powers but "owing to the operation of the 'ten-year-decision' and the clamant [something urgently demanding attention] need for economy, our absolute strength also has ... been so diminished as to render the fleet incapable, in the event of war, of efficiently affording protection to our trade". Field also claimed that the navy had fallen below the standard required for keeping open Britain's sea communications during wartime and that if the navy moved to the East to protect the Empire there would not be enough ships to protect the British Isles and its trade from attack and that no port in the entire British Empire was "adequately defended".

Indeed, in 1933 when the Nazis were tightening their grip on Germany, Britain's stocks of armour, munitions and materiel were looking embarrassingly thin on the ground, thin in the air and thin on the waves. All this despite a frightening awareness of Germany's territorial ambitions and the knowledge that, whatever happened, in the event of hostilities, nothing could stop Britain being bombed by a burgeoning Luftwaffe. Orders for barrage balloons were placed and the Air Raid Precautions Department was established at the Institute of Mechanical Engineers in 1935 to supervise civil defence measures throughout the UK.

The sexism, prejudice and misogyny continues

Memories were short. Despite the sterling work women did in World War I – just 21 years before- many employers were still reluctant to hire women, in spite of the urgent need for manpower replacement and extra demands for more and more labour in many traditionally male-orientated industries. Here is what one personnel manager at a Birmingham engineering company wrote in his diary in January 1942, objectifying two female interviewees and pedalling stereotypes:

> "See two more girls sent down from London. A striking blonde from a beauty parlour and a brunette from a gown shop, both in the West End. Capstan shop foreman afraid to put them on his machines; said they were too good a type. I was seriously concerned myself as our factory is an old shabby place and its sanitary arrangements of a very low standard… Local factory class girls are used to them."[3]

As a defence mechanism to shore up male dominance and superiority, the unions dreamt up *The Extended Employment of Women Agreement* to protect men's pay and conditions by ensuring that women's employment was temporary, so that men would not be permanently replaced and women's wages were 'kept under control'[4].

The 1937 Factories Act stated that women could not be employed for more than 48 hours a week and were not allowed to be employed on night shifts. This was all relaxed in 1939: employers were once again permitted to employ women for a maximum of 60 hours a week, and they were allowed to work nights, Sundays and on seven day rotas. Three years later, the Government's report into women's welfare, the *Third Report from the Select Committee on National Expenditure – Women's Welfare, 1942 – 1943* said that "Many married women are of necessity now doing the equivalent of two full-time jobs and, though they do this willingly and cheerfully, the strain of this must inevitably reduce their power of endurance." True enough but it would be interesting to know how many really did 'do this willingly and cheerfully'. Domestic economic necessity may have been a factor?[5]

Women going out to work was of undoubted inestimable value to the nation, as they once again filled the gaps in the labour force while the men of the country upped and left their occupations and sailed off to war. To a large extent it liberated women again and demonstrated once again that they could do most things a man could do and that they could do it very well. Their war employment went a long way to changing the dusty old perceptions of women's place in the workplace and allowed them to project themselves forwards and upwards in post war British society. However, it did also present two unique problems: child care provision, and the replenishment of food supplies to feed the family.

Childcare: who looks after the children?

Before World War II, childcare provision by the government was virtually non-existent, despite the experience gained from World War I and the constrictions on vital women's employment it caused then. The feeling, again, was that women would and indeed *should* be pre-occupied with housework in their own homes from the day they were married and that all care would fall to the mother when the children came along. For mothers who had to go out to work, the options were:

Day Nurseries

The Ministry of Health provided Day Nurseries for women for children under the age of five, but only where the work was deemed 'necessary' and the women were the sole adult wage-earners: in essence they were for unmarried, separated or widowed women. But these nurseries were few and far between - in 1938 there were only 104 Day Nurseries in Great Britain, providing care for a mere 4,291 children. In addition to the (subsidised) fees, mothers would often have to provide essential items such as nappies and a change of clothes.

Nursery Schools

Provided by the local authorities, for 2-5 year old children; however, local authorities were not obliged to provide this option so provision was patchy to say the least. In 1938, there were 118 Nursery Schools, but these only provided care for children between 9am until 3.30pm which did not correspond with the clocking on and off needs of many working women. Newspaper archives held at Valence House Museum in Dagenham give one glimmer of enlightenment when they reveal that breastfeeding mothers who worked at Ford Motor Company were allowed to take four-hourly breaks to go to the nursery at nearby Eastbury Manor and feed their babies.

Elementary Schools

Where it fitted age-wise, this was the preferred choice of many working women as it meant that older siblings could escort the younger children to and from school. In 1938, 170,000 children between 3-5 years old were attending school, which was more than either of the nursery institutions took at that time.

Child-minders

Women workers, where they could afford it, often paid for relatives or friends to care for their children. Although this offered them greater flexibility in terms of obtaining care for the hours needed, the care was more unreliable with greater risk of no-shows due to the minders' own commitments, and was often more expensive than the government-funded care options.

Perversely, middle and upper-class nannies were hailed as wonderful carers for children, but for the working classes, child-minding was deprecated because apparently it just caused juvenile delinquency.

But when do I do the shopping?

Another problem facing factory girls and women was something as routine, simple and essential as, 'When do I do the shopping?' One reason why women took uncontracted time off work was to do their shopping and attempt to get in the queue for rationed goods before they sold out. The only free time women had to shop was during their lunch hour, which meant they had no time for a meal or a rest break themselves. One woman, Connie Hayball, who worked in a Brass Foundry in Birmingham during the war explains the shopping difficulties many women faced:

> "Shopping was a problem, and they used to have to go out in their dinner hour, and I mean, they hardly had any dinner hour, because they would be going, seeking food for their families. And then they would have to go home and have to cook it. And they would be working all day.[6]"

As Penny Summerfield (1989) writes: 'To overcome this problem, some factories paid for professional shoppers, but women preferred to do their own shopping. Eventually many factories conceded a regular extended lunch break or 'shopping hour' to meet this need'.

Eventually the government recognized that happy workers were productive workers and that something as simple as minimum standards of welfare could provide 'a congenial working environment'. So the government built canteens providing cheap, nourishing hot food, washrooms and other facilities. The popular BBC radio programme 'Music While You Work' was switched on to help the long, tedious hours pass.

Respirators by the million

In the mid 1930s the Chemical Defence Research Department contacted the Defence Requirements Committee with a demand for 30 million respirators (gas masks) to protect Britain's civilians. They were to be issued free of charge to people in all areas that were considered to be vulnerable.[7]

Companies better known for their peace-time products and brands were commandeered to produce these respirators. They included the Avon Rubber Company at Melksham (usually producing tyres, golf balls and bath mats); Henley Tyre & Rubber Company, Gravesend (rubberised cables, tennis balls and tyres), and Leyland & Birmingham Rubber Company (swimming hats and rubber flooring). Women made up significant parts of the workforce in each. J.B. Baxter of Leyland were charged with providing and filling the filters, which they did in a converted Blackburn mill. In January 1937 what would eventually become the Government Respiratory Factory had 300 staff, mostly young women, rising to 500 as they turned out 40 million respirators at the rate of 500,000 per week. Time and motion studies revealed that 30,000 respirators could be assembled by twenty-nine workers every eight hours. The kudos of being the first company devoted to the mass provision of wartime PPE for the protection of the civilian population soon evaporated when the particulate layer was changed to merino wool impregnated with asbestos. Many workers suffered chronic illness and early death as a result of breathing in asbestos particles[8].

To warn people that there was a gas around, the ARP would sound the gas rattle.

Aircraft manufacture and shadow factories

The manufacture of aircraft was one of the main beneficiaries of the many shadow factories instituted under the Shadow Scheme, a government plan devised in 1935 and developed in the build up to World War II to try to meet the critical need for more aircraft; in this case, it was technology transfered from the motor industry which was deployed to implement additional manufacturing capacity, that is, to build many more planes.

Astonishingly, General Erhard Milch, chief administrator of the Luftwaffe, was in Britain in 1937 inspecting new shadow factories in Birmingham and Coventry, RAF aeroplanes and airfields. No doubt he was eager to milk this opportunity to observe our aviation preparations with impunity.

The first car makers selected for engine shadows were: Austin, Daimler, Humber (Rootes Securities), Singer, Standard, Rover and Wolseley. Unsold cars were converted into ambulances by removing the rear half and adding an ambulance body.

Central to the plan was the development of nine new factories which the government would build and equip; car companies would gain experience in making aeroplane engine parts so that, if war broke out, the new factories could immediately go into full production. Extensions were to be added to existing factories to facilitate either an easier switch to aircraft industry capability, or an extension of production capacity. As an example, the new factory in Castle Bromwich was contracted to deliver 1,000 new Supermarine Spitfires to the RAF by the end of 1940; in all they manufactured 11,989 Spitfires and Avro Lancasters there. By 1939, 31 shadow factories were complete or under construction; the Air Ministry was responsible for sixteen, of which eleven were working to full capacity. By 1943, 473 establishments employed over 100 employees, many of which were women. The aircraft manufacturing labour force had grown by over 4,000 per cent with 1.8 million men and women employed.

The "shadow factories" were government funded but staffed and run by private companies.

Shipbuilding

Despite the strides made by women in the shipyards and boatyards during World War I, misogyny was still thriving in 1939. As a result, compared with other industries, the number of women allowed to be taken on was comparatively small at the beginning of the war, at ten percent. Those that did make it onto the payroll were engaged in all manner of jobs with a wide range of complexity. Women were particularly occupied in the manufacture of landing craft for the Normandy invasion, which were built in numerous boatyards.

Irene Wonders started at Swan Hunter's in 1940 aged seventeen; she tells us what life there was like for a young working woman, in Ron Curran's *North Tyneside During the Second World War* (pp. 42-43):

> The men I worked with were super. If they swore in front of me, they would always say, 'Sorry pet, I didn't know you were there'. Our forelady used to say, 'You understand how men swear. But if it's not said at you, just ignore it'. Which we did. But there was very little swearing really, they were real gentlemen'.

Munitions: ROFs and RFFs

Fifty or so UK Royal Ordnance Factories (ROF) and Royal Filling Factories (RFF) were set up under the Ministry of Supply before and during World War II[9].

The Royal Ordnance Factories were established with six generic types of factories; most of the employees were women.

In February 1944 there was a tragic fatal accident at the Royal Ordnance Factory in Kirby, Lancashire. In one building 19 workers, mainly women, were filling trays of anti-tank mine fuses when one of the fuses exploded, setting off the rest of the fuses in the tray. *The Daily Telegraph* takes up the gruesome story:

> The girl working on that tray was killed outright and her body disintegrated; two girls standing behind her were partly shielded from the blast by her body, but both were seriously injured, one fatally. The factory was badly damaged: the roof was blown off, electric fittings were dangling precariously; and one of the walls was swaying in the breeze.

The Second Gunpowder Plot, 1942?

We know that munitions work was carried out in hundreds of locations such as converted factories, underground railway shelters and private basements. One of the more unusual examples was the Palace of Westminster's Munitions Factory, documented in files MF/1-6 in the House of Lords Records Office. Volunteers, including members of the Houses of Commons and Lords as well as staff, were invited to sign up for a regular shift assembling instruments. Initially this was done at the Westminster Technical Institute, but when the accommodation there was needed for full-time workers, attempts were made to find space within the Palace itself, causing great alarm to the Lord Great Chamberlain who supposed that explosives would be involved and ruled that 'under no circumstances will he, as being responsible for the safety and well-being of the Palace, allow this scheme to be carried out' (MF/2 15 December 1942). Only the personal intervention of the Minister of Production changed his mind. The scheme became successful, with more than a hundred part-time workers by 1944. All were paid, unless they were civil servants of the higher grades. Some produced torque amplifiers for anti-aircraft guns, some assembled detonator holders and fuses, and others inspected shell fuse parts.

Sources for the History of London 1939-45 - https://archives.history.ac.uk/history-in-focus/War/londonWork.html

Birmingham Small Arms (BSA)[10]

BSA produced the .303 Lee Enfield rifle at Small Heath and at various shadow factories in the West Midlands and Worcestershire along with machine guns, 2-pounder gun carriages, Hispano and 20mm Oerlikon cannons and, of course, their famous motorcycles and bicycles. During the war BSA produced 1,250,000 Lee–Enfield .303 service rifles, 404,383 Sten sub-machine guns, 468,098 Browning machine guns plus spares equivalent to another 100,000, 42,532 Hispano cannon, 32,971 Oerlikon cannon, 59,322 7.9 mm Besa machine guns, 3,218 15 mm Besa machine guns, 68,882 Boys Anti-tank guns, 126,334 motorcycles, 128,000 military bicycles (over 60,000 of which were folding paratrooper bicycles), 10,000,000 shell

Women in the war factories

fuse cases, 3,485,335 magazines and 750,000 anti-aircraft rockets were supplied to the armed forces.

BSA turned out over 60,000 folding bicycles: equal to half the total production of military bicycles during World War II. BSA also manufactured folding motorcycles for the Airborne Division.

Small Arms Ammunition (SAA) was made up of four factories, rising to twenty-four all involved in manufacturing components or filling shells, bombs, grenades and the like. They were just a fraction of the 1,500 or so firms busy filling and producing ordnance. These employed 100,000 workers, of whom 70,000 were women. During the war the factories delivered some 12 million rounds of ammunition of various calibres.

Wilkinson Sword, Acton had a long arms and armour history from the 18th century when they started producing bayonets and swords for the British Army. The company was founded as a manufacturer of guns, which were made in Shotley Bridge in County Durham, by Henry Nock in London in 1772[11]. Over the years the company has also produced typewriters, garden shears, scissors and motorcycles. 1940 saw them winning the contract to supply the first 1,500 Fairbairn Sykes 'FS' fighting knives (which masqueraded as 'hunting knives') for Royal Marine commandos. Fairbairn and Sykes had become knife specialists working for the Shanghai Riot Police and they had returned to Britain earlier that year to train Commandos. Early batches were largely made by hand until Wilkinsons were able to mechanise the process. In October 1942, Wilkinson received an order for 38,000 all black finish F-S knives from the Ministry of Supply. Wilkinson's bulletproof vests were instrumental in the design and early construction of 'flak vests' used by USAAF aircrew.

Wilkinson Sword was soon joined in the war effort by the Sheffield company **John Clarke & Son** who also made F-S fighting knives; the knife is still used by Royal Marine Commandos to this day and so iconic has the knife become to the regiment that it features on the Commando regimental badge. The John Clarke website states 'It is inconceivable to think that the Commandos would ever enter a conflict without carrying their trusty F-S knife as their predecessors did in World War II. **Sanderson Bros.** produced paravane units for minesweepers, torpedo parts, clutch plates for armoured vehicles, gun and rifle parts and over 1 million bullet proof plates[12]. The paravane is a towed winged (hydrofoiled) underwater object – a water kite.

In World War I, the **Singer Manufacturing Company's** sewing machine production gave way to munitions. The Singer Clydebank factory benefited from over 5000 government contracts, and made 303 million artillery shells, shell components, fuses, and aeroplane parts, as well as grenades, rifle parts, and 361,000 horseshoes. The labour force of 14,000 was about 70% female by 1918. Between 1941 and 1942 Singer again suspended production of sewing machines and took on the manufacture of No. 4 Mark I bayonets for Lee Enfield rifles; the initial order was for 75,000; altogether over 3 million 'pig stickers' were produced by Singer in Clydebank and by other companies. Again, women made up the majority of workers. The modified Mark IIs were produced by **Howard & Bullough** of Accrington (the world's biggest manufacturer of power looms in the

167

1860s), along with shells, gun carriages, mine sinkers and aircraft components; at its peak, Howard and Bullough employed over 6,000 people from Accrington and surrounding areas. **Prince-Smith & Stells** of Keighley, makers of textile machinery for wool-combing, drawing and spinning produced 1,057,515 spike bayonets at their Burlington Shed; **Lewisham Engineering** was built on a bomb site at 9 & 11 Malyons Road, Ladywell in 1943, the smallest maker of the No. 4 Mk. II, with approximately 84,566 reportedly produced from 1943–1945. The factory later made cylinder heads for Davey-Paxman landing craft engines. **Baird Manufacturing** of Belfast turned out approximately 101,103 bayonets from 1942– 1944. Scabbards were important too: **Sheffield Steel Products** produced 670,000 Mk. 1 scabbards while Vanden Plas (Eng) 1923 Ltd. of Kingsbury Rd., London manufactured approximately 950,000 Mk. 1 scabbards.

In Sheffield, during the war and into the 1920s and 30s, buffing was the main occupation of women; in nearly every house there was a buffer girl. Viners and Dixons were the main employers of buffer girls with 900 alone at Dixons. File cutting was another woman's trade; with many of the women working at home because they had to look after children and elderly parents.

The Keighley district was big in World War II manufacturing: 204 million munition components rolled out of the Royal Ordnance Factory at Steeton; **George Hattersley and Sons** of Northbrook Works, makers of looms and other textile machinery, produced tapes, metal ribbons and webbing for the services: during World War II they manufactured 28,000 miles of webbing. In 1931 Nuernberg Schwachstrom Fabriken (NSF), a German manufacturing company, set up British NSF Co as its UK agents. In 1932 A radio factory was established by the British NSF at Croydon; 23 German technicians were brought in for six months to train the workers. In 1934 The Home Secretary gave permission for women and young people to be employed on two day shifts in the Wire Winding Dept, at Croydon. In an air raid around 30 employees were killed and several wounded. The Ministry of Aircraft Production relocated the factory to Keighley; **the British NSF** made radio parts for the Resistance movement in occupied Europe. **Keighley Bagcraft** was the London branch of a German leather goods manufacturer until the outbreak of World War II when it became an independent company in its own right and had substantial factories in Airedale Mill in Keighley. Bagcraft supplied webbing for the first 50,000 American troops posted to Britain. During World War II 100 lathes a month, produced by **Dean, Smith and Grace**, were mainly used aboard repair ships. The company financed their own Spitfire as part of a nationwide drive to raise money for fighter planes. They produced lathes for all branches of the armed forces, the government's Ministry of Supply and for the Admiralty, and became one of the first traditionally all-male firms to employ women. At their output peak they were producing 107 machines per month, meaning one-fifth of all the lathes manufactured in this country were coming from Dean, Smith & Grace. The marine engines of **H. Widdop and Co** were "just what the Admiralty and Ministry of Shipping required". Their larger engines enabled Chinese river boats to evade the Japanese by sailing to India non-stop.

Women in the war factories

Fireworks companies

World War II had serious consequences for fireworks manufactures. In 1939 storage magazines were full to capacity with fireworks ready for that November's Bonfire Night; however they had to remain in storage until the end of the war in Europe. Standard Fireworks still made indoor fireworks and sold them for at least a season but also made blinds and lampshades out of black paper for the mandatory "blackout" for protection against aerial attack. The Ministry of Defence contracted Standard Fireworks to manufacture items such as practice ammunition, Verey pistol stars, Thunderflash sticks and parachute flares. Brock's Fireworks in Berkhampstead made signal rockets, parachute flares and Verey lights.

But that was not all: Cooper's sheep dip factory at Berkhamsted developed anti-louse powder during the war. They tested many different formulas – the 63rd was found to be the best – and so it was given the name AL63. Troops dusted AL63 into their clothes to exterminate lice, which could spread diseases such as typhus and diphtheria. Thousands of these tins were found by the Belgian Government in a large hangar in Flanders.

The Mills Bomb

The "Mills bomb" was the first modern fragmentation grenade used by the British Army and saw widespread use in the First and Second World Wars. William Mills (1856-1932), a hand grenade designer from Sunderland, patented, developed and manufactured the "Mills bomb". Early in 1915 Mills converted the Atlas Aluminium Works at Grove Street and Bridge Street West, Birmingham into the **Mills Munitions Factory**. Before then, grenades had often proved just as deadly to the thrower as to the target. Mills did not have an exclusive production contract but the factory made about four million of the seventy-five million supplied to the British and Allied armies throughout the war. Shortly after the outbreak of war it became common for an engineering shop to be staffed almost entirely by women 'hands', and it was usual to find women tool-setters, and women gaugers who tested the grenades.

Initially the grenade was fitted with a seven-second fuse but in the Battle of France in 1940 this delay proved to be too long, giving the enemy time to escape the explosion, or much worse, to throw the grenade back with potentially fatal consequences. The delay was reduced to four seconds. The No. 36 fragmentation grenade was made in prodigious quantities at the **Mills Munition Factory** in Birmingham; contractors manufactured the bodies and base plugs. Finished grenades would then be sent to the Filling Factories. The perforated edges caused it to fragment into many pieces of cast iron on explosion, creating maximum trauma and damage. Troops were taught to throw Mills bombs as if they were cricket balls.

At the start of World War II the firm came under government control and was required to produce medium and large aero engine castings. Products included the aluminium blocks for the Merlin engine used in the Spitfire.

The No. 69 Mills fragmentation grenade, made from Bakelite, was produced by **De La Rue Plastics Ltd**, London. During World War II at the Avenue Works - probably the largest plastics moulding group in Europe - they also produced Bakelite communications equipment and shaped mouldings for Wellington bombers as well as plastic non-metal toilet seats for minesweepers. They were leaders in injection moulding, using new polythene resins for radar and radio. By 1945 the company had over 3,000 workers, and quickly moved into new plastics such as nylon and polystyrene.

Webbing

1937 Pattern Web Equipment ('37 Webbing') was an essential item of military load-carrying kit. It replaced the 1908 Pattern and 1925 Pattern – on which it was based – and was standard issue for British and Commonwealth troops from its introduction in 1937 throughout World War II. **The Mills Equipment Company** of London's Victoria Street was the manufacturer in both wars with the help of 31 different companies. Modern warfare meant that '37 Webbing' had to be versatile: it would consist of interchangeable components, which could be modified to suit the individual needs of a soldier based on his role. Standard components included a belt, cross straps ('braces'), cartridge pouches for .303 ammunition (which gave way to 'universal' pouches to carry ammunition for an array of infantry weapons then used by the British Army, in addition to grenades), a water bottle carrier and a small pack. The large (1908) pack and entrenching tool carrier were retained from World War I issue. Various items were issued for use by officers and armoured vehicle crewmen, such as pouches for binoculars, pistol ammunition and compass as well as a 'valise' side pack and holster for the .38 revolver. The theoretical weight of the fully loaded equipment was 56 pounds for an infantryman in full marching order, including a rifle but not a helmet or gas cape, and 42 pounds for an officer.

The Wool Control

World War II khaki is a felted woollen uniform cloth, worn extensively as an official uniform by the British military forces and made with pure worsted wool which is lighter than the felted uniforms of World War I. The shortcomings experienced with wool supply in 1914 were not to be repeated in 1939, and to that end the Wool Control was set up well in advance and able to start operations the day that war broke out[13]. Essentially it gave the Ministry of Supply control over the production of yarns and fabrics and made it the only importer and supplier of wool in Britain. Rationing was introduced to prioritise uniforms and other clothing for the armed forces with civilian clothing third in the pecking order after exports. Leaving nothing to chance the Ministry bought the entire clips from Australia, New Zealand and South Africa every year up to 1945. It was not cheap, the cost of this monopoly for 1943-1944 was over £ 100 million. Cotton was dealt with similarly with over one third of output going to production for military use.

In 1943, 10,325,000 battle dress jackets and trousers were produced by Britain's wool and textile industry, (British War Production 1939 - 45). Davina Blake (*Wool, Women and World War II*) tells how clothes rationing for civilians was introduced in 1941, and the following year the government set maximum prices. The Board of Trade permitted only a few styles, made only from specified cloths, the ones that were not being used for battledress. Stockings were only available made in lisle or wool, as silk was needed for parachutes. Women painted their legs with potassium permanganate to give a somewhat streaky tan. A black eyebrow pencil was used to give the impression of a seam. By saving on stockings, clothing coupons could be reserved for more essential purchases, such as shoes and coats.

Montague Burton

We have described Montague Burton's contribution to the World War I war effort with his prodigious output of British military uniforms and demob suits ("The Full Monty"), comprising jacket, trousers, waistcoat, shirt and underwear. Burton repeated the feat in World War II with a rapid conversion to the production of greatcoats and battledress. Sir Montague not only dressed many British men, he also introduced a pioneering welfare system for his workers. He could boast fourteen factories and a labour force of 1,000 men and 9,000 women producing 30,000 suits every week. Overall, Burton's produced 13.6 million garments for all three services -25% of the total UK war manufacturing in this area.

Other forces kit makers included the **Fifty Shilling Tailors** founded in Leeds in 1905 with its 399 nationwide stores - a made-to-measure suit of clothes, a matching jacket, vest and trousers for 50/-. Less obvious was the Dunlop Rubber Co.

Dunlop Rubber Company

On 3 March 1945 a V2 made a direct hit on the **Dunlop Rubber Company** at Edmonton, London, starting a fire which burnt down buildings where forces clothing was manufactured. Photographs (held by the IWM) show factory workers salvaging bales of khaki. The connection between rubber and khaki originated when Dunlop began investing in Malayan rubber estates in 1909 and with the establishment of a cotton mill in Rochdale to protect the company's supply of tyre cord and other fabrics. According to the *Manchester Evening News* (20 March 2006) the 'Tyre Yarns and Fabric Weavers Association was formed, which started to make cotton cloth for insertion into Dunlop pneumatic tyres. The cloth was to form a bond with the special rubber so that an air-filled tyre could be made which would make road transport better for goods and more comfortable for passengers'. Dunlop Rubber Co. also designed and licensed the production of joysticks and joystick components on British and other allied aircraft - most notably the joystick grip and head on early Merlin engine Spitfires.

When the Dunlop story began in 1914 the company employed 500 workers. This had risen to 1,650 by 1922, 3,400 in 1929 and 3,270 in 1939, many of them women.

Shadow factories and the Group System

This was an arrangement which allowed any company which could supply a product to standard design and on time could pitch for a contract. Companies as diverse and seemingly unfitting as **Princess Silk Shade** (silk lampshade makers – webbing shoulder straps) and **Crown Bedding** (later Slumberland) who began producing tank parts in 1940, started to win Government contracts which not only involved the making of beds for the military, but also parachutes, emergency rubber water tanks, military webbing, repairing of RAF aircraft gantries, and much more materiel.

Established in 1760, **Barrow Hepburn & Gale Ltd** is a luxury British leather goods company, famous as the manufacturer of the iconic Government red Despatch Boxes; they produced goods for British and Empire troops during World War I, supplying leather for items such as saddles, belts and cases for officers and soldiers. During World War II they were making leather goods and webbing for soldiers, sailors and airmen.

When Mary Harris (the Yves St Laurent of the North East) said goodbye to her husband as he went off to war with the RAF she decided to devote all her efforts to the war effort, converting her four **Mary Harris Gowns** factories in Gateshead, and enlisting her near on 1,000 employees (mostly women), to produce something a little less frivolous than the latest fashions. Instead, she started producing haversacks, webbing and hospital equipment. South Shields-born Mary was also one of the few civilians to know about the D-Day landings before they happened: How? She was given the contract to make flags for the D-Day convoys and also pyjamas, anticipating the thousands of inevitable casualties.

Teddy bears had become very popular amongst the upper classes during World War I, with many companies set up to manufacture them, including Ealon Toys, or **The East London Federation Toy Factory,** which was founded by suffragette Sylvia Pankhurst. It was at about the same time that the **Teddy Toy Company** was founded by B.C. Hope and Abe Simmonds.

In 1920, Rupert Bear first appeared in the *Daily Express*, while A.A Milne published *Winnie the Pooh* in 1926: Pooh Bear toys and games were produced by Chad Vally and Teddy Toy Co. During World War II Teddy Toy Co made leather

Women in the war factories

'bayonet frogs' and helmet liners. Bayonet frogs - a device used to attach a bayonet to a leather belt - were also made by **Marks & Spencer**, among others.

The Railways at War

The railways were amongst the first to form their Home Guard units with hundreds of thousands volunteering. Railway personnel were particularly in demand for work in the Docks Groups, Movement Control Units, and the Railway Construction companies attached to the Royal Engineers. Before the war there were 26,000 women employed on the railways, mainly in clerical jobs or as carriage cleaners, office cleaners, crossing keepers, cooks or waiting room attendants. As the war progressed they took on more roles and were trained in a wide range of functions left vacant by men. Interestingly, they were paid the same wages, after an agreed time, as the men whose positions they filled. Women turned their hands to all manner of jobs, including loaders and porters, oilers, greasers and firelighters, on track maintenance and as coppersmiths, welders, concrete mixers and turners.

Tanks and other armoured vehicles

It did not take long for the potential synergy in working practices between the motor industry, railway engine construction and the building of tanks and similar armoured fighting vehicles to be realised. Companies such as Vickers, Vauxhall, Nuffield, Leyland and Rolls Royce were all involved. During the war this versatile British industry produced 27,528 tanks and self-propelled guns, 26,191 armoured cars and 69,071 personnel carriers – all with women workers heavily involved; the London, Midland and Scottish Railway (LMS) were particularly prolific producers working round the clock to turn out 70,000 steel castings and four million stampings for war equipment such as shells, aircraft and tanks. **Birmingham Railway Carriage and Wagon Co** alone made the A10 Cruiser tank, Churchill, Valentine, Cromwell and Challenger tanks. The company also built Hamilcar gliders[14], invaluable at the D Day landings and at the battle of Arnhem in September 1944.

Vauxhall in Luton also produced Churchill tanks, pulling out all the stops when the British army was down to its last 100. Its 12,000 workforce also delivered 1,000 lorries every month during the course of the war, including 209,906 Bedfords. Over 5,000 Churchill tanks were built in total; these tanks even saw action in Russia with the Red Army. Fake inflatable vehicles, which were used to confuse German pilots into wasting ammunition, were also made there. Also coming off the production line were 5 million sheet metal sides for jerry cans, four million rocket venturi tubes, numerous 6-pounder armour piercing shells, and 750,000 steel helmets[15]. The Venturi tube or venturimeter is an instrument for accurately measuring the flow rate of fluids in pipes.

York Carriage Works had been busy and significant contributors to the World War I war effort, as might be expected. Horse drawn vehicles were particularly important; these were augmented by 984 general service wagons for the Army Service Corps, Officers Mess Carts and 412 General Service Limbers. York also helped the French army when it built 400 twenty-ton covered wagons which ran on French railways. Less obviously, 1,850 stretchers came out of York, entrenching tools, pack saddles for artillery horses and 400 clarifying reels for use in water purification. The construction of tank transporters must have been an unexpected contract; the revolutionary twenty-ton mobile war machine needed a very special vehicle for transportation and the railways were an obvious answer to at least part of the challenge. Existing flat wagons were inadequate and unsuitable: they could only be loaded at the ends and they could not bear the weight of a tank. York produced forty of the new RECTANKS, themselves weighing thirty-five tons with the crucial design feature that they could be loaded from the side. So good were they that they were used in World War II as well.

The London Rubber Co and Durex[16]

https://archives.history.ac.uk/history-in-focus/War/londonWork.html reports how

The Public Morality Council (PMC) became concerned in 1943 that '....young girls, some of them just leaving school, aged 14-15, were being enticed into the blind alley occupation of the manufacture, testing and packing of contraceptives, by large wages offered'. They were earning £2.5.0. a week, very good pay for their age at a time when adult female munitions workers got £2.16.0. The PMC tried to get a minimum age limit set on this work but the government refused, pointing out that the girls took up the work of their own accord, often because an older relative in the same firm had got them the job (LMA A/PMC/1 0. 16.9.43). The flourishing state of the London Rubber Company, would have annoyed the formidable birth control reformer, Marie Stopes, as she tried to run her free contraception clinics. Her papers, in the Wellcome Institute Contemporary Medical Archives Centre, document her ceaseless skirmishes with the 'enraging' Rubber Control at the Ministry of Supply which was unwilling to divert supplies for her clinics. She wrote to the London Rubber Co in December 1944, '...the position I maintain is that the commercial trade, touting in garages and barbers shops, should have no supplies at all while we are short' (PP/MCS/B.29).

– Extract from *Sources for the History of London 1939-45*
Chapter 5, pages 83-84[17]

In 1839, Charles Goodyear discovered the vulcanisation of rubber, the process that makes rubber - which is naturally hard when cold and soft when warm. This enabled condoms to be made from rubber, but the first rubber condoms were as thick as bicycle tyre inner tubes and had seams protruding down the sides, so they would not have given a particularly pleasurable sexual experience for either partner. Latex, made from rubber suspended in water, was invented in 1920. The US Youngs Rubber Company was the first to manufacture a latex condom which was an improved version of their Trojan brand. In the 1930's the London Rubber Company manufactured the first condoms using the latest liquid latex dipping technology. By the end of World War II, London Rubber was Britain's biggest condom manufacturer. Re-usable sheaths, such as the Durex Paragon, provided a money-saving alternative to single-use condoms and could last for three months if properly maintained using rolling devices and dusting powders (at extra cost). The Durex brand, launched in 1929, gets its name from **'Dur**ability, **re**liability and **ex**cellence.

The LRC website tells us (https://sites.google.com/view/london-rubber-company/home/) that LRC had a long tradition of employing women and girls, and, come the war, a good number of the employees were women who worked shifts on the various production and testing lines. Girls as young as 14 worked on the condom production lines in Chingford, Essex. Many women stayed on after the war: mothers, daughters, sisters and aunts had jobs at Chingford and lots of them ended up working for the company for generations citing the camaraderie and family atmosphere as reasons for their longevity[18].

The company was indeed very family orientated: the London Rubber Co had its own in-house magazine *London Image*, that featured appointments, promotions, weddings, retirements, deaths and other family matters. There was a Social Club with dances, parties and outings, including one year taking 1100 children to see, *Dick Whittington* in the West End.

The December 1941 National Service Act required unmarried women between the ages of twenty and thirty to be conscripted to help the war effort in whatever way possible so LRC's workforce must have fallen outside of these age groups. As noted, Watch Committees had reservations about 14 year old girls straight out of school handling Durex contraceptives; the Public Morality Council attempted to have the matter raised in Parliament but the Minister of Labour was having none of it and the girls stayed.

An example of the many women who stayed for many years is Mrs L.R. Stevenson a supervisor, who lived 200 yards from the Chingford factory and clocked up twenty-eight years service[19]. Miss A. Want joined the Surgical Testing Department and stayed for thirty-two years[20]; Minnie Skingley started in 1939 and she too worked there for twenty-eight years while her daughter later worked in Data Processing[21]. Mrs Alice Sleap, a charge hand in production tooling in the North Circular Road factory started there in 1941 and remained for twenty-six years. Joyce Idell, her daughter, joined later as a secretary 'and met her husband over condoms in the AP plant'[22]. Anyone who had to take a bus to and from work had the option of paying their fare in condoms.

Which brings us on to…

Chapter 17

Prostitution in the World Wars

Prostitution was often, but by no means always, women's work [1]. And even when it was a female occupation, it was an activity, like many other forms of war work, shared, to a greater or lesser extent, with men who usually had at least a fifty per cent involvement and a 100 per cent investment in the sexual activity offered by prostitutes. Prostitution, however, should not, as it sometimes is in the modern world by various religious and moralist groups, be confused or lumped in with women and girls just having a good time, enjoying their world war independence and new freedoms. However, files released in 2005 suggest that in World War 2.

Prostitutes preyed on American soldiers stationed in Britain during World War II, causing fears that Nazis would seize on this to portray Britain in a negative light, according to wartime police files. The files reveal that United States and British officials were so concerned that they held a series of high-level crisis meetings during the war in an attempt to defuse the issue.

https://mg.co.za/article/2005-11-02-london-prostitutes-pestered-wwii-troops/

Letters opened by military censors from American troops to their families painted a "very adverse picture" of London's West End, unnamed officials said in the papers. "They describe how rife accosting is, and also tell stories of men who have been robbed by these women," one official wrote. The British authorities rejected the claim suggesting that the Americans should not be flashing their money around in the first place: Air Vice Marshall Sir Philip Game asserted that

> "I pointed out that in these days it was quite impossible to distinguish many over-painted possibly respectable persons from the professionals, and that to me, at any rate, they all looked the same."

In this chapter we are concerned with those women who regarded prostitution as a full or part-time occupation for which they got paid either in cash or in kind – their's was a remunerative profession.

The World Wars, as any war, disrupted traditional familial behaviour and challenged family and societal norms and values. Makepeace, for example, says "I would say a 'significant minority' of British soldiers engaged in extramarital sex." History tells us that, since time immemorial, wherever there is a gathering of (male) military personnel, prostitutes will not be far away. Indeed, prostitutes could be extremely tenacious and resourceful, following armies as camp followers: they constituted a vital part of the baggage train. In the 20th century the more enlightened and pragmatic Western governments accepted that, do what you may, soldiers were always going to have sex with prostitutes, so they routinely opened brothels conveniently near garrisons to please the troops and mitigate exposure to such venereal diseases (VD) as gonorrhoea and syphilis, for example (STIs today). After all, any circumspect commander will tell you that a happy soldier is a good soldier[2].

We learn from the online 1914-1918-online *International Encyclopedia of the First World War*[3] https://encyclopedia.1914-1918-online.net/article/prostitution#:~:text=The%20mass%20mobilization%20of%20troops,to%20venereal%20disease%20(VD) that in 1914, many continental European countries practiced variations on the French regulatory system that A.J.B. Parent-Duchâtelet (1790-1836) had developed in the early nineteenth century. The "French System" required that tolerated prostitutes register with the vice police and ply their trade in "closed" brothels. A key element of this system was the mandatory regular medical examination of prostitutes, which was meant to limit the spread of venereal disease among their clients.

The French set up an extensive network of legalised brothels, *maisons tolérées*, in towns in the northern part of the country.

The various concentrations of troops assembling to depart for the fronts were an easy target - not just for the prostitutes but for other women just seeking a good night out in what has been termed 'clandestine sex' with soldiers, airmen and sailors, British and foreign, particularly cash rich Americans later in the war. The *Encyclopedia* suggests that ' Civilian and military authorities suspected these women of being infected with particularly virulent forms of VD because they were able to avoid the medical exams that were compulsory for registered prostitutes'.

In the British Army, as in other armies, rank is everything and it is this which led to the British High Command insisting that brothels should be kept 'in bounds' for most of the war. Officers went to Blue Lamps; the other ranks to Red Lamps.

Rates of clandestine prostitution in Great Britain increased dramatically between 1914 and 1918 because the war created more opportunities for illicit sex. "Khaki fever," which refers to women and girls seeking soldiers and having illicit sex with them on the home front, concerned civilian leaders who desired tight control over women's sexual behavior. The concern about women's sexuality led to the creation of a **Women Patrols Committee.**

Indeed, we have seen how the Women's Police Service was originally established in World War 1; one of the main responsibilities of the Women's Patrols - as they were first known - was to monitor women's activities around factories or hostels and to attempt to prevent clandestine prostitution by reducing contact with the military personnel. We have noted how the presence of prostitutes caused trouble for Belgian and French refugees arriving in London, particularly the danger of their being groomed for prostitution at railway stations - sex trafficking in modern parlance. A breakthrough came with the approval of a pragmatic Sir Edward Henry, Commissioner of Police of the Metropolis, to train up women, who would then patrol the streets of London on a voluntary basis offering advice and support to women and children, primarily to help prevent sexual harassment and abuse.

A proven and effective way to limit the contagion of STIs is the issuing of condoms for prophylactic purposes; they obviously had the additional benefit of (sometimes) preventing pregnancy[4]. Condoms were distributed to German soldiers even before 1914. But the British government – and the Americans when the U.S. entered the war in 1917 – initially resisted their distribution, with moralists at home arguing that this would encourage fornication and further disrupt societal and family norms - another example of British 'not invented here syndrome'. When US soldiers and airmen flooded into Britain from 1942 they came not only with nylons and lipstick in their kitbags – they had also been issued with under the counter condoms.

The Wall Street Journal website https://graphics.wsj.com/100-legacies-from-world-war-1/contraception provides some very interesting and important facts relating to VD and World War I[5]:

> Up to 5% of British and Empire soldiers – of an army that at its peak reached four million men – suffered from venereal disease during World War I.
>
> Sexually transmitted diseases caused 416,891 hospital admissions among troops from Britain and its Empire during the war – though some of these admissions were due to relapses. At one time in 1918, 11,000 troops were estimated to be in hospital. (The rate of venereal disease among British soldiers in 1916 was 3.7%; for the better-paid Canadians, it was more than 20%.)
>
> *Each syphilis sufferer spent five weeks in recovery and each gonorrhoea sufferer four weeks–a significant drain on military resources.*
>
> In World War I, the U.S. Army lost nearly 7 million man-days and discharged more than 10,000 men because of STDs. Only the influenza pandemic of 1918-19 accounted for more lost days during the war.
>
> By 1917, U.K. soldiers had started receiving condoms from the army – many British Empire soldiers had received them from volunteers and in some officially sanctioned brothels anyway – but they were never distributed to U.S. troops.

Infection figures for 1917 were not encouraging, however: 55,000 British soldiers ended up in hospital with one STI or another[7]. Military men, of course, are more prone to VD because of their intinerant lifestyle, their social freedoms when away from home and, most alarmingly, they are thus likely to pass it on to others – abroad and at home when they return to wives and girlfriends. So concerning was the problem that VD Hospitals were established in 1915 with patients clocking up an average stay of between fifty and sixty days. Over the four or so years of the war there were 400,000 cases of VD with gonorrhoea the most frequent with sixty per cent of cases [8]. Working prostitutes would have made a major contribution to this terrible toll which took so many solders out of the line for so long.

Back at home confusion, controversy and procrastination prevailed: there were those who preached abstinence - moral prophylaxis – or post-infection treatment[9], but this was seen as encouraging permissiveness and as a doorway to vice[10]. The National Council for Combating Venereal Disease (run by women) saw prophylaxis as a form of contraception which was seen to result in 'uncontrolled passion'[11].

So, what did the British government do in the midst of all the clamour and controversy ? It procrastinated until the final months of the war when a prophylaxis programme for the armed forces was finally implemented – but the programme did not include condoms, proven, as stated, as an effective barrier against the spread of venereal contagion[12]. In the meantime, prostitutes continued to ply their trade wherever and whenever they could find a receptive market and soldiers continued to find themselves unfit for combat duty, thus depleting the strength of the British army. What, then, was issued to our troops? American inspired prophylaxis packs which contained no condoms but instead topical treatments to rub into the penis and groin[13].

If anything was going to help the allied armies win the war then it was clearly the provision of condoms for prophylactic purpose. The *Journal* continues:

> Instead, U.S. troops received a "Dough Boy Prophylactic" kit, to treat the disease after it was contracted [6]. An offer from France to create "special houses" for American soldiers to have access to registered prostitutes is said to have led Secretary of War Newton Baker to explode "My God, if [President Woodrow] Wilson sees this he'll stop the war."
>
> While the U.S. was almost alone at the end of World War I in not distributing condoms, it learned its lesson, distributing prophylactics to soldiers during World War II. According to many public-health specialists, World War I also opened the path for sex-education programs for military personnel in the U.S. [and in schools].

The Royal Navy was so frustrated by the lack of guidance that they simply produced and distributed their own packs in 1917. Amongst many other sailors 2,000 men at Portsmouth barracks received packs containing: disinfectant (Condy's Fluid or potassium permanganate/potash, cotton wool, swabs and capsules of calomel ointment [14].

With remarkable foresight this cohort of 2,000 was closely monitored with the astonishing result that there was only seven cases. Potash was clearly the answer in the absence of condoms which continued to be left out in the cold regarding their efficacy, even by such eminences as Frank Kidd in 1916 addressing the Royal Commission of Venereal Disease.

The Royal Navy was consequently ahead of the game and in 1933 the Admiralty signed a contract with the London Rubber Company for the supply of condoms, becoming in 1937 the official supplier to the Admiralty[15]. This, obviously, was an attempt to mitigate the contagion potential of the 'one in every port' scenario.

World War II

In World War II prostitution and brothel keeping was one of the four most frequent social issues in World War II which had increased significantly and had to be dealt with by female prisoner officers and their male colleagues. They were: shoplifting – a reaction to clothes rationing; neglect of children – with many fathers away fighting and mothers forced out to work; brothel keeping; and industrial absenteeism[16].

World War II brought with it another surge in permissiveness and sexual activity, what with muster points with concentrations of troops awaiting embarkation, a flood of American GIs and the mass mobilisation of women for war work all increasing sexual opportunities for the man and woman in, and on, the street[17]. Between 1939 and 1942 cases of VD shot up 70 per cent[18], while Watch Committees complained of 'immoral conduct in air raid shelters, an increase in streetwalkers and the solicitation of the Forces in Shepherd Market and St John's Wood by aggressive prostitutes' [19]. Not surprisingly, London Rubber Company, the market leader, saw a marked rise in demand for their products. But it took until 1942 before LRC started providing condoms for British troops, thanks to the rationalisation of industry scheme, and the threat to rubber supplies following the Japanese invasion of Malaya.

As in World War 1, a syphilitic soldier in World War 2 was a non-soldier, out of action for months. Cari Romm in *The Atlantic* explains why VD (STIs) were militarily such an elemental problem which to a greater or lesser extent weakened all armies involved in the conflict [20]: in 1942 the US authorities were well aware of the impact VD was having on their fighting capabilities and declared it "military saboteur number one."

In practice, though, the real saboteurs were considered to be the women who carried them. Over the course of the United States' involvement in World War II, federal authorities detained hundreds of women in quarantine centres across the country, determined to protect the country's fighting men from sex workers and other women who flocked to the towns that housed army bases, known as "Khaki Wackies," "good-time Charlottes," "camp followers," and – in a portmanteau coined by a the U.S. Public Health Service – "patriotutes."

These so-called 'patriotutes' were ready and waiting for the GIs wherever they were posted and that, of course, included the towns and cities of Britain, particularly London where the city's prostitutes welcomed the new influx of business with open arms.

Prostitution in the World Wars

"Controlling these women was considered important to the defense effort," said John Parascandola, a medical historian and the author of *Sex, Science, and Sin: A History of Syphilis in America*. In 1939...the War Deparment, the Navy, the Federal Security Agency, and state health departments crafted the Eight-Point Plan, a set of measures intended to curb the spread of STDs "in areas where armed forces or national-defense employees are concentrated."

Treating VD was no simple or quick affair – treatment pre wide penicillin availability was lengthy and depended on the compliance of the patient – always a problem: that problem was treating STDs at the time was often a lengthy and involved process. Penicillin was first used as a treatment for syphilis in 1943, but it was scarce for civilians during the war – the more common treatment at that time was a regular injection of arsenic-based drugs, administered once a week for up to a year. Gonorrhea could be cured with a round of pills, but even that required careful adherence to the dosing schedule in order to work. Counting on such a high degree of cooperation was too much of a gamble.

Chapter 18

The Day the war ended

What happened in and after the summer of 1945? Women usually continued to be paid less than men and many employers still had neither compulsion nor desire to train women up or to delegate skilled work to them - they were still often regarded as temporary workers, as temporary men. Men expected to come back home, be de-mobbed and resume their place as the undisputed and inviolable head of the household. Some men insisted that their wives should stop working now that they had returned; others did not like the fact that their wives had gone out to work in the first place. It was often assumed that women would want to return to the home (even though they had never really left it), along with self-serving dogmatic view that young children should never be separated from their mothers in any way.

– Charlene Price, *Women Factory Workers in Birmingham during the Second World War* https://sheroesofhistory.wordpress.com/2017/08/24/women-factory-workers-in-birmingham-during-the-second-world-war/

During the war young women were able to enjoy themselves on an unprecedented scale: some were able to use their wages to go to the cinema, go dancing or roller skating or for clothes shopping and seaside trips. This mostly evaporated in 1945; with demand for women's labour drying up, the government stopped funding nurseries and so most closed down thus resurrecting the barrier to women going out to work. By 1945 the dramatic fall in the birth rate produced a 'moral panic' about the falling population. Women were now told to go home and have babies.

Demob – *one more time*

Peace in Europe brought with it an end to women's second stint as temporary men in just over 30 years. As combatants and PoWs flooded back from Europe and the Middle East, and later from the Far East, women had to stand aside and allow men to resume their jobs and careers in the relative peacefulness of 'civvy street'. No doubt, many women were happy to do this, but a significant number surely regretted and missed the loss of independence, income, and cameraderies they had enjoyed for up to six years. They will also have missed the respect they earned from many men and other women for a job superbly well done, and the confidence and self respect which war work had given them, be it fusing a shell, nursing a suppurating wound, fighting a conflagration, training a searchlight, milking a cow,

The Day the war ended

cracking a code, knitting a sock, delivering a baby, flying a Lancaster bomber, or simply serving a nice cup of tea.

For most, the time had come for demobilisation.

Many of the services, however, carried on – the war, if nothing else, having convinced the doubters and cynics and the morbidly insecure in Whitehall and the military hierarchies something that women, and some enlightened men, knew all along, that of course there was a place for women in the services, be they military or civilian, paid or voluntary, in industry, on the land or in the emergency services. So from now on, whenever a woman decided that her place was not in the home, she was, slowly but surely, able to choose more options for herself. And not just in the absolutely invaluable caring professions where, given the chance she always did excel anyway; and not just in catering even though the offer of a cup of tea can be a veritable life-saver in itself. No - opportunities to serve in the womens' Army, Air Force or Navy were gradually opening up, as were careers in scientific research and industry and academia, in agriculture, teaching, the GPO and the Civil Service, in medicine, surgery, dentistry and veterinary science and in what were then called professions allied to medicine: physio- and occupational therapy and in psychology, all fuelled and amplified by the inordinate demands caused by the war disabled, psychologically as well as physically.

The new Labour government, having seen the potential lying unrealised in 50 percent of its voters, were finally minded in 1945 to enable and elevate women, not just in domestic science, mothercraft and home-making courses – it went much further than how to make a salad, burp a baby, or distemper a wall – by way of courses in office practice, budgeting and carpentry, for example.

Women and women's war work had enabled and expedited all of that.

Sadly, nearly 80 years after the end of World War II, we still have some way to go; women need a more influential presence in boardrooms and in areas such as engineering, surgery, policing, the military, the law and in government. And the gender pay gap still goes on, and on. Nevertheless, the alacrity, the speed of learning, the astonishing versatility and the proficiencies which women demonstrated in World War I and II show that, indubitably, none of this is beyond a woman's capabilities any more than it is a man's.

Appendix 1

Marie Curie's War Effort

It would be remiss not to mention the wonderful efforts Polish born and Nobel Prize Winner Maria Skłodowske (1867-1934) made to help the war effort by assisting in the care of allied soldiers in France. On the outbreak of war in 1914 she soon saw how she could apply her unique expertise to help save the lives of countless wounded soldiers. Marie realized that the electromagnetic radiation of X-rays could allow surgeons first to see bullets and shrapnel embedded in soldiers' bodies and so facilitate their removal, and also locate broken bones. Many hospitals in France already had X-ray equipment, but those machines were often far from the battlefields.

In order to bring the technology closer to the soldiers, Curie and her daughter, Irène, assembled a fleet of vehicles equipped with X-ray machines and set up 200 radiological units in more permanent posts near the frontlines in the first two years of the war. The IEEE takes up the story: https://spectrum.ieee.org/how-marie-curie-helped-save-a-million-soldiers-during-world-war-i

Curie was living in Paris in 1914 when the war began. As founding director of France's Red Cross Radiology Service, she was in the midst of setting up her laboratory at the Radium Institute, a new center in the city for the study of radioactivity. Construction was complete, but many of her researchers were off fighting the war. Just before the German army's invasion, the French government moved the country's capital to Bordeaux. Curie transported France's only sample of radium in a safe-deposit box to the city, 600 kilometers southwest, but she quickly returned to Paris, determined to apply her scientific knowledge to aid the war effort.

Curie approached her wealthy friends and colleagues to donate automotive vehicles which when modified could be used as mobile X-ray units. And she persuaded French manufacturers of X-ray equipment to donate it along with portable electric generators. She also asked local body shops to voluntarily outfit the vehicles with the equipment so it could be positioned in field hospitals close to the front. By October 1914, the first of 20 vehicles, which French soldiers dubbed petites Curies (little Curies), were ready.

. The IEEE goes on to reveal that Although Curie had lectured about X-rays at Sorbonne University (now Paris Sorbonne University), she had no practical experience working with them. So she took crash courses on how to operate the equipment and on human anatomy so she could learn how to read the film. She also learned to drive a car and how to fix it if necessary. Accompanied by a military doctor and her 17-year-old daughter, Irène, for an assistant, Curie made her trip to the battlefront in October 1914. In less than two years, the number of units had grown substantially, and the Curies had set up a training program at the Radium Institute to teach other women to operate the equipment.

> Curie also opened her wallet to aid the war effort…. She offered to donate her gold medals to the French government to aid the war effort, but the French National Bank turned her down. Instead, she used most of her Nobel Prize money to buy French war bonds.

In 1919 her laboratory at the Radium Institute was finally ready. There, she would dedicate herself to research until she tragically died in 1934 aged 66 of aplastic anaemia—ironically attributed to having no protection from radiation exposure when she operated the mobile X-ray units, as well as the radon gas tubes she carried in her pockets during her research.

Appendix 2

Stamford Military Hospital, Dunham Massey and The Carrel-Dakin Treatment

With the outbreak of the World War 1 the British Red Cross and the Order of St John of Jerusalem joined forces to create the Joint War Committee in which they pooled resources to provide services in support of the war effort. Auxiliary Hospitals were a major part of this provision: over 5,000 properties were offered involving private houses like Dunham and public buildings such as village halls and schools. The marvellous result was that 3,000 auxiliary hospital administered by the Red Cross county directors were established to help the growing numbers of war wounded.

Dunham Massey Hall is a Georgian country house near Altrincham, Greater Manchester. Penelope Grey, Countess of Stamford, wife of the 9th Earl of Stamford, made the house available to the Red Cross as a military hospital, becoming known as the Stamford Military Hospital from April 1917 to January 1919. In that time it looked after 182 injured soldiers' cases ranging from gas poisoning to those presenting with bullets in the brain. Lady Stamford was Commandant; the matron was Sister Catherine Bennett. Lady Stamford's daughter, the tireless Lady Jane Grey (*later* Turnbull), trained as a nurse at the hospital. The medical officers were a Dr Harry Gordon Cooper and Dr Percy Robert who used the foot of the Grand Staircase as an 'extremely unhygienic' operating theatre.

From 1 March 2014 until 11 November 2016, the main ward at Stamford Military Hospital (known as "Bagdad"), along with the operating theatre, nurses' station and the recreation room were brilliantly recreated to commemorate the 100-year anniversary of the start of World War I, along with actors playing the role of characters who worked, lived and recovered at the hospital.

Liz Webb, Dunham's Visitor Experience Manager said at the time:

> "Everyone will be given (as the soldiers were) a hospital admission ticket on arrival. Each ticket will carry the name and short history of a particular soldier, whose progress they'll be able to follow as they journey through the hospital." "Apart from one original bed, each of the hospital beds in Bagdad Ward will represent a named soldier who illustrates a particular war injury – such as shell shock or trench foot. His story, the medical treatment he received and what happened to him when he left the hospital will be told through archive photographs, letters and records kept by nursing staff."

'One of the real soldiers to have been treated at Dunham Massey was Private William Johnstone, who arrived with two pieces of shrapnel in his brain. The doctor, assisted by Lady Jane, had to drill through his skull in the makeshift operating theatre under the great stairs. "Surgery was performed there because it was next to the billiards room, which had a toilet. Sadly, they managed to remove the first bit of shrapnel, but he died at Manchester Royal Infirmary before they could remove the second piece."'[1]

The Carrel-Dakin Treatment

This groundbreaking infection control method in the fight against sepsis was developed by French surgeon Alexis Carrel (1873-1944): his approach consisted of removing debris from the wound and debriding the necrotic tissue. The surgeons would then irrigate the wound with Dakin's solution, developed by English chemist Henry Dakin (1880-1952). The treatment was used at Dunham Massey to good effect, saving many lives and amputations.

Alan J. Hawk goes on to tell us how

> The diluted sodium hypochlorite solution chemically sterilizes the wound and acted as a solvent against remaining necrotic tissue and pus. Unlike iodine or carbolic acid, Dakin's solution does not damage healthy tissue. Under the Carrel-Dakin method, closure would only occur after the bacterial count of the wound showed that it was sterile[2].

In short, 'the Carrel-Dakin technique was a major breakthrough for fighting infection. During the Battle of Champagne in 1915, 80% of the wounded were infected with gas gangrene bacteria. A year later, when surgeons applied the Carrel-Dakin technique during the Battle of the Somme, that number was 20%'.

Indeed, 'Despite deadlier weapons, as well as more severe and contaminated wounds, an injured soldier was less likely to undergo a limb amputation during WWI than during the U.S. Civil War. Only 35% of soldiers who sustained a femur fracture in WWI underwent amputation, compared with 56% of similarly injured combatants during the U.S. Civil War. A large part of this success can be credited to the Carrel-Dakin technique'.

> See: *Sanctuary from the Trenches: The Stamford Hospital at Dunham Massey*, National Trust, 2014
>
> Gaydos J. History of Wound Care: A Solution to Sepsis: The Carrel-Dakin Method. *Today's Wound Clinic* . 2017;11:2 .
>
> Keen WW. *Treatment of War Wounds*. Philadelphia, 1918

Notes

Introduction

1. Nancy Witcher Langhorne Astor, Viscountess Astor, CH (1879 – 1964) was an American-born British politician who was the first woman to take a seat as Member of Parliament for Plymouth Sutton in 1919, serving from 1919 to 1945. Astor is noted for her anti-semitism and sympathetic view of National Socialism.
2. See, amongst many others, Pankhurst, Emmeline. *"My own story"* 1914; Purvis, June. *"Emmeline Pankhurst (1858–1928), Suffragette Leader and Single Parent in Edwardian Britain";* Romero, Patricia W. E. *"Sylvia Pankhurst: Portrait of a Radical"*; Smith, Harold L. *The British women's suffrage campaign, 1866–1928* (2nd ed. 2007); Winslow, Barbara, *Sylvia Pankhurst: Sexual politics and political activism* (1996).
3. Brittain (1933)
4. Nielson, 2015
5. Having witnessed the highly effective deployment of women in engineering work during World War I, Lady Parsons was robustly critical of the removal of many women from such work under the terms of the Restoration of Pre-War Practices Act 1919 that restored many returning male combatants to their pre-war responsibilities. In a widely publicised speech on 9 July 1919 from her 'Women's Work and Shipbuilding during the War' she deplored the way that women had been required to produce the 'implements of war and destruction' but then be denied 'the privilege of fashioning the munitions of peace'.
6. For the ATS signallers see /www.royalsignalsmuseum.co.uk/women-secrets-and-signals.

PART ONE: WORLD WAR I

Chapter 1: Women at work in World War I – women as temporary men

1. For a graphic picture of the social and domestic conditions prevailing at the time see Rowntree, Seebohm, *Poverty*; Chrystal, *The Rowntree Family of York*; ibid, *History of Chocolate in York*.

Notes

2. The first women factory inspectors were appointed in 1893. Until 1921 they operated as a separate section of the Factory Inspectorate with special responsibility for inspecting the working conditions of women. See Spurgeon, 2012, *The Contribution of the Women's Factory Inspectorate (1893-1921) to improvements in women's occupational health and safety.*

3. The Act specified that men from 18 to 41 years old were liable to be called up for service in the army unless they were eligible for exemptions listed under this Act, including men who were married, widowed with children, serving in the Royal Navy, a minister of religion, or working in one of a number of reserved occupations, or for conscientious objection. A second Act in May 1916 extended liability for military service to married men, and a third Act in 1918 extended the upper age limit to 51.

4. The Derby Scheme was introduced in the autumn of 1915 by Kitchener's new Director General of Recruiting, Edward Stanley, 17th Earl of Derby (1865–1948) after which it was named. Since the 'over by Christmas war' was lasting longer than had been anticipated and the British military required more recruits, 'Derby's scheme' was a survey to determine how many could be obtained, via the use of appointed canvassers visiting eligible men at home to persuade them to 'volunteer' for war service. The scheme was undertaken in November and December 1915 and obtained 318,553 medically fit single men. However, 38% of single men and 54% of married men had resisted the mass orchestrated pressure to enlist in the war, so the British Government, determined to ensure a supply of replacements for the mounting casualties overseas, passed The Military Service Act of compulsory conscription into the war, 27 January 1916.

5. The guild was established in 1882 as The London Guild by Lady Wolverton after being asked to provide garments for a London orphanage. In 1914, the charity was renamed Queen Mary›s Needlework Guild and began to supply troops during World War I, with branches being established throughout the Empire and other areas of the world, including China and Argentina.

6. The War Emergency Workers National Committee was a joint Labour organisation established to protect the interests of the working classes on matters such as employment, wages and conditions of service and supply of essential commodities in the war-time situation. See Harrison *The War Emergency Workers' National Committee*, 1914–1920.

7. Seebohm Rowntree (1871-1954) served as Director of the newly-established Welfare Department at the Ministry of Munitions, and worked on the implementation of the principles of 'scientific management' in the munitions factories. See Chrystal, *The Rowntree Family of York*; Chrystal, Paul, *History of Chocolate in York.*

8. Both quoted in Southwick, 2021, *Newcastle-upon-Tyne: Fragments of the Past Volume 1* p. 60, Newcastle.

9. See, amongst others, *"SWH Scottish Women's Hospital"* (PDF). Library at the Royal College of Surgeons of Edinburgh. 17 February 2016; Weiner, M-F. "The Scottish Women's Hospital at Royaumont"; Morrison, E (2013). "The

Scottish Women's Hospitals for Foreign Service – the Girton and Newnham Unit, 1915–1918" (PDF). *Medical History*. 38 (2): 160–177.
10. See Noakes, *Women's Military Service*.

Chapter 2: Women in the services

1. See Baker, Chris. "Women and the British Army in the First World War". *The Long, Long Trail*. Shipton, Elisabeth, *Female Tommies: women in the First World War,* 2014
2. See Popham, Hugh, 2002, *The FANY in Peace and War*
3. See Storey, *WRNS*
4. See Escott, *Women in Air Force Blue*; Beauman, *Partners in Blue*

Chapter 3: Women nurses, physiotherapists and doctors

1. Dick Robinson, Edie's great nephew, explained in 2012:
'A lot of the references are quite brief and trivial but, as a whole, I believe they show that Edie had a positive view of the VADs with whom she worked so closely in often very stressful situations. I hope this collection sheds some light on a working relationship which is often misunderstood or – worse – misrepresented'.
My thanks to Dick Robinson for permission to use these excerpts from Edie's diaries.
2. For details of Borden's fascinating life, see https://spartacus-educational.com/Wborden.htm
3. For a near comprehensive list of British women who made a contribution in World War I see https://en.wikipedia.org/wiki/Category:British_women_in_World_War_I
4. See Geddes, *The Women's Hospital Corps;* idem, *Deeds and words in the suffrage military hospital in Endell Street*; idem, *Louisa Garrett Anderson (1873-1943), surgeon and suffragette.*
5. Wendy Moore, A Hospital 'Manned by Women'; Wendy Moore is author of *Endell Street: The Trailblazing Women Who Ran World War One's Most Remarkable Military Hospital*
6. See Cornelis, M.E. The *Scottish Women's Hospitals.*
7. Albrinck, 1998, *Borderline Women* examines the confusion in this famous episode. See also Mitton, 2011, *The Cellar-House of Pervyse*; Atkinson, 2010, *Elsie and Mairi Go to War;* Souttar, *A Surgeon in Belgium, http://www.greatwardifferent.com/Great_War/Surgeon_in_Belgium/Surgeon_in_Belgium_00.htm, 8.*
8. *May Sinclair and the First World War, Suzanne Raitt, 1999, http://www.nhc.rtp.nc.us:8080/ideasv62/raitt.htm,*

Notes

9. Ian Hay, *One Hundred Years of Army Nursing* p. 337; Elizabeth Haldane, *The British Nurse in Peace and War*, p. 179.

10. Grace McDougall wrote an anonymous 1917 account of her experiences *Nursing Adventures: A FANY in France*, retitled *A Nurse at War: Nursing Adventures in France for America*. In 1919 Pat Beauchamp wrote *Fanny Goes to War* about her experiences serving with the Corps.

11. St Clair Stobart, *War and Women*; Shipton, *Female Tommies*; Smith, *British Women of the Eastern Front*; London, *Inspirational Women Of World War One: Mabel St. Clair Stobart*.

12. See Chrystal, *York and its Railways*; Peart, *Trains of Hope: ambulance trains in times of conflict*

13. From the archives of the Young Women's Christian Association: MSS.243/14/22/4

14. https://combatstress.org.uk/about-us/our-history

15. See Claire Hilton (2021). *Civilians, Lunacy and the First World War*. The abstract for the article reads:

> [During the war] the entire population faced hardships, but for those people designated "pauper lunatics" in public asylums, life became very harsh. At the beginning of the war, the asylums were a story of good intentions gone awry, the failed dreams of social reformers and psychiatrists. They had become "vast warehouses for the chronically insane and demented."
>
> Richard Hunter and Ida Macalpine, in their history of Colney Hatch Asylum, commented about the gloomy picture: "Custodial care was forced on asylums as a way of life....paralysed by sheer weight of numbers of patients" and financial constraints. "Nothing", they said, showed "more blatantly how relentless pressure for more and more beds forced the asylum further and further away from the idea of a hospital".

16. See Bogacz, War Neurosis and Cultural Change in England, 1914-22: The Work of the War Office Committee of Enquiry into 'Shell-Shock'. https://www.jstor.org/stable/260822 p. 23

17. An ill-defined medical condition characterized by lassitude, fatigue, headache, and irritability, associated chiefly with emotional disturbance. The ICD-10 system of the World Health Organization categorizes neurasthenia under "F48 - Other neurotic disorders". For details relating to Dorothy L. Sayers, see Newman, *Changing Roles*, pp. 118-123.

Chapter 4: Women working on the land: farms, forage and forests

1. See, for instance, Warwickshire County Record Office. The Women's Land Army Handbook. Document; Land Girls and their Impact; Twinch, *Women on the Land*

2. Carol Twinch (*Women on the Land* p.2): 'German strategists had noted Britain's increasing dependence on imported food, and were confident a submarine blockade would starve her into submission. Indeed, there were many in Britain itself who believed that the German intelligence network was better informed as to the true state of British agriculture than was the British Government'.
3. Twinch, *ibidem.*
4. https://www.bbc.co.uk/news/uk-wales-26238755: *How Land Girls helped feed Britain to victory in WW1* by Neil Prior 26 February 2014
5. Quoted in Gullace, N.F. 2002, *Reinventing Womanhood.*

Chapter 5: Other wartime women's organisations

1. Swedish drill was a series of movements performed slowly and gently (for the most part), with an emphasis on balance and complete muscle control.
2. See Dunn, *Not Far from Brideshead*, pp. 15, 23, 37-38, 81
3. Vera Brittain, *Testament of Youth,* p. 436

Chapter 6: Women in industry in World War I

1. Issue 4129 Vol CLII June 8th 1918.
2. For industrial health and occupational disease see the chapter in Chrystal, *Factory Girls* (2022).
3. See https://www.royalgunpowdermills.com/archive for details.
4. See Bryder, Mobilising Mothers: The 1917 National Baby Week, *Medical History* 2019 Jan; 63(1): 2–23
5. See Newman, *Changing Roles,* pp. 125-128
6. A number of the images are in G.R. Griffiths, *Women's Factory Work in World War One* (2014).

Chapter 7: Small arms manufacturing

1. See Moore, 2014, *The Production of Muskets and Their Effects in the Eighteenth Century*
2. See Musson,1957, 'James Nasmyth and the Early Growth of Mechanical Engineering'. *The Economic History Review.* 10 (1): 121–127.
3. Burton, *The Workers' War* p. 86
4. Pam, David, (1998). *The Royal Small Arms Factory Enfield & Its Workers. Enfield*: Published by the author.
5. Burton, *The Workers' War,* p. 94
6. See Vickers, Sons and Maxim Limited, 1898, *Their Works and Manufactures*; Ellis, 1976. The Social History of the Machine Gun; Goldsmith, 1989. The

Notes

Devil's Paintbrush; McCallum, 1999. Blood Brothers: Hiram and Hudson Maxim.
7. Grant, 2014, *The Lewis Gun.*

Chapter 8: Munitionettes – the canary girls

1. Burton, *The Workers' War*, p. 12.
2. *Ibid*, pp. 12-13
3. See Woollacott, *On Her Their Lives Depend*
4. See, for example, Brader, (2001). *Timbertown girls*; Ministry of Munitions of War (1919). *H.M. Factory, Gretna;* Rayner-Canham, (1996). *"The Gretna Garrison";* Ritchie,(1988). *The Gretna Girls;* Routledge, *Gretna's Secret War;* Routledge, (2003). *Miracles and Munitions.*
5. *See* Cocroft, (2000), *Dangerous Energy*
6. Potts, 2017, *The Canary Girls, The workers the war turned yellow;* https:// www.bbc.co.uk/news/uk-england-39434504
7. Haber, (1986). chapter 10. *The Poisonous Cloud;* "Gas Girls – acta – Bristolacta – Bristol". Acta-bristol.com. 28 May 2014.
8. https://war-work.com/national-projectile-factory-lancaster/; https://api. parliament.uk/historic-hansard/written-answers/1920/aug/10/national-projectile-factory-lancaster; Page, Michael, June 28, 2017, *A Munitionette in the National Projectile Factory, Lancaster;* https://www.surreyinthegreatwar. org.uk/story/a-munitionette-in-the-national-projectile-factory-lancaster/
9. https://www.walesonline.co.uk/news/wales-news/hidden-bunkers-thousands-women-secretly-15731403
10. "London's explosion was at Silvertown". *New York Times*. 29 January 1919
11. See Chrystal, *Leeds's Military Legacy*, 2017, pp. 38ff
12. Billings, 1993, *Ashton Munitions Explosion, 1917*

Chapter 9: Balloons and policewomen

1. See *Observation Balloons on the Western Front"*. The Western Front Association. 29 June 2008; Ege, L. *Balloons and Airships*; *Kite Balloons in Escorts*. Naval History and Heritage Command.
2. See, for example, Emsley, 2010, *The Great British Bobby*; Lock, 1979, *The British Policewoman;* Jackson, 2006, *Women Police*
3. It took only four days after war against Germany was declared for the government to pass the emergency legislation that was the Defence of the Realm Act 1914 (DORA). Enacted without debate, this allowed the government to exercise a wide range of powers during wartime to ensure the defence of the realm and the security of the nation. See https://www.parliament.uk/about/

living-heritage/transformingsociety/private-lives/yourcountry/collections/the-outbreak-of-the-first-world-war/dora/

The original DORA) was little more than a paragraph long. The second revised and expanded version outlined a wider range of possible wartime offences against the British state, such as the power to requisition buildings or land needed for the war effort, or to create criminal offences. Trivial peacetime activities now *verboten* included flying kites, starting bonfires, buying binoculars, feeding wild animals bread, discussing naval and military matters or buying alcohol on public transport. Alcoholic drinks were watered down and pub opening times were restricted to 12pm–3pm and 6:30pm–9:30pm. The requirement for an afternoon gap in permitted hours lasted in England until the Licensing Act 1988. DORA imposed censorship of journalism and of letters from the front line. The press was subject to controls on reporting troop movements, numbers or any other operational information that would potentially be exploited by the enemy. People who breached the regulations with intent to assist the enemy or not would have been sentenced to death. Ten people were executed under the regulations.

4. The Contagious Diseases Act was first passed in 1864. It was extended in 1866 and 1869, before being repealed in 1886. The Acts were introduced as a (clumsy) attempt to regulate 'common prostitutes', in order to reduce the prevalence of sexually transmitted infections within the British army and navy. The Contagious Diseases Act made it mandatory for women suspected of prostitution to register with the police and submit to an invasive medical examination. The Act gave the police the power to determine who was a prostitute. If the woman was found to be suffering from an STI, she would be confined to a 'lock hospital' until pronounced 'clean'. The alternative to the examination was three months' imprisonment (extended to 6 months in the 1869 Act) or hard labour. The Acts did not enforce the examination of men to detect any STIs.

The Act caused outrage among the British public because it led to the unjust and prejudicial treatment of women. It was eventually repealed after an impressive grassroots movement led by Josephine Butler, who founded the *Ladies' National Association (LNA) to* campaign against the implementation of the Act.

– https://navigator.health.org.uk/theme/contagious-diseases-act#:~:text=The% 20Contagious%20Diseases%20Act%20was, the%20British%20army%20and%20navy.

Chapter 10: Between the wars

1. This is reminiscent of the mantra elite ancient Roman men trotted out to their womenfolk from 753 BC to AD 410: *'Domum servavit, lanam fecit'* – *'she looked after the home and made the wool'*. Not much change then in 1,700 years.

Notes

PART TWO: WORLD WAR II

Introduction

1. It superseded the Military Training Act 1939. See Broad, (2006), *Conscription in Britain, 1939-1964.* For the Act see https://vlex.co.uk/vid/national-service-act-1941-808185561. From the blurb for Broad:
'Compulsory military service in Britain can be traced back to Anglo-Saxon times, but it was only in the twentieth century that it became universal. Conscription occurred during both world wars with a total of eight million men in total being conscripted into the army, navy and air forces, and after the end of World War II compulsory service continued for another eighteen years to meet overseas commitments and under the threat of the Cold War'.
Under the Military Training Act only single men 20 to 22 years old were liable to be called up; they were to be known as 'militiamen' to distinguish them from the regular army. To emphasise this distinction, each man was issued with a suit in addition to a uniform. The intention was for the first intake to undergo six months of basic training before being discharged into an active reserve. They would then be recalled for short training periods and attend an annual camp.
2. Women who had one or more children 14 years old or younger living with them. This included their own children, legitimate or illegitimate, stepchildren, and adopted children, as long as the child was adopted before 18 December 1941.
3. Fox, Lynne, *South Yorkshire Women in Industry: A Study of the Last 100 Years* (2008), p. 2 and Chrystal, *Doncaster at Work,* for details.

Chapter 11: Women workers in the military services – here we go again

1. Lynsey Ann Lord: extracted from a University of St Andrews honours project. Last Update July 2008. https://mathshistory.st-andrews.ac.uk/Biographies/Clarke_Joan/. See also Dunlop, *The Bletchley Girls*
2. For more information see Hinsley, *Codebreakers*; Hodges, *Alan Turing*; Sebag-Montefiore, *Enigma*; Smith, *Station X.* For a list of women in Bletchley Park, see *https://en.wikipedia.org/wiki/List_of_women_in_Bletchley_Park.*
3. James, Lawrence, Tantrums, Cigars and Budgerigars, *Sunday Times* May 11 2019
4. See Picardie, Justine, *Miss Dior: A Story of Courage and Couture* (2021)

Chapter 12: Women workers in the civilian services

1. http://eng.world-war.ru/the-womens-voluntary-service-in-britain/
2. Figures for 1938 from the NFWI magazine, *Home and Country*, p. 113. NFWI Archives, The Woman's Library.

3. https://www.iwm.org.uk/history/what-did-the-womens-institute-do-during-the-second-world-war.
4. Frances White, The WI in World War II: How British women kept the countryside running, *History of War*, May 2015.
5. See Robinson, *A Force to be Reckoned With*, 2011; Stamper, *Countrywomen in War Time*
6. See Brown: *Put That Light Out!: Britain's Civil Defence Services at War 1939–1945*. 1999
7. Part of Charity Bick's George Medal citation:
   WITH ALL THE OTHER ARP WARDENS ELSEWHERE SHE BORROWED A BICYCLE AND FINDING HER WAY BLOCKED OR HAVING TO SHELTER FROM EXPLOSIONS AND FALLING DEBRIS MADE REPEATED ATTEMPTS TO REACH THE CONTROL ROOM.
   - https://www.thegazette.co.uk/London/issue/35074/supplement/870
8. Chain Home (CH), was the codename for the ring of coastal Early Warning radar stations built by the RAF before and during World War II to detect and track aircraft. Chain Home was the first early warning radar network in the world, and the first military radar system to reach operational status.
9. For example, https://en.wikipedia.org/wiki/List_of_World_War_II_war_correspondents_(1942%E2%80%9343) which lists 69 correspondents, all male, from James Aldridge, *The New York Times* to Harry Zinder, *TIME*. Another list redeems the situation by including a number of women war correspondents - https://en.wikipedia.org/wiki/Category:War_correspondents_of_World_War_II
10. For Clare Hollingworth, see Mackrell, *Going With the Boys* which traces 'six extraordinary women writing from the Front Line'; they are:
11. Anne Sebba, 10 January 2017. "Clare Hollingworth obituary". *The Guardian*. "Obituary: Clare Hollingworth". *BBC News*. 10 January 2017.
12. Yeung, A.; Hoenig, E., 2000. "Clare Hollingworth". *Far East. Econ. Rev.* 79.
13. Alan Stafford, 2015, *Wilson, Keppel and Betty: Too Naked for the Nazis* – Fantom Publishing (2015) pp 5-7
14. Freda Utley, 1948, *The High Cost of Vengeance*, Chapter 7, pp 188–189

Chapter 13: Nursing and other health care workers

1. See Piggott, *Queen Alexandra's Royal Army Nursing Corps*.
2. *See* Mackie*: Sky Wards - A History of the Princess Mary's Royal Air Force Nursing Service* 2001*;* Mackie*: Wards in the Sky – the RAF's Remarkable Nursing Service,* 2014
3. See Cohen, *The District Nurse;*
4. For details, see Crossland,, 2014, *Britain and the International Committee of the Red Cross, 1939–1945*; Oliver, 1966, *The British Red Cross in Action*
5. See Wankhade, (2015). *Ambulance Services;* White, (2018) *Ordinary Heroes*.

Notes

Chapter 14: The emergency Services

1. Sarah Hands, Gloucester Police Archives, https://gloucestershirepolicearchives.org.uk/
2. https://gmpmuseum.co.uk/collection-item/history-of-women-in-policing/
3. See Johnston, Helen, *Gendered Prison Work*
4. Creaton, 1998, *Sources for the History of London,* p. 99

Chapter 15: Women on the farms, in the fields and in the forests

1. Foat, pp. 124-6, 128
2. Sne(e)dding is stripping the side shoots and buds from a branch or shoot, usually of a tree or woody shrub. This process is often performed during hedge laying and before the felling of trees on plantations ready for cropping.
3. Foat, pp. 40-41
4. Vickers, 2011, p. 137
5. Swanston, 1946, p. 3
6. Vickers 2011, p. 108; Hendrie 2009, p. 41.
7. Vickers 2011, p. 109.
8. Gazeley 2008, p. 658.
9. Vickers 2011, p. 112
10. Regulation 2A provided that "If, with intent to assist the enemy, any person does any act which is likely to assist the enemy or to prejudice the public safety, the defence of the realm or the efficient prosecution of the war, he shall be liable to penal servitude for life."
    In 1940 amendments to the regulations created two capital offences: "forcing safeguards" (crashing through roadblocks etc.) under regulation 1B, and looting under regulation 38A. A third new capital offence, called treachery, was created soon afterwards by the Treachery Act 1940.

Chapter 16: Women in the war factories

1. Barnett, *The Collapse of British Power*, p. 278.
2. The Geddes Axe: consecutive cuts by the Committee on National Expenditure.
3. Mass Observation Archive (MO-A), FR 1298, *People in Production,* June 1942
4. There were moves in parliament which were successful in securing equal pay in some areas, for example for teachers; but unfortunately not for the majority of women workers. See Smith, *'The Problem of "Equal Pay for Equal Work" in Great Britain during World War II',* p. 659

5. The Third Report from the Select Committee on National Expenditure – *Women's Welfare, 1942 – 1943* (19) III.331 (1942 – 1943). For more balanced appraisals of the burden on women see *Women Workers in the Second World War: Production and Patriarchy in Conflict* by Penny Summerfield; *Out of the Cage: Women's Experiences in Two World Wars* by Gail Braybon and Penny Summerfield; *Working for Victory: A Diary of Life in a Second World War Factory* by Sue Bruley.

6. TUC Library Collections, Interview with Connie Hayball, 2005, http://www.unionhistory.info/workerswar/voices.php

7. Later the Chemical and Biological Defence Establishment, Porton Down. See Chrystal, Paul, 2023, *Bioterrorism and Biological Warfare.*

8. The Chemical Defence Establishment at Porton Down released a report in 1989 Asbestos in World War II Respirator Canisters - detailing the use of asbestos in the manufacture of respirator filter canisters prior and at the start of the second world war. Filters were made with 80% carded wool and 20% asbestos. Sometime in 1940 this asbestos wool was replaced by resin-impregnated wool. However, some 40 million respirators containing the asbestos wool had been issued by 1939.

9. The ROFs included: ROF Chorley (Filling Factory No. 1); ROF Aycliffe (# 8); ROF Thorp Arch (# 9)

10. See Ryerson, 1980, *The Giants of Small Heath - The History of BSA.*

11. See *Fairbairn-Sykes Commando Dagger* by Leroy Thompson (2011); *Wilkinsons and the F.S. Fighting Knife* by Robert Wilkinson-Latham (2009)

12. *Grace's Guide*, https://www.gracesguide.co.uk/Sanderson_Brothers_and_Newbould

13. See Briggs, *The Framework of the Wool Control;* Zimmern, *The Wool Trade in Wartime.*

14. For more details see Hypher, Stephen (1996), *Birmingham Railway Carriage and Wagon Company - A Century of Achievement, 1855-1963.*

15. See David. D. Jackson, https://usautoindustryworldwartwo.com/General%20 Motors/vauxhallmotors.htm

16. See Borge, Jessica, *Protective Practices: A History of the London Rubber Company and the Durex Business*, Montreal, 2020

17. According to the National Archives
'The London Council for the Promotion of Public Morality, later the Public Morality Council, was formed in 1899 to combat vice and indecency in London and to assist in their repression by legal means, already existing but neglected. Its members included representatives of the Church of England, Roman Catholic and Non-conformist churches and of the Jewish faith, leaders in education, medicine and charitable associations and others supporting reform. It continued until 1969, concentrating latterly on opposition to sexual immorality and pornography in general and in the theatre, cinema, radio and television. Its functions were taken over by the Social Morality Council, constituted in 1969'.

https://discovery.nationalarchives.gov.uk/details/r/4fa412a8-cdd3-493d-86b3-f308e68aefbc
Idem, 43-44
18. *London Image*, August 1968, 29
19. Borge, 63
20. *London Rubber Company International People*, Chingford, 3 April 1973
21. *London Image*, Spring 1968, 11
22. *Ibid*, Winter 1967, 29; Borge, 63
https://theconversation.com/durex-condoms-how-their-teenage-immigrant-inventor-was-forgotten-by-history-152497 and others

Chapter 17: Prostitution in the World Wars

1. See, for example, Makepeace, Clare: Male heterosexuality and prostitution during the great war. British soldiers' encounters with Maisons Tolérées, in: *Cultural and Social History* 9/1, 2012, pp. 65-83. Steward, Journey: Prostitution, in:1914-1918-online. *International Encyclopedia of the First World War*, ed. by Ute Daniel, Freie Universität Berlin, Berlin, 2017.
2. See, amongst the copious literature on the subject: Harris, Victoria: *Selling sex in the Reich. Prostitutes in German society, 1914-1945*, Oxford, 2010; *Hirschfeld, Magnus: The sexual history of the world war*, New York 1941: Cadillac.; Le Naour, Jean-Yves: Le sexe et la guerre. Divergences Franco-Américaines pendant la Grande Guerre (1917-1918), in *Guerres Mondiales et Conflits Contemporains* 197, 2000, 103-116.Röger, Maren, From control to terror. German prostitution policies in eastern and western European territories during both world wars, in *Gender & History* 28/3, 2016, 687-708. Wingfield, Nancy M.: The enemy within. Regulating prostitution and controlling venereal disease in cisleithanian Austria during the Great War, in *Central European History* 46/3, 2013, pp. 568-598.
3. Article by Journey Steward, Northern Illinois University.
4. The condom obviously also had huge implications for birth control at the time. For example, the work done by Marie Stopes: the scientific nature of her efforts had an ideological purpose, and the Society of Constructive Birth Control and Racial Progress that she founded in 1921 reflected this.
5. *100 Years, 100 Legacies > 13/97 Contraception* by Stephen Fidler; Borge, Jessica, *Protective Practices: A History of the London Rubber Company and the Durex Business*, Montreal, 2020
6. A University of California website https://calisphere.org/item/7cee94b02bfe031b4dc921aa679bca1d/: 'When draft examinations for World War I revealed infections for nearly a quarter of all recruits, military policy was altered to accept some soldiers with pre-existing Venereal Disease. Over the next two years, around 380,000 American soldiers would be diagnosed

with some form of VD, eventually costing the U.S. more than $50 million in treatment... The idea behind these kits was that soldiers who "went out on a weekend furlough and had sexual contact would then clean themselves up afterwards with antiseptics and urethral syringes and so forth." Edmonson points out that this method was like "closing the gate after the horse is out of the barn; not very effective." This half-hearted prevention program resulted in a complete epidemic of sexually transmitted infections. Sarah Forbes says nearly 18,000 soldiers a day were unable to report for duty because of these illnesses. Starting with the pro-kit, which Forbes describes as "glorified soap that was completely ineffective."

7. Weeks, J., Sex, Politics and Society: The Regulation of Sexuality Since 1800, 188
8. Harrison, Mark, The British Army and the Problem of VD in France and Egypt during the First World War, Medical History, 39(1995), 140.
9. See Davenport-Hines, Richard, Sex, Death and Punishment, Chapter 5: Venus Decomposing, London 1990
10. Simpson, David, The Moral Battlefield: Venereal Disease and the British Army in the First World War, PhD thesis, University of Iowa 1999, 11, 183; Davenport Hines, 196-198
11. Devenport-Hines, 234-235
12. Simpson, 183; 403
13. Hall, L.A, 1999, "'War always brings it on': War, STDs, the military, and the civilian population in Britain, 1850-1950", Clio Medica, 55, 214
14. Simpson, 120, 122
15. Borge, Protective Practices, 41
16. See also, for example, Rose, Sonya O. "Sex, Citizenship, and the Nation in World War II Britain." The American Historical Review 103, no. 4 (1998): 1147–76.
17. Laite, Julia, 2012, Common Prostitutes and Ordinary Citizens 1885-1960: Commercial Sex in London, London
18. Levine, Josua, 2015 The Secret History of the Blitz, London, 211-236
19. Borge, J. Protective Practices, 42
20. Romm, Cari, During World War II, Sex Was A National-Security Threat, The Atlantic, October 8 2015

Appendix 2: Stamford Military Hospital, Dunham Massey and The Carrel-Dakin Treatment

1. https://www.independent.co.uk/life-style/history/first-world-war-centenary-dunham-massey-hall-reconverted-into-a-hospital-9169187.html
2. Clin Orthop Relat Res. 2019 Dec; 477(12): 2651–2652. Published online 2019 Oct 25.

Further Reading

This is divided into General, World War I and World War II

General

Abbott, Pamela, 1987, *Women and Social Class*, London

Achterberg, Jeanne, 1991, *Woman as Healer: A Panoramic Survey of the Healing Activities of Women from Prehistoric Times to the Present*, Boston.

Adam, Ruth, 1977, *A Woman's Place*, Norton

Adams, Virginia, 'Jane Crow in the Army'. Obstacles to Sexual Integration', *Psychology Today*, October 1980.

Adie, Kate, 2003, *Corsets to Camouflage: Women and War*, London

Allen, Mary S., 1925, *The Pioneer Policewoman*, London

Anderson, A., 1919, *'Johnnie' of Queen Mary's Army Auxiliary Corps*

Arbogast, Kate A., 'Women in the Armed Forces: A rediscovered Resource', *Military Review* November 1973

Bamfield, Veronica, 1975, *'On The Strength', Story of the British Army Wife*, Knight (Charles) & Co Ltd

Barton, E.M, 1918, *Eve in Khaki; the Story of the Women's Army at Home and Abroad,*

Beachamp, P., 1940, *Fanny Went to War*, London

Beard, Mary R., 1946, *Woman as a Force in History. A Study in Traditions and Realities*, New York

Beauman, Katherine, 1971, *Partners in Blue, The Story of Women's Service with the Royal Air Force*

Beauman, Katherine, 1977, *Greensleeves: The Story of the WS/WRVS,*

Bidwell, Shelford, 1977, *The Women's Royal Army Corps*, Barnsley

Bigland, Eileen, 1946, *Britain's Other Army - Story of the ATS*, Nicholson & Watson

Bigland, Eileen, 1946, *The Story of the WRNS*, Nicholson & Watson

Binkin, Martin, 1977, *Women and the Military*, The Brookings Institute

Black, C., 1915, *Married Women's Work*, London

Bolin-Hort P., 1989, *Work, Family, and the State*, Lund

Braybon, Gail, 1987, *Out of the Cage, Women's Experiences in Two World Wars*, London

Brooks, Jane, ed., 2015, *One Hundred Years of Wartime Nursing Practices, 1854-1953*, Manchester

Burman, Sandra, (ed), 2012, *Fit Work for Women*, London

Burke, Colin, 2010, From the Archives: A Lady Codebreaker Speaks: Joan Murray, the Bombes and Perils of Writing Crypto-history from Participants' Accounts, in *Cryptologia* 34, 4, 359-370

Burke, Joanna, 2000, *An Intimate History of Killing: Face-to-Face Killing in Twentieth Century History*, Basic Books

Chapkis, W., (ed), 1971, *Loaded Questions, Women in the Military*, Amsterdam

Chauncey, A., *Women of the Royal Air Force*, WRAF Old Comrades Association) undated.

Chrystal, Paul, 2015, *York and Its Railways 1839-1950*, Catrine

Chrystal, Paul, 2017, *Leeds's Military Legacy*, Barnsley

Chrystal, Paul, 2017, *Women at War in the Classical World*, Barnsley

Chrystal, Paul, 2021, *A History of the World in 100 Pandemics, Plagues and Epidemics*, Barnsley

Chrystal, Paul, 2022, *A History of Britain in 100 Objects*, Darlington

Chrystal, Paul, 2022, *Factiry Girls: Women and Children at Work*

Chrystal, Paul, 2023, *Bioterrorism & Biological Warfare: Disease as a Weapon of War*, Barnsley

Clarke, Linda, 2006, 'Omitted from History: Women in the Building Trades in Dunkeld', M.. ed., *Proceedings of the Second International Congress on Construction History Cambridge,*, 35–59

Clarke Linda, 2006, 'Women in Manual Trades', in A. Gale ed., *Managing Diversity in the Construction Sector*, London

Cocroft, Wayne D., 2000, *Dangerous Energy: The archaeology of gunpowder and military explosives manufacture.* Swindon

Cohen, Susan, 2010, *The District Nurse*, Oxford

Cohen, Susan, 2016, *The Midwife*, Oxford

Cohn, Carol, 1993, "War, Wimps, and Women: Talking Gender and Thinking War", in Cooke (ed.), *Gendering War Talk*, Princeton, pp. 227-246

Collett Wadge, D., 2003, *Women in Uniform*, London

Collins Weitz, Michel, ed, *Behind the Lines: Gender and the Two World Wars*, New Haven, CT

Conway, Jane, 2010, *A Woman of Two Wars – The Life of Mary Borde*, Munday Books

Cooper, Helen, M. ed. (1989). *Arms and the Woman: War, Gender, and Literary Representation.* Chapel Hill, NC.

Cooper, Tim, 2008, Challenging the "Refuse Revolution": War, Waste and the Rediscovery of Recycling, 1900–50, *Historical Research* 81

Cowper, J., 1957, *A Short History of the QMAAC*, London

Cowper, Col. J.M., 1957, 'Summary Punishment f or Women', *Journal of the Royal United Service Institution* 606, 1957.

Criado Perez, Caroline, 2019, *Invisible Women: Exposing Data Bias in a World Designed for Men*, London

Curti, Merle, 1963, *American Philanthropy Abroad.* Transaction Publishers

Further Reading

Davidoff, Leonore, ed, 1986, *Our Work, Our Lives, Our Words,* Barnes & Noble

Davidson, Caroline, 1982, *A Woman's Work is Never Done*, London

Davies, M.L., ed., 1975, *Life as We Have Known It, by Co-operative Working Women*, New York

Dawson Scott, 1915, *Official Handbook of the Women's Defence Relief Corps*

Dixon, N., 1994, *The Psychology of Military Incompetence*, Pimlico

Doerr, Paul W. (2006), "Great Britain, Women in Service during World War II", in Cook, Bernhard A. (2006), *Women and War: a Historical Encyclopedia from Antiquity to the Present,* Santa Barbara, pp. 241-244

Donnison, J., 1977, *Midwives and Medical Men: A History of Interprofessional Rivalries and Women's Rights*

Douglas, R.M., 1999. *Feminist Freikorps: The British Voluntary Women police, 1914-1940,* Westport

Dowell, William Chipcase, 1987, *The Webley Story*, Washington

Drake, B., 1917, Women in the Engineering Trades, *Fabian Research Papers*, London

Drummond, J.D., 1960, *Blue for a Girl; the Story of the WRNS,* London

Du Cros, Rosemary, 1983, *ATA Girl: Memoirs of a Wartime Ferry Pilot*, London

Dunlop, Tessa, 2021, *Army Girls,* London

Ege, L., 1973, *Balloons and Airships,* Blandford

Ellis, John, 1976, *The Social History of the Machine Gun*. London

Ellis, Mary, 2016, *A Spitfire Girl,* Barnsley

Elshtaln, Jean Bethke, 1987, *Women and War*, Brighton

Emsley, Clive, 2010, *The Great British Bobby. A History of British Policing from the C18th to the Present,* Quercus

Enloe, Cynthia, 1980, 'Women - The Reserve Army of Army Labour', *The Review of Radical Political Economics* 12

Enloe, Cynthia, 1988, *Does Khaki Become You? The Militarisation of Women's Lives,* Pandora Press

Escott, B.E., 1989, *Women in Air Force Blue: the story of women in the Royal Air Force from 1918 to the Present Day,* London

Ewing, Elizabeth, 1975, *Women in Uniform through the Centuries,* London

Feld, M.D.,1978, 'Arms and the Woman. Some general considerations.' *Armed Forces and Society* 4

Fernandez, R., 2007. 'Women, work and culture', *Journal of the European Economic Association* 5

Fletcher, Marjorie H., 1989, *The WRNS: A History of the Women's Royal Naval Service*. London

Fortescue, John, 1928, A *Short Account of Canteens in the British Army*, Cambridge

Fountain, Nigel (ed), 2002, *Women at War*, London

Fox, Lynne, 2008, *South Yorkshire Women in Industry: A Study of the Last 100 Years*

Gasson, Ruth, 1980, *The Role of Women in British Agriculture*, Women's Farm and Garden Association

Giles, M.J, 1989, *Something That Bit Better: Working-Class Women, Domesticity and 'Respectability' 1919–1939,* York

Giles, M.J., 1995, *Women, Identity and Private Life in Britain*, 1900–1950 (Women's Studies at York Series)

Glaister, Lt. Colonel G., 1977, *'Servicewomen in the British Army'*, unpublished paper, Royal Military College of Science

Glew, Helen, 2016 *Gender, Rhetoric and Regulation: Women's work in the Civil Service and the London County Council, 1900-55,* Manchester

Glick, Stephen P., 1983, War, Games and Military History, *Journal of Contemporary History,* 4

Goldin, Claudia, 1990, *Understanding the Gender Gap*, New York

Goldman, Nancy, 1973, 'The Changing Role of Women in the Armed Forces', *American Journal of Sociology*

Goldman, Nancy L., 1978, *'The Utilization of Women in Combat: The Armed Forces of Great Britain, World War I and World War II',* (Typescript; Research supported by US Army Institute for Behavioral end Social Sciences).

Goldman, Nancy L. *'British Women in Two World Wars - and After'*, Typescript, presented at Inter-University. Seminar on Armed Forces and Society's National Conference, October 23 - 25, 1980, Chicago

Goldman, Nancy Loring (ed.), 1982, *Female Soldiers - Combatants or Noncombatants? Historical and Contemporary Perspectives*, Greenwood

Goode, Jackie (ed), 2019, *Clever Girls: Autoethnographies of Class, Gender and Ethnicity*, London

Gooding, N.G., 1984, Awards of the Military Medal to Women. *Orders & Medals Research Society Journal*, Vol 23, No 4, Winter 1984, pp 225-228

Gordon, Peter, 2001, *Dictionary of British Women's Organisations, 1825–1960,* London

Gould, Jennifer Margaret, 1988, *The Women's Corps: The Establishment of Women's Military Services in Britain*. A thesis presented for the Degree of Ph.D, University College London, 1988

Grant, Neil, 2014, *The Lewis Gun,* Oxford

Graves, Robert, 1941, *The Long Weekend: A Social History of Great Britain 1918-1939*, Newton Abbott

Grieg, G.A., 1916, *Women's Work on the Land*, Norwich

Gwynne Vaughan, Helen, 'How Britain Can Avoid War - The WAACs on Active Service', *British Legion Journal* 6, July 1935.

Hacker, Barton C. ed., 2012, *A Companion to Women's Military History*, Leiden

Haldane, Elizabeth, S., 1913, *The British Nurse in Peace and War*, London

Hareven, Tamara, 1982, *Family Time and Industrial Time*, Cambridge

Hartman, Heidi, 1976, 'Capitalism, patriarchy, and job segregation by sex'. *Signs.* 1(3, pt. 2), 136–69

Hay, Ian, 1953, *One hundred Years of Army Nursing: The Story of the British Army Nursing Services from the Time of Florence Nightingale to the Present Day.* London

Heren, Louise (2016), *British Nannies and the Great War: How Norland's Regiment of Nannies Coped with Conflict and Childcare in the Great War*, Barnsley

Hetherington, Angela (2018), *British Widows of the First World War: The Forgotten Legion:* Barnsley

Further Reading

Higonnet, Margaret Randolph, ed, 1987, *Behind the Lines. Gender and the Two World Wars,* London

Holloway, Gerry, 2007, *Women and Work in Britain Since 1840*, London

Hore, Peter (2021), *Bletchley Park's Secret Source: Churchill's Wrens and the Y Service in World War II*, Barnsley

Horwood, Catherine, *Gardening Women: Their Stories from 1600 to the Present*, 2010

Hudson, Pat, 2011, *Women's Work,* https://www.bbc.co.uk/history/british/victorians/womens_work_01.shtml

Hunt, Cathy, 2012, 'Sex versus class in two British trade unions in the early twentieth century', *Journal of Women's History*. 24 (1): 86–110

Hunt, Cathy, 2014, *The National Federation of Women Workers, 1906–1921*, Stuttgart

Hunter, Edna I., 1978, 'Women in the Military, An annotated Bibliography', *Armed Forces and Society Vol 4*

Jackson, Louise, A. 2006, *Women Police: Gender, Welfare and Surveillance in the Twentieth Century*, Manchester

Johnston, Helen, 2014, Gendered Prison Work: Female Prison Officers in the Local Prison System, 1877–1939, *The Howard Journal of Criminal Justice* 53, pp. 193-212, 2014

Joyce, P., 1987, *The Historical Meanings of Work*, London

Jowitt, J.A.,(ed) 1988, *Employers and Labour in the English Textile Industries, 1850–1939*, London

Kramer, Ann,2008, *Land Girls and their Impact,* Barnsley

Lewenhak, Sheila, 1977, *Women and Trade Unions: An Outline History of Women in the British Trade Union Movement,* London

Light, Sue. *VAD Life*, at: http://www.scarletfinders.co.uk/183.html

Lock, Joan, 1979, *The British Policewoman. Her Story,* London

Mackie, Mary, 2001, *Sky Wards - A History of the Princess Mary's Royal Air Force Nursing Service,* Stroud

Mackie, Mary, 2014, *Wards in the Sky – the RAF's Remarkable Nursing Service*, Stroud

Mackrell, Judith, 2021, *Going with the Boys: Six Extraordinary Women Writing from the Front Line*, London

McCarthy, Helen, 2020, *Double Lives: A History of Working Motherhood*, London

Mason, Ursula Stuart, 1992, *Britannia's Daughters: the story of the WRNS.* London

Mason, Stuart, (2012) *Britannia's Daughters: The Story of the WRNS*, Barnsley

Meredith, Anne, 2003, *Horticultural Education in England, 1900-40: Middle-Class Women and Private Gardening Schools, Garden History* 31

Meyer, Jessica, 2015, "Neutral Caregivers or Military Support? The British Red Cross, the Friends' Ambulance Unit, and the Problems of Voluntary Medical Aid in Wartime. *War & Society* 34, 105–120.

Mill, John Stuart, 2006, *On Liberty and the Subjection of Women*, London

Moore, Frank, (repr. 1966), *Women of the War: Their Heroism and Self Sacrifice*

Newman, Vivien (ed), (2023) *Nursing through Shot and Shell: A Great War Nurse's Story – Beatrice Hopkinson's Memoirs*, Barnsley

Noakes, Lucy, 2006, *Women in the British Army: War and the Gentle Sex, 1907–48*, London

Oakley, Annie, 1976, *Housewife*, London

Oliver, Dame Beryl, 1966, *The British Red Cross in Action*, London

Opitz, Donald, L. 2013, A Triumph of Brains over Brute: Women and Science at the Horticultural College, Swanley 1890-1910, *Isis* 104

Oren, L., 1973, The Welfare of Women in Labouring Families: England 1860–1950, *Feminist Studies*

Pam, David, 1998, *The Royal Small Arms factory Enfield & Its Workers*, David Pam

Pattinson, Juliette, 2021, *Women of War: Gender, modernity and the First Aid Nursing Yeomanry*, Manchester

Pennington, Reina, 2003, *Amazons to Fighter Pilots - A Biographical Dictionary of Military Women (Volume 2)*. Westpoint, CT

Piggott, Julie, 1975, *Queen Alexandra's Royal Army Nursing Corps*, London

Popham, Hugh, 1984, *FANY: The Story of the Women's transport Service, 1907 - 1984*

Popham, Hugh, 2002, *The FANY in Peace and War*, Barnsley

Pugh, Martin, 1993, *Women and the Women's Movement in Britain, 1914–1959*, New York

Purvis, June, ed., 1995, *Women's History in Britain, 1850–1945*, London

Quester, George, 'Woman in Combat', *International Security*, Spring 1977

Reid, F., 2007, Distinguishing between Shell-shocked Veterans and Pauper Lunatics: The Ex-Services' Welfare Society and Mentally Wounded Veterans after the Great War. *War in History* 14, 347–371.

Roberts, Elizabeth, 1995, *A Woman's Place: An Oral History of Working Class Women, 1890–1940*, Chichester

Roberts, Hannah, 2018, *The WRNS in Wartime: the Women's Royal Naval Service 1917–1945*. London

Robinson, Jane, 2011, *A Force to be Reckoned With: A History of the Women's Institute*, London

Rosen, Sherwin, 1990, 'Male-Female Wage Differentials in Job Ladders', *Journal of Labor Economics* 8, 106–23

Sackville West, Vita, 2016 repr., *The Women's Land Army*, London

Shewell-Cooper, W.E.,undated, *Land Girl: A Handbook for the Women's Land Army*, English Universities Press

Simonton, Deborah, 1998, *A History of European Women's Work: 1700 to the Present*, London

Southwick, Michael, 2021, *Newcastle-upon-Tyne: Fragments of the Past Volume 1* p. 60, Newcastle.

Spring-Rice, M., 1939, *Working-Class Wives: Their Health and Condition*, London

Spurgeon, Anne, 2012, *The Contribution of the Women's Factory Inspectorate (1893-1921) to improvements in women's occupational health and safety*. MPhil thesis, University of Worcester

Sterling, Christopher H., 2008, *Military communications: from ancient times to the 21st century*. ABC-CLIO

Storey, Neil, R. 2017, *WRNS: The Women's Royal Naval Service*, Oxford
Sub Cruce Candida, 2002, *A Celebration of one hundred years of Army Nursing 1902-2002*, QARANC Association
Summerfield, Penny, 1998, *Reconstructing Women's Wartime Lives*, Manchester
Summers, Anne, 1988, *Angels and Citizens - British Women as Military Nurses 1854-1914*, London
Tate, Tim, 2016, *Girls with Balls,* John Blake
Terry, Roy, 1988, *Women in Khaki*, Columbus, OH
Thomas, Patricia I., 1978, 'Women in the Military: America and the British Commonwealth. Historical Similarities', *Armed Forces and Society* 4
Tilly, Louise, 1987, *Women, Work, and Family*, London
Twinch, Carol, 1990, *Women on the Land: Their story during two world wars,* London
Vickers, 1898, *Vickers, Sons and Maxim Limited: Their Works and Manufactures.* (Reprinted from '*Engineering*') London
Wankhade, Paresh, 2015, *Ambulance Services: Leadership and Management Perspectives*. Springer
Ward, Irene, 1955, *FANY Invicta,* London
Way, Twiggs, 2006, *Virgins, Weeders & Queens: A History of Women in the Garden,* Stroud
Wheelwright, Julie, 1999, *Amazons and Military Maids*, London
Wightman, Clare, 2017, *More Than Munitions: Women, Work and the Engineering Industries, 1900-1950,* London
Wood, Emily, 1995, *The Red Cross*, London
Zimmern, D.P., 1918, The Wool Trade in Wartime. *The Economic Journal* 28

World War I

Abbott, Edith, 1917, 'The War And Women's Work in England', *The Journal of Political Economy* 7
Albrinck, Meg, 1998, Borderline Women: Gender Confusion in Vera Brittain's and Evadne Price's War Narratives. *Narrative 6*
Andrews, Irene Osgood, 1918, *Economic Effects of the War Upon Women and Children in Great Britain* (Carnegie Endowment for International Peace, Oxford
Anonymous Diary of a Nursing Sister on the Western Front, 1915, Edinburgh
Atkinson, Diane, 2010, *Elsie and Mairi Go to War: Two Extraordinary Women on the Western Front,* London
Baker, Chris, *Women and the British Army in the First World War. The Long, Long Trail. http://www.longlongtrail.co.uk/army/regiments-and-corps/women-and-the-british-army-in-the-first-world-war/*
Berry, Paul, 1985, *Testament of a Generation; The Journalism of Vera Brittain and Winifred Holtby,* London
Billings, John, 1913, *Ashton Munitions Explosion, 1917,* Tameside Leisure Services

Binyon, Laurence, 1918, *For Dauntless France - An Account of Britain's Aid to the French Wounded and Victims of War*, London

Bogacz, T. (1989). War Neurosis and Cultural Change in England, 1914-22: The Work of the War Office Committee of Enquiry into "Shell-Shock." *Journal of Contemporary History*, 24(2), 227–256. http://www.jstor.org/stable/260822

Bourke, Joanna, 1999, *Dismembering the Male: Men's Bodies, Britain and the Great War*, London

Bowser, Thekia, 1917, *The Story of British VAD Work in the Great War*, London

Brader, Christopher, 2001, *Timbertown girls: Gretna female munitions workers in World War I* (PhD thesis), University of Warwick

Braybon, Gail, 1981, *Women Workers in the First World War*, London

Braybon, Gail, ed., 2003) *Evidence, History and the Great War: Historians and the Impact of 1914- 1918*, Oxford

Brennan, Patrick, 2007, *The Munitionettes: A History of Women's Football in North East England During the Great War*, Denmouth

Brittain, Vera, 1933, *Testament of Youth: An Autobiographical Story of the Years 1900-1925*, London

Condell, Diana, 1987, *Working for Victory? Images of Women in the First World War*, London

Cornelis, M.E., The Scottish Women's Hospitals: the first World War and the careers of early medical women. Cornelis ME. *Med Confl Surviv.* 2020 ;36(2):174-194

Cosens, Monica, 1916, *Lloyd George's Munition Girls*, London

Cowen, Ruth, 2013, *A Nurse at the Front: The First World War Diaries of Sister Edith Appleton*, London

Crofton, Eileen, 1997, *The Women of Royaumont: a Scottish Women's Hospital on the Western Front*, Tuckwell Press

Crosthwait, Elizabeth, *'The Girl Behind the Man Behind the Gun': The Women's Army Auxiliary Corps 1914 – 1918*

Dakers, Caroline, 1987, *The Countryside at War* 1914-1918, London

Donner, H.,1997, Under the Cross: Why V.A.D.s Performed the Filthiest Task in the Dirtiest War: Red Cross Women Volunteers, 1914-1918. *Journal of Social History*, *30*(3), 687–704.

Dunn, Daisy, 2022, *Not Far from Brideshead: Oxford between the Wars*, London

Fitzharris, Lindsey, 2022, *The Facemaker: One Surgeon's Battle to Mend the Disfigured Soldiers of World War I*, London

Gould, Jennifer Margaret, Women's Military Service in First World War Britain, in Higonnet, *Behind the Lines*, 1987, 114-125

Geddes Jennian F. The Women's Hospital Corps: forgotten surgeons of the First World War. *J Med Biogr.* 2006, 14(2):109-17.

Geddes, Jennian F. Deeds and Words in the Suffrage Military Hospital in Endell Street, *Med Hist.* 2007 Jan; 51(1):79-98.

Geddes, Jennian F. Louisa Garrett Anderson (1873-1943), Surgeon and Suffragette. *J Med Biogr.* 2008 Nov; 16(4):205-14.

Further Reading

Grayzel, Susan, R., 1997, 'The Outward and Visible Sign of Her Patriotism: Women, Uniforms and National Service During the First World War', *Twentieth Century British History, Vol. 8, No. 2*

Grayzel, Susan, R., 1999, *Women's Identities at War: Gender, Motherhood, and Politics in Britain and France During the First World War,* Chapel Hill NC

Grayzel, Susan, R., 2002, *Women and the First World War,* Harlow

Greenwood, Maj., 2018, *An Inquiry Into the Prevalence and Aetiology of Tuberculosis Among Industrial Workers, With Special Reference to Female Munition Workers – 18 Feb. 2018,* Patala Press

Griffiths, G.R. 2014, *Women's Factory Work in World War One*, Stroud

Haber, L. F., 1986, *The Poisonous Cloud: Chemical Warfare in the First World War*. Oxford

Hallett, Christine, 2011, *Containing Trauma, Nursing Work in the First World War;* Manchester

Hallett, Christine, 2014, *Veiled Warriors; Allied Nurses of the Great War;* Oxford

Harrison, R., 1971, The War Emergency Workers' National Committee, 1914–1920. In: Briggs, A., ed, *Essays in Labour History 1886–1923*. London

Haste, Cate, 1977, *Keep the Home Fires Burning: Propaganda in the First World War,* London

Hay, Ian (Maj.Gen. John Hay Beith, CBE, MC) (1949). R.O.F. *The Story of the Royal Ordnance Factories, 1939-1948*. London

Heald, Henrietta, 2019, *Magnificent Women and their Revolutionary Machines*. London

Higgs, Edward, 1986, 'Domestic Service and Household Production', in Angela John, ed., *Unequal Opportunities: Women's Employment in England*, 1800–1918, Oxford

Higonnet, Margaret Randolph, ed, 1987, *Behind the Lines: Gender and the Two World Wars,* Yale

Hilton, Claire, 2021, *Civilians, Lunacy and the First World War.* In: Hilton, Claire, *Civilian Lunatic Asylums During the First World War,* London

HMSO, 1921, *Reports by the Joint War Committee and the Joint War Finance Committee of the British Red Cross Society and the Order of St. John of Jerusalem in England on voluntary aid rendered to the sick and wounded at home and abroad and to British prisoners of war, 1914–1919*

House, Euan, The Impact of the Great War on the Woods and Forests of Scotland, *Forestry Memories*

John, Angela, ed., 1986, *Unequal Opportunities: Women's Employment in England 1800–1918*, Oxford

Kenyon, David, 2015, *"First World War National Factories: An Archaeological, Architectural and Historical review"*. Historic England

Kozack, M., *'Women Munition Workers During the First World War, with special reference to Engineering'*, PhD, University of Hull, 1976.

Krippner, Monica, *The Quality of Mercy - Women at War in Serbia 1915-18*; Newton Abbott, 1980

Lee, Janet, 2005, *War Girls: The First Aid Nursing Yeomanry in the Great War,* Manchester

Levine, Phillipa, 1994, Walking the Streets in a Way No Decent Woman Should: Women Police in World War I.', *The Journal of Modern History 1994*; 66: 34-78

London, Lucy, 2018, *No Woman's Land: A Centenary Tribute To Inspirational Women Of World War One,* Posh Up North

MacDonald, Lyn, 1980, *The Roses of No Man's Land*, London

Marwick, Arthur, *Women at War 1914-1918*, London

Marlow, Joyce (ed), 1998, *The Virago Book of Women and the Great War,* London

McCalman, J., 1971, The Impact of the First World War on Female Employment in England. *Labour History, 21,* 36–47

McEnroe, Natasha, ed., 2014, *The Hospital in the Oatfield; The Art of Nursing in the First World War;* Florence Nightingale Museum, 2014

Ministry of Munitions of War, 1919, *H.M. Factory, Gretna: Description of Plant and Process,* Dumfries

Mitchell, David, 1966, *Women on the Warpath - The Story of the Women of the First World War*, London

Mitton, G.E., 2011, *The Cellar-House of Pervyse: The Incredible Account of Two Nurses on the Western Front During the Great War,* Bibliolife

Moore, Wendy, 2020, *Endell Street: The Trailblazing Women Who Ran World War One's Most Remarkable Military Hospital,* London

Morgan, Vivien, 2020, *Dressed to Kill: Women who went to war disguised as men.*

Murray, Flora, 1920, *Women as Army Surgeons: Being the history of the Women's Hospital Corps in Paris, Wimereux, and Endell Street September 1914–October 1919,* London

Navarro, Antonio de, 1917, *The Scottish women's hospital at the French abbey of Royaumont,* London

Newman, Vivien, 2014, *We Also Served: The Forgotten Women of the First World War*, Barnsley

Newman, Vivien, 2012, *Changing Roles: Women after the Great War,* Barnsley

Newman, Vivien, 2019, *Children at War 1914-1918: 'It's my War too!',* Barnsley

Nielsen, Jan, 2015, Women and the First World War, *Socialist Review Archive* 400, March 2015

Noakes, Lucy, 2005, Women's Military Service in the First World War, *Women, War and Society,* https://www.gale.com/binaries/content/assets/au-resources-in-product/wwsessay_noakes_womens.pdf

Osborne, Mile, 2012, *Grandad's Army: Volunteers Defending the British Isles in the First World War,* Stroud

Pam, David, (1998). *The Royal Small Arms Factory Enfield & Its Workers.* Enfield: Published by the author.

Parsons, Katharine, 1919, "Katharine Parsons, 'Women's Work in Engineering and Shipbuilding during the War'" (PDF). *NECIES Proceedings* 35 (1918–19)

Patterson, Edward, Gunpowder Manufacture at Faversham: Oare and Marsh Factories, *Faversham Papers No 42*

Further Reading

Percival, Arthur, 1985, The Great Explosion at Faversham by Arthur Percival, *Archaeologia Cantiana* Vol. C. (1985).

Percival, Arthur, The Faversham Gunpowder Industry and its Development, *Faversham Papers No 4*

Powell, Anne, 2013, *Women in the War Zone: Hospital Service in the First World War*, Stroud

Putman, T. (1992). *A Short History of the Royal Small Arms Factory, Enfield*, Centre for Applied Historical Studies, Middlesex University

Rawlins, Michelle, 2020, *Women of Steel: The Feisty Factory Sisters Who Helped Win the War*, London

Rayner-Canham, Marelene, 1996, The Gretna Garrison, *Chemistry in Britain* 32, 37–41.

Reid, F. 2017, *Medicine in First World War Europe: Soldiers, Medics, Pacifists,* London

Riley, Denise, Some Peculiarities of Social Policy concerning Women in Wartime and Postwar Britain, Higonnet, *Behind the Lines*, 1987, 260-271

Ritchie, E., 1988, *The Gretna Girls,* Wigtown

Routledge, Gordon L., 1999, *Gretna's Secret War: The Great Munitions Factory at Dornock, Eastriggs, Gretna and Longtown and an Account of the Quintinshill Railway Disaster,* Carlisle

Routledge, Gordon L., 2003, *Miracles and Munitions: A Concise History of Munitions Manufacture from the time of Alfred Nobel to the building of H.M. Factory Gretna during World War I.* Longtown: Arthuret Publishers.

Stobart, Mabel Annie St Clair, 1913, *War and Women, From Experience in the Balkans and Elsewhere,* London

Shipton, Elisabeth, 2014, *Female Tommies: The Frontline Women of the First World War,* Stroud

Smith, Angela K., 2016, *British Women of the Eastern Front: War, Writing and Experience in Serbia and Russia, 1914-20.* Oxford

Storey, Neil, R.2010, *Women in the First World War,* Oxford

Tate, Trudi, ed, 1995, *Women, Men and the Great War*, Manchester

Taylor, Eric, 2001, *Wartime Nurse - One Hundred Years from the Crimea to Korea 1854-1954,* London

Tennyson, Jesse, F., 1919, *The Sword of Deborah. First hand impressions of British Women's Army in France,* Wentworth Press

Thom, Deborah, *'Women Munition Workers at Woolwich Arsenal in the 1914 - 18 War'*, MA, University of Warwick, 1975

Unwin, Stanley, 1920, *The Work of VAD During the War*, London

Vellacott Newberry, Jo, 'Anti-War Suffragists', *History* 62, October 1977.

Waddell, Pat B., *FANY Went to War. The FANY 1914 - 1918.*

Waites, B.A., 1976, 'The effect of the First World War on Class and Status in England', *Journal of Contemporary History* 11, 1, 1976

Watson, Janet S.K. 2002, Wars in the Wards: The Social Construction of Medical Work in First World War Britain, *Journal of British Studies* 41

Watson, Janet S.K. 2004, *Fighting Different Wars - Experience, Memory and the First World War in Britain,* Cambridge

White, Jerry, 2015, *Zeppelin Nights: London in the First World War,* London

White, Sally, 2018, *Ordinary Heroes: The Story of Civilian Volunteers in the First World War*, Stroud

Woollacott, Angela, 1994, *On Her Their Lives Depend: Munitions Workers in the Great War,* Berkeley

Wynn, S., 2017, *Women in the Great War.* Grub Street Publishers

Yates, L.K., 1918, *The Woman's Part: A Record of Munitions Work*, New York

World War II

Addison, Paul, 1994, *The Road to 1945. British Politics and the Second World War,* Pimlico

Aldrich, Richard J.(ed), *Allied Propaganda in World War II: The Complete Record of the Political Warfare Executive (FO898) from the Public Record Office,*

Babington Smith, Constance, 1957, *Evidence in Camera: The Story of Photographic Intelligence in the Second World War,* London

Baden-Powell, Dorothy, 2005, *They Also Serve: an SOE agent in the WRNS,* London

Barnett, Correlli, 2002, *The Collapse of British Power,* London

Bates, H. E., 1946, *The Tinkers of Elstow: the Story of the Royal Ordnance Factory run by J. Lyons and Company Limited for the Ministry of Supply for the World War of 1939–1945.* Privately published

Bergel, Hugh, ed, 1972, *Flying Wartime Aircraft; ATA Ferry Pilots' Handling Notes for Seven World War II Aircraft*, Newton Abbot

Bergel, Hugh, 1982, *Fly and Deliver: A Ferry Pilot's Log Book,* Shrewsbury

Berriman, Geoffrey, 2002, *They Swept the Skies: A Story of British Searchlight Units of the Second World War*, Seaham

Bigland, Eileen, 1946, *Britain's other army: The story of the A.T.S, an official history,* Nicholson & Watson

Brayley, Martin J., 2001, *World War II Women's Allied Services,* Oxford

Briggs, Asa, "The Framework of the Wool Control." *Oxford Economic Papers*, no. 8, 1947, pp. 18–45.

Briggs, Asa, 2000, *Go to It ! Working for Victory on the Home Front 1939-1945,* London

Brigstock, Keith, 2007, *Royal Artillery Searchlights.* Royal Artillery Historical Society

Broad, Roger, 2006, *Conscription in Britain, 1939-1964: the militarisation of a generation,* London

Brown, Mike, 1999, *Put That Light Out!: Britain's Civil Defence Services at War 1939–1945,* Stroud

Burman, Annie, 2013, *Gendering Decryption – Decrypting Gender: The Gender Discourse of Labour at Bletchley Park, 1939–1945,* (M.A.) Uppsala Universitet

Further Reading

Bruley, Sue, 2001, *Working For Victory, A Diary of Life in a Second World War Factory,* London

Bryan, Tim, 2011, *The Railways in Wartime,* Shire

Christie, Agatha 2017, Agatha: An Autobiography, London

Chrystal, Paul, *Gunners from the Sky: 1st Airlanding Light Regiment RA in Italy and at Arnhem,* Barnsley, 2023

Costello, John, 1985, *Love, Sex and War - Changing Values 1939 - 45*, London

Cowper, J. M., 1949, *The Auxiliary Territorial Service, an official history,* Nicholson & Watson

Crang, Jeremy A., 2008, 'Come into the Army, Maud': Women, Military Conscription, and the Markham Inquiry," *Defence Studies 8*, 381–395

Crang, Jeremy A., 2010, "The revival of the British women's auxiliary services in the late nineteen-thirties," *Historical Research 83*, Issue 220, 343–357

Creaton, Heather, 1998, *Sources for the History of London 1939-45, A Guide and Bibliography,* British Records Association

Crossland, James, 2014, *Britain and the International Committee of the Red Cross, 1939–1945,* Palgrave Macmillan

Curtis, Lettice, 1985, *The Forgotten Pilots: A Story of the Air Transport Auxiliary, 1939-45,* Olney, Bucks

Dady, Margaret, 1986, *Women's War: Life in the Auxiliary Territorial Service*

de Courcy, Anne, 2006, *Debs at War: 1939-1945,* London

de Groot, Gerard J., 1997, "'I love the scent of cordite in your hair': Gender dynamics in mixed anti-craft batteries" *History 82* 73–92

Douie, Vera, 1950, *Daughters of Britain. An Account of the Work of British Women during the 2nd World War*, George Ronald

Downing, Taylor, 2011, *Spies in the Sky,* London

Duchen, Claire, 2001, *When the War Was Over: Women, War, and Peace in Europe, 1940-1956,* Leicester

Dunlop, Tessa, 2015, *The Bletchley Girls: War, secrecy, love and loss: the women of Bletchley Park tell their story,* London

Escott, Beryl, 1989, *Women in Air Force Blue,* Patrick Stephens

Escott, Beryl, 1995, *Our Wartime Days, The WAAF in World War II*, Stroud

Escott, Beryl, 2003, *The WAAF: A History of the Women's Auxiliary Air Force,* Oxford

Fazio, Teresa, 2019, Writing Women at War, *Foreign Policy*, April 13, 2019

Foat, Joanna, 2019, *Lumberjills: Britain's Forgotten Army*, Stroud

Foot, Michael, R.D., 1966, *SOE in France,* London

Foot, Michael R. D., 1981, "Was SOE Any Good,?" *Journal of Contemporary History,* Vol. 16, 174

Gane Pushman, Muriel, 2006, *We All Wore Blue: Experiences in the WAAF,* London

Gardiner, Juliet, *Wartime Britain 1939-1945,* London

Gazeley, Ian, 2008, "Women's Pay in British Industry during the Second World War". *The Economic History Review 61:* 651–671

Gillies, Midge, 2004, *Amy Johnson, Queen of the Air,* London

Gillies, Midge, 2006, *Waiting for Hitler, Voices From Britain on the Brink of Invasion,* London

213

Gowing, Margaret, 1972, 'The Organisation of Manpower in Britain during the Second World War', *Journal of Contemporary History* 7

Gubar, Susan, 'This my rifle, this is my gun'. World War II and the Blitz on Women, in Higonnet, *Behind the Lines*, 1987, 227-259

Halsall, Christine, *Women of Intelligence. Winning the Second World War with Air Photos,* Stroud

Harrison, Ada, 1944, ed., *Grey and Scarlet - Letters from the war areas by army sisters on active service;* London

Hay, Ian, 1949, *R.O.F. The story of the Royal Ordnance Factories, 1939-1948,* HMSO

Heath, Nick, 2015, *Hacking the Nazis: The secret story of the women who broke Hitler's codes.* TechRepublic

Hendrie, James, 2009, Lumberjills, *Forestry Journal,* 40-41

Herbert-Davies, Amanda, 2017, *Children in the Second World War: Memories from the Home Front,* Barnsley

Hill, Marion, 2004, *Bletchley Park People,* Stroud

Hill, Stephen, n.d., *Stockport Air Raid Shelters and the Blitz,* Stockport

Hinsley, F.H., 1993, *Codebreakers: The inside story of Bletchley Park,* Oxford

Howe, Ellic, 1982, *The Black Game: British subversive operations against the Germans during the Second World War* London

Hyams, Jacky, 2012, *The Female Few: Spitfire Heroines of the Air Transport Auxiliary,* Stroud

Hyams, Jacky, 2013, *Bomb Girls*, London

Inman, P. 1957, *Labour in the Munitions Industries,* London

Irving, Henry, 2016, "Paper salvage in Britain during the Second World War", *Historical Research* 89 (244): 373–93

Kerr, Dorothy Brewer, 1990, *Girls Behind the Guns: With the Auxiliary Territorial Service in World War II*, London

Lee, John 2012, "'Station X': The Women at Bletchley Park" in Lee, Celia and Paul Strong (2012), Women in War, Barnsley

Lopez, Beatriz, Muriel Spark and the Art of Deception: Constructing Plausibility with the Methods of WWII Black Propaganda, *The Review of English Studies,* 71, Issue 302, November 2020, 969–986,

Meiggs, Russell, *1949, Home Timber Production 1939-1945*, Crosby Lockwood

National Archives. 1938–1973 *"Political Warfare Executive and Foreign Office, Political Intelligence Department: Papers (Ref: FO 898)"*. Discovery. nationalarchives.gov.uk.

Nesbitt, Roy, 1988, "What did Happen to Amy Johnson?" *Aeroplane Monthly (Part 1),* Vol. 16,, *(Part 2)* Vol. 16, no. 2, February 1988.

Peart, Mike (2017), *Trains of Hope: ambulance trains in times of conflict,* York

Picardie, Justine, *Miss Dior: A Story of Courage and Couture,* London, 2021

Pile, Frederick, 1949, *Ack-Ack: Britain's Defence against Air Attack during the Second World War,* London

Pollard, Robert S.W. 1942, *You and the Call-up: A Guide for Men and Women*

Further Reading

Price, Charlene, *Women Factory Workers in Birmingham During the Second World War* https://sheroesofhistory.wordpress.com/2017/08/24/women-factory-workers-in-birmingham-during-the-second-world-war/

Priestley, J.B., *1943, British Women Go to War*, Glasgow

Rawlins, Michelle, 2020, *Women of Steel: The Feisty Factory Sisters Who Helped Win the War*, London

Richards, Lee, 2010, *The Black Art: British Clandestine Psychological Warfare against the Third Reich* London: www.psywar.org

Richards, Lee, 2010, *Whispers of War: Underground Propaganda Rumour-mongering in the Second World War* London: www.psywar.org

Routledge, Brig N.W., 1994, *History of the Royal Regiment of Artillery: Anti-Aircraft Artillery 1914–55,* London

Ryerson, Barry, 1980, *The Giants of Small Heath - The History of BSA,* Sparkford

Sebag-Montefiore, H., 2004, *Enigma: The battle for the code,* London

Smith, Harold, 1981, 'The Problem of "Equal Pay for Equal Work" in Great Britain during World War II', *The Journal of Modern History* 53, 652 – 672

Smith, M., 2004, *Station X: The Code Breakers of Bletchley Park,* London

Stamper, Anne, 2003, *Countrywomen in War Time: Women' Institutes 1938-1945*

Starns, Penny, 2000, *Nurses at War; Women on the Frontline 1939-45*, Stroud

Stelzer, Cita, *Working with Winston: The Unsung Women Behind Britain's Greatest Statesman,* London, 2019

Stewart, Paul, 2020, https://rafa.org.uk/blog/2020/10/28/raf-medmenham/ *RAF Medmenham – The Clearest View*

Stone, Tessa, 1998, *The Integration of Women into Military Service, WAAF in WWII,* Cambridge

Stone, Tessa, 1999, "Creating A (Gendered?) Military Identity: The Women's Auxiliary Air Force in Great Britain in the Second World War", *Women's History Review* 8, 605–624

Sugden, Philip, 2015, *Amy's Last Flight: The Fate of Amy Johnson in 1941,* Beverley

Summerfield, Penny, 1989, *Women Workers in the Second World War: Production and Patriarchy in Conflict,* London

Summerfield, Penny, 2000, Women in the firing line: the home guard and the defence of gender boundaries in Britain in the second world war, *Women's History Review* 9, 231-255

Swanston, Catherine, 1946, "The Health of Forestry Workers: A Survey of the Women's Timber Corps of Great Britain". *Occupational and Environmental Medicine. BMJ.* 3 (1): 1–10.

Taylor, Eric, 1997, *Front-Line Nurse - British Nurses in World War II,* London

Taylor, Leonard, 1943, *Airwomen's Work,* London

Taylor, Philip M., 1995, *Munitions of the mind: a history of propaganda from the ancient world to the present era,* Manchester

Thomas, Lesley, 2002, *WRNS in Camera: the Women's Royal Naval Service in the Second World War,* Stroud

Thompson, Leroy, 2011, *The Fairbairn-Sykes Commando Dagger,* Oxford

Times, The, 1945, *British War Production 1939-1945*, London

Turner, John Frayn, 2011, *The WAAF at War*, Barnsley

Vickers, Emma, 2011, "'The Forgotten Army of the Woods': The Women's Timber Corps during the Second World War", *Agricultural History Review 59*: 101–112.

Wailer, Ian, 1987, *Women in Wartime: The Role of Women's Magazines 1939 - 1945*, London

Waller, Jane, 1989, *Women in Uniform 1939-1945*, Basingstoke

Wheeler, Jo, 2018, *The Hurricane Girls: The Inspirational True Story of the Women who Dared to Fly*, London

Whittell, Giles, 2007, *Spitfire Women of World War II*, London

Wilkinson-Latham, Robert, 2009, *Wilkinsons and the F.S. Fighting Knife*, Air Pilot Publisher

Williams-Ellis, Amabel, 1943, *Women in War Factories*, London

Wubs, Ben, 2003, *International Business and National War Interests: Lever Brothers and Unilever during World War II*, BHC-EBHA Meeting

Index

Abuse, verbal, sexual and physical against women, xvii, 2-3, 4, 12, 17
Academia, women in, 72-73
Aircraft manufacturing, 75, 112, 164
Air Raid Precautions, 136, 139-142
Women as, 141
Air Transport Auxiliary (ATA), 116, 134-135
Allied Central Interpretation Unit (CIU), Medmenham, 121-123
Almeric Paget Military Massage Corps (APMMC), The, 27-28
Amazon Defence Corps, 143-144
Ambulance trains and ambulance train nurses, 54-56
American Ambulance, Great Britain, 123, 152-153
Anderson, Louisa Garrett, 40-42
Animals in war, *Plates* 13 and 14, xi, 67-68, 88
Appleton, Edith Elizabeth OBE RRC *Plate 2*, ix, 36
Armistice November 1918: what happened to the working women ? 108-110
Armistice September 1945: what happened to the working women ? 182-183
Astor, Nancy, xv
Auxiliary Fire Service (AFS), 154
Auxiliary Hospitals, 186
Auxiliary Territorial Service (ATS), 110, 124, 126-128
ATS personnel at an anti-aircraft gun station, *Plate 28,* xii
ATS and Princess Elizabeth, 128

ATS and the Royal Signals, 127-128
ATS Searchlight detachments, *Plate 27,* 128-130
Auxiliary Territorial Service (ATS) personnel attacking a Centurion tank, *Plate 31*, xii
Auxiliary Territorial Service (ATS) Signal Corps, *Plate 12*, x, xii, xix
Auxiliary Territorial Service (ATS) West Indian woman, *Plate 29*, xii

Baby Week 1917, 82-83
Bastions, male, xv-xvi, 4, 12, 14-15, 72-73, 117-121
Bick, Charity, 141
Black, Catherine and plastic surgery, PTSD
Bletchley Park, see Government Code and Cypher School
Body image, women's, 20, 83-84
Borden, Mary, 38-39
Boy Scout's Association, 81-82
Bradford, May, 39
Britain, unprepared for war in 1914, 62, 88-89
British War Relief Society, 135
British Women's Hospital, Richmond, 52
Brittain, Vera, xvi, xvii-xviii, 37, 109-110
Building trade and women, 7-8
Bullying of women, xvii
Bundles for Britain, 135-136
Burton, see Montague Burton

217

Cambridge Military Hospital, Aldershot, 33

Canary Girls, Canary Babies and TNT tainted yellow skin, 93-94

Canteens in the field, 56-57

Careswell, Alma, *Plate 12,* xi, 127

Carrel-Dakin treatment, 187

Caswell, Margaret, 21

Carriage cleaning, *Plate 19*, xi

Central Army Clothing Depot in Pimlico, 78

Central Committee on Women's Employment, 5-6

Chapple, Phobe Dr MM, QMAAC, 21

China and earthenware trades, 79

Chauvinism against women, 3, 12

Chemical Defence Research Department, 164

Chemical warfare, *Plate 13, 14, 23,* xi

Chemico Body Shield ('the greatest invention of the age'), 26

Child mortality, 2

Childcare and child welfare in WWI, xii, 112-113, 162-163

Children in war work, 81-82

Christie, Agatha, 39

Churchill, Winston, 160-161

Churchill, Winston, women working with, 123

Civil Hospital Reserve Nurses, 30

Clarke, Joan, Bletchley, 118-119

Clerical work and women, 14-15

Coats Mission, the, 128

Combat Stress – see PTSD

Combat Stress – the charity, 57

Community spirit and friendship between working women, 2-3, 182

Conditions of women's work, dreadful, xvii, 2-3, 7, 110

Conscription, 3, 112
of women 1941, 112

Corps of Village Forewomen, 62-63

Correspondents, women war, 145-148
Clare Hollingworth OBE (1911 – 2017), 145-146

Betty Knox, (1906-1963), 146

Erika Mann, (1905 –1969), 147

Evadne Price (1888 – 1985), 147

Muriel Audrey Russell, MVO (1906 – 1989), 147

Elizabeth "Lee" Miller (1907 –1977), 147-148

Curie, Marie, 184-185

Curie, Irène, 184-185

D-Day, *Plate 36,* xii, xiii, 127

Dead Nurses blog, 25

Demobilisation 1945, and women, 182-183

Derby Scheme, The 3

Devil's Porridge Museum, *Plate 4*, ix

Dilution, 16-18

Dior, Catherine, resistance fighter, 133

Discrimination against women, *passim* but particularly: xv, xix, 2-3, 12, 16-18, 20, 90, 119-120, 155, 161-162, 182-183

District (Queen's Nurses), 150-151

Diversification, Racial, *Plate 29*, xii, 42

Doctors, 25ff

Domestic service, 4, 11, 14, 16, 63, 90, 109

Domestic service crisis back home and moaning, xvii, 16

Drivers, women, 31, 130-131

Dunham Massey, see Stamford Military Hospital

Dunlop Rubber Company, Edmonton, 171-172

Durex, *Plate 8*, x, 174-175

Economic benefits to domestic budget through women's war work, 3

Eder, M.D and PTSD, xviii

Education, women restricted in, xv-xvi, 14-15, 72-73

Employment, women's pre-1914, 2

Employment, women's after 1914, 3-4, 6-7, 18, 19

Endell Street Military Hospital, 41-42

Index

Engineering and chemicals industries, women in, 7-8, 13, 15, 16, 75-77, 79-80, 112

Entertainments National Service Association (ENSA), 145

Exploitation of women, xvii, 2-3

Explosives Loading Company, Faversham, 100-101

Factories/companies, converted to war work, xix, 164
  Birmingham Small Arms (BSA), 166-167
  Wilkinson Sword, Acton, 167
  Singer Manufacturing Company, 167
  Vauxhall, 173
  York Carriage Works, 174

Factories, opportunities for women in, 3-4, 16

FANY, see First Aid Nursing Yeomanry

Farmborough, Florence, 38

Fashion, hair and cosmetics changes during WW1, 83-84

Fatalities, women in military service, *Plate 7*, 17, 21

Feeding the family, 163

Female unemployment in 1914, 3

Feminism, 42

Fire Watcher Service, 154-155

Fireworks companies, 169

First Aid Nursing Yeomanry (Princess Royal's Volunteer Corps) (FANY) (PRVC), 19, 47-51, 109, 110, 129-130
  FANY London Motor Companies, 110
  FANY and the SOE, 132
    Noor Inayat Khan
    Odette Sansom
    Violette Szabo
    Lise de Baissac
    Nancy Wake

Flax, in aircraft manufacture, 69

Flying Nightingales, 116

Food and drink industries, 80

Football, Women's, *Plate 10,* x
  Lionesses, 84
  Munitionettes, 95

Fraser, *Women and War Work*, 14, 15-16

Free FANYs, 131

Friends Ambulance Unit, 54-56

Garrod, Dorothy, 122-123

Gas and gas masks, *Plate 13*, 14, 23, xi, xii, 164

Gillies, Harold, xviii, 33-34

Girl Guides, 81

Girls' Nautical Training Corps, 125

Girls' Training Corps, 124-125

Girls' Venture Corps Air Cadets (GVCAC), 126

Gonorrhea and syphilis, *Plate 26*

Government Code and Cypher School, Bletchley Park, xix, 117-118, 127
  Women at, 118-120

Greatorex, Agnes, 63-64

Gretna, HM Factory, *Plate 4, 5,* ix, 90, 91-93
  Sir Arthur Conan Doyle, 92

Hackett-Lowther Ambulance Unit, 31-32

Hadfields Limited of Hecla and East Hecla, Sheffield, 91

Hadfield-Spears Ambulance Unit, 124, 152

Harrogate, xi, xix, 115, 127, 128

Hartlepool, *Plate 3*, 22, xi, 70, 83, 95

Health of Munitions Workers Committee, 94

Helmsley, York, 64

Hitler Youth, 124

Home-sickness in women workers, xvii

Hooley Hill Rubber and Chemical Works, Ashton-under-Lyme, 104

'Hush WAACs', 21

Independence, new, of women xix

Industry, women in, 7, 75ff

219

Inglis, Elsie Maud Dr, and the Scottish Women's Hospitals Units (SWH), 8-9, 42-44
Isle of Man, 127

Japan, women in war with, 127-128
Johnson, Amy, 135
Joint War Organisation, 34-35, 151-152, 186

Lancet, The: August 12 1916 as 'Observations on the effects of tri-nitro-toluene on women workers', by Agnes Livingstone-Learmouth M.B., CH.B. EDIN., and Barbara Martin Cunningham M.D. EDIN.
Land Girls/Land Lassies, 63
Landswoman, The, 63
Leather trades, 79
Leeds, 77, 78, 79, *81, 101-104, 171*
Lens grinding, *Plate 34*, xiii
Lewis, May Winifred, *Plate 3*, ix
Lewis, Maud Elizabeth, *Plate 3*, ix
Lewis, Dorothy Evelyn, *Plate 3*, ix
Living conditions for women, squalid, 2
London Rubber Company (LRC), *Plate 8*, x, 174-175
London Society for Women's Suffrage, 76
Lumberjills, 158-159

'Mannish', women seen as, 17
Marriage bar, 2, 3, 109
Medicine, women in, 109-110
Barred entry to study and train, 110-111
Maxillofacial, plastic and trauma surgery, xviii, 33
Maxwell, John. Chief Constable, 155-156
Mechanised Transport (Training) Corps (MTC), 123-124
Men, enlightened, 62, 76, 115, 155-156, 183

Middle class women, 34
Midwives, 32
Military Service Act, 1916, 3
Mills bomb, the, and Mills Munitions Factory, 169
Ministry of Munitions, 89
Misogyny, 8-9, 16, 41, 53-54, 64, 72-73, 83-84, 161-162
Montague Burton, Leeds, 78-79, 171
Morris, William, 115
Munitionettes, *Plate 22*, x, xi, xviii, xix, 88-104
Football teams, 95
Long-term occupational diseases, xix, 93-94
Moral indignation against, 95
Sexism against, 94-95
Sexual slurring, 95
Sidelined post-war and shabby treatment of, 25, 84, 93
Social life, 94-95
Munitions work, 11, 76, 84, 88-104, 165-166
Munitions factories, disasters, xix, 97, 99-104, 165-166
Munitions of War Act 1915, xix, 89
Munro Ambulance Corps, The, 52
Munro, Hector (aka "Saki" (1870 - 1916)), 52
Murray, Flora, 40-42
Murray, Gilbert, 73

NAAFI, The *Plate 33*, xiii, 56-57, 144-145
National Balloon Factory, Finchley, 105
National factories, 96
National Filling Factories (NFFs), 95-96, 165-166
Barnbow, Leeds, 1011-104
Chilwell, Nottinghamshire, 101
Morecambe, 97
Pembury, 99
Silvertown, West Ham, 99-100

Index

National Fire Service (NFS)
 firefighters, *Plate 35*, xiii, 154
National Political League (NPL), 66
National Projectile Factory, Birtley,
 Gateshead, 98-99
National Projectile Factory, Lancaster,
 96-97
National Savings Campaign, 139
National Service (No 2) Act, 1941, 112
Navy, Army and Air Force Institutes
 (NAAFI), see NAAFI
Neurasthenia, see Post traumatic stress
 disorder
Newcastle-upon-Tyne, *Plate* 16, xi,
 76-77
Northern Area Clothing Depot, Leeds,
 77-78
Nurses, 19, 25ff
 Theatre Nurses, 32-33

Observation balloons, 105
Oliver, Sarah, 122
Opposition and antipathy towards
 women working in the war effort,
 passim, but particularly xv, vvii,
 xix, 11, 12, 16-18, 19, 22, 41,
 53-54, 61-64, 72-73, 90, 90-91
Oxbridge and women students, 73, 77,
 109-110, 118, 122-123

Pacifism, 54-56
Palace of Westminster Munitions
 Factory, 166
Pankhurst, Christabel, xv
Pankhurst, Emmeline, xv
Pankhurst, Sylvia, 7, 11
Parsons, Lady Katharine (1859 – 1933)
 and Rachel Mary Parsons, Rachel
 Mary(1885–1956), 76-77
 and PTSD, xviii, 8
Patriotism and heightened self esteem
 in women through war work, xix, 3,
 4, 9, 11, 14-15, 17, 84
Patronisation by men of women, 3

Pay differential between men and
 women, *passim*, but particularly
 xvii, 12, 13-14, 16, 17, 89, 93,
 116, 183
Photographic Intelligence (PI), 121-122
Physiotherapists, 25
Political Warfare Executive (PWE),
 Woburn Abbey, xix, 120-121
 Quentin Bell
 Graham Greene
 Muriel Spark
 Stephen Spender
 AJP Taylor
Post Office, The, 15
Post traumatic stress disorder (PTSD)
 and women, xvii-xix, 25, 41, 57-60
 Stigma, 57-60
 Treatment, 57-60
 Punishment, 57-60
 and Dorothy L. Sayers, 60
Preston Army Pay Office Ladies'
 Football Team, x
Princess Christian's Army Nursing
 Service Reserve (PCANSR), 29-30
Princess Mary's RAF Nursing Service
 (PMRAFNS), 150
Printing and paper industries, 80
Prison officers, women, 156
Propaganda, 82, 139
Prostitution, 176-181
Psychological impact of war work on
 women, 71-72, 71-72
PTSD see Post traumatic stress
 disorder

Quakers, 54-56
Queen Alexandra's Imperial Military
 Nursing Service (QAIMNS), *Plate*
 2, 36, xiii, 28-29, 149
Queen Alexandra's Imperial Military
 Nursing Service Reserve
 (QAIMNSR), 29
Queen Alexandra's Royal Army
 Nursing Corps (QARANC), 150

221

Queen Alexandra's Royal Naval Nursing Service (QARNNS), 29, 149

Queen Mary's Army Auxiliary Corps (QMAAC), *Plate 6, 7*, x, 17, 21

Queen Mary's Hospital, Sidcup, 33

Queen Mary's Needlework Guild, 4-6

Queen's Nurses, 150-151

Queen's Work for Women Fund, 6

RAF Air Ambulance Unit, 116

RAF Menwith Hill, 128

Railways, 173

Red Cross, The *Plate 21*, xi, 35, 115, 184, 186

Refugees, 136

'Report on the Replacement of Men by Women in Industry', 13

Reserved occupations, 112

Resistance fighters, women as, 133 Catherine Dior

Respirators, see gas, 164

Restoration of Pre War Trade Practices Act, 1919, 14, 108

Rowntree, Seebohm, 7

Royal Filling Factories (RFFs), see National Filling Factories

Royal Gunpowder Factory, Waltham Abbey, 80

Royal Observer Corps (ROC), 142-143

Royal Ordnance Factories (ROFs), 165-166
Maltby, 112

Royal Small Arms Factory (RSAF), Enfield, 86

Salvage drives, 136-137, 159

Sanitary towels, 115

Scottish Women's Hospitals Units (SWH), or Scottish Women's Hospitals for Foreign Services, 8-9, 42-44

Sayers, Dorothy L. 60

Segregation of women, 17

Selborne, Lord, 62

Sex Disqualification (Removal Act), 1919, 73-74

Sexism, *passim* but particularly, 8-9, 16, 41, 53-54, 64, 72-73, 83-84, 94-95, 119-20, 156, 161-62

Sexually transmitted infections (STIs), 176-181

Sexual slurring of women, xix, 17, 18, 74, 83-84, 176-181

Shadow factories, 164-165, 172

Sheffield's Women of Steel, *Plate 1*, ix; 91

Shell Crisis, The, 88-89

Shell shock see PTSD

Shipbuilding, *Plate 30*, 75, 112, 165

Shopping: who does the ? 163

Sister Susie's Sewing Shirts for Soldiers, 78

Small arms manufacturing, 85-87, 166-167

Special Military Probationers, 51

Special Operations Executive (SOE), xix, 117, 120, 132

Stamford Military Hospital, Dunham Massey, 186-187

St Clair Stobart, Mabel Annie, 53

Stereotyping of women, *passim*, but particularly 3

Stockport Air raid tunnels, *Plate 24*, xii, 142

Substitution jobs, 6-7, 9

Suffragettes/suffragists, xv, 9, 10, 77

Syphilis and gonorrhea, *Plate 26*

STIs, *Plate 26*, xii

Tanks and other heavy armour, 173

Teachers, 17, 72, 109

Temporary workers, women were always to be, 11, 12, 14, 16, 18, 108, 182-183

Ten Year Rule, The, 160

Territorial Army Nursing Service (TANS), 149-150

Index

Territorial Force Nursing Service (TFNS), 45-47

Tetley's, Leeds, 81

Trade Unions and women, xix, 5-6, 12, 16-18, 90

Transport, women in, 12, 15-16

Trauma surgery and gangrene, 40

Typewriter, the, impact of on women's employment, 14-15

Underwear, class sensitive, 20, 115-16

Uniforms, dislike of, 20, 115-116

University degrees, women finally awarded, xv-xvi

US military personnel, *Plate 26*

VD, see Sexually transmitted infections (STIs)

Viner's Sheffield, and disgusting conditions for women, 110

Voluntary Aid Detachments, VADs, *Plate 3*, 15, ix, xi, 19, 34ff, 150
Famous VADs, 39

Voluntary organisations, 17-18

Volunteer Motor Mobilisation Corps (VMMC), 71

War Cabinet Committee on Women in Industry, 93

War Hospital Supply Depots, *Plate 18*, xi, 25-26

Watson, William, 62

Weapons, women not allowed to fire, 129

Webbing, manufacture of, 170

Welding, women, *Plate 31*, 17

Welfare supervisors, loathed, xix

West Indian women, *Plate 29*, xii

Wimereux Hospital, 40-41

Window cleaners, *Plate 16,* xi

Woman and changes in social norms, 83-84

Women, decorated, 21

Women gardeners, 61-62

Women, invisible in WW2, 118-120

Women, just getting on with it, carrying on, *passim* but particularly xvi, xix, 16, 25, 42-43, 94

Women, health care workers and the medically qualified, 8-9, 21, 25ff, 40, 42-45, 109, 183

Women, quick learners and quality of work, *passim*, but particularly xvi, 16, 19, 76-77, 84, 108f, 154, 182-183

Women and the shortage of men after 1918, 109

Women, unprepared for the tasks ahead in 1914, xvi

Women's Agricultural and Horticultural International Union (WAHIU), 66

Women's Army Auxiliary Corps, WAAC *Plate 11*, x, 17, 18, 19, 23, 109

Women's Auxiliary Air Force (WAAF), parachute packing, *Plate 32*, xii, 116

Women's Auxiliary Force, 70

Women's Auxiliary Police Corps (WAPC), 155-156

Women's Defence Relief Corps, 65-66

Women's Emergency Corps (WEC), 10, 19
Motor Department
Women's Motor Manual, 10

Women's Farm and Garden Union, 63, 66

Women's Forage Corps (WFC), 67-68

Women's Forestry Corps (also WFC), 68-69

Women's Health Enquiry 1933: verdict: no improvement pre- 1914-1933

Women's Home Defence /The Home Guard, 143-144

Women's Hospital Corps, 19, 40

Women's Institute (WI), 137-139

Women's Junior Air Corps (WJAC), 125

Women's Land Army (WLA), *Plates 9, 25*, x, xii, 61- 63, 157-158
  Lilly Chitty,
  Ethel Thomas
  Macaulay, Dame Emilie Rose
Women's Legion, 71
Women's Mounted Emergency Corps, *Plate 20*, xi
Women's National Land Service Corps (WNLSC), 62, 66-67
Women's National Service League, 39
Women Patrols Committee, 177
Women's Police Volunteer (WPV)/ Women's Police Service (WPS), 102, 105-107
Women's Reserve Ambulance Corps (WRAC, aka the Green Cross Corps), 30-31
Women's Royal Air Force (WRAF), *Plate 17*, xi, 18, 23, 109, 115
Women's Royal Naval Service (WRNS), 18, 21-23, 109, 114
Women's Service Bureau, 17
Women's Sick and Wounded Convoy Corps (WSWCC), 52-54

Women's Signaller Corps, 21-22
Women's Social and Political Union (WSPU), xv, 9-10, 41, 42
Women's Timber Corps, 158-159
Women's Voluntary Services for Air Raid Precaution (WVS), 136-137
Women's Volunteer Reserve (WVR), 70
Women, votes for, xv, 84, 90-91
Women in war work 1943, 112
Women's War Register, 10-11
Women's War Work Subcommittee photographic archive of women's war work 10, 84
Wool Control; the, 170, 171
Wright, Dr Helena Rosa MRCS (Eng.) and LRCP (Lond.), 44-45

YMCA National Women's Auxiliary (WA), 143
York Carriage Works, 54-56, 174
York Minster, 103
Yorkshire Shoddy Works, 77-78
Young Women's Christian Association (YWCA), 143